GREEN ARROW

CRAWLING THROUGH THE WRECKAGE

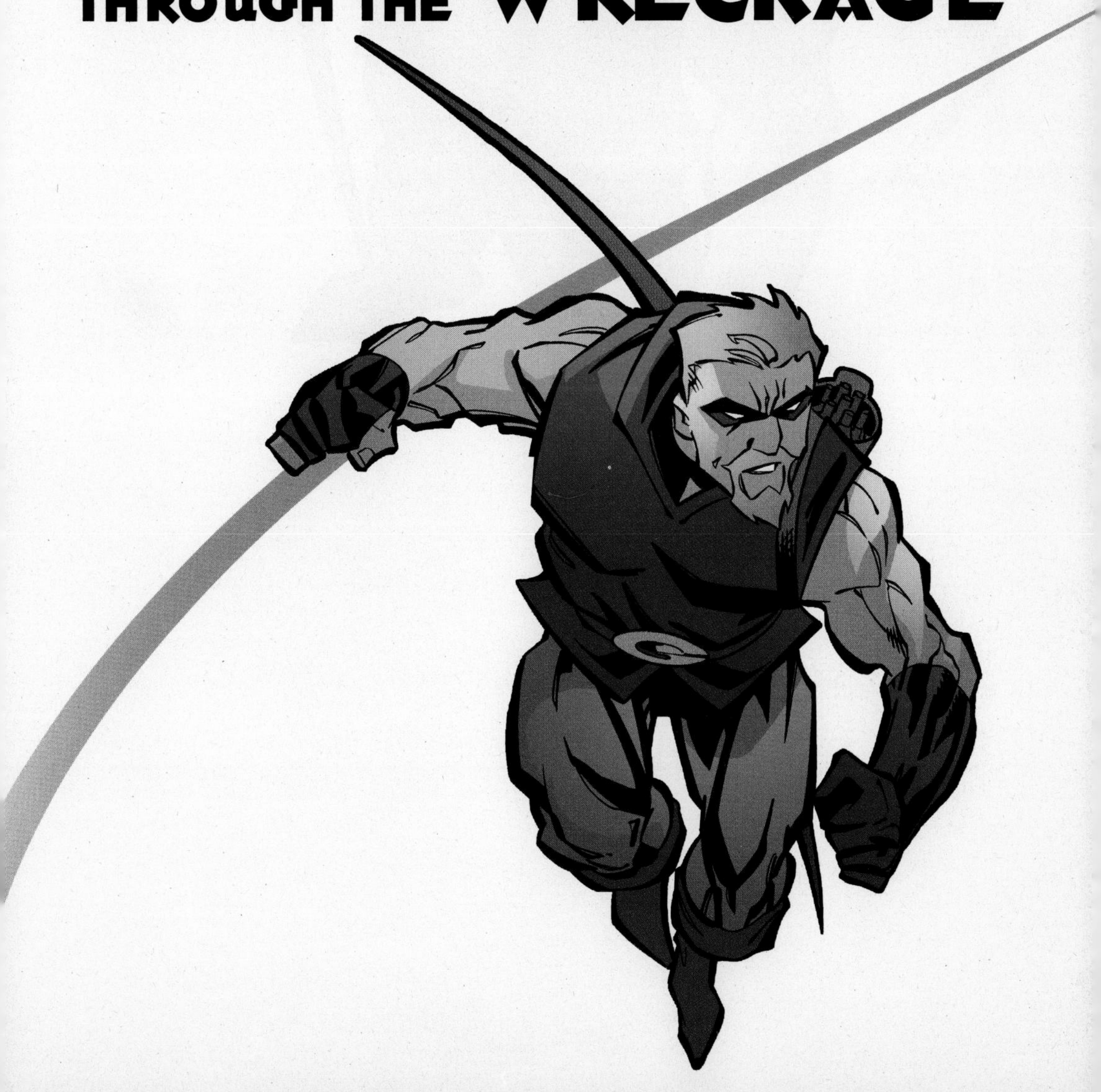

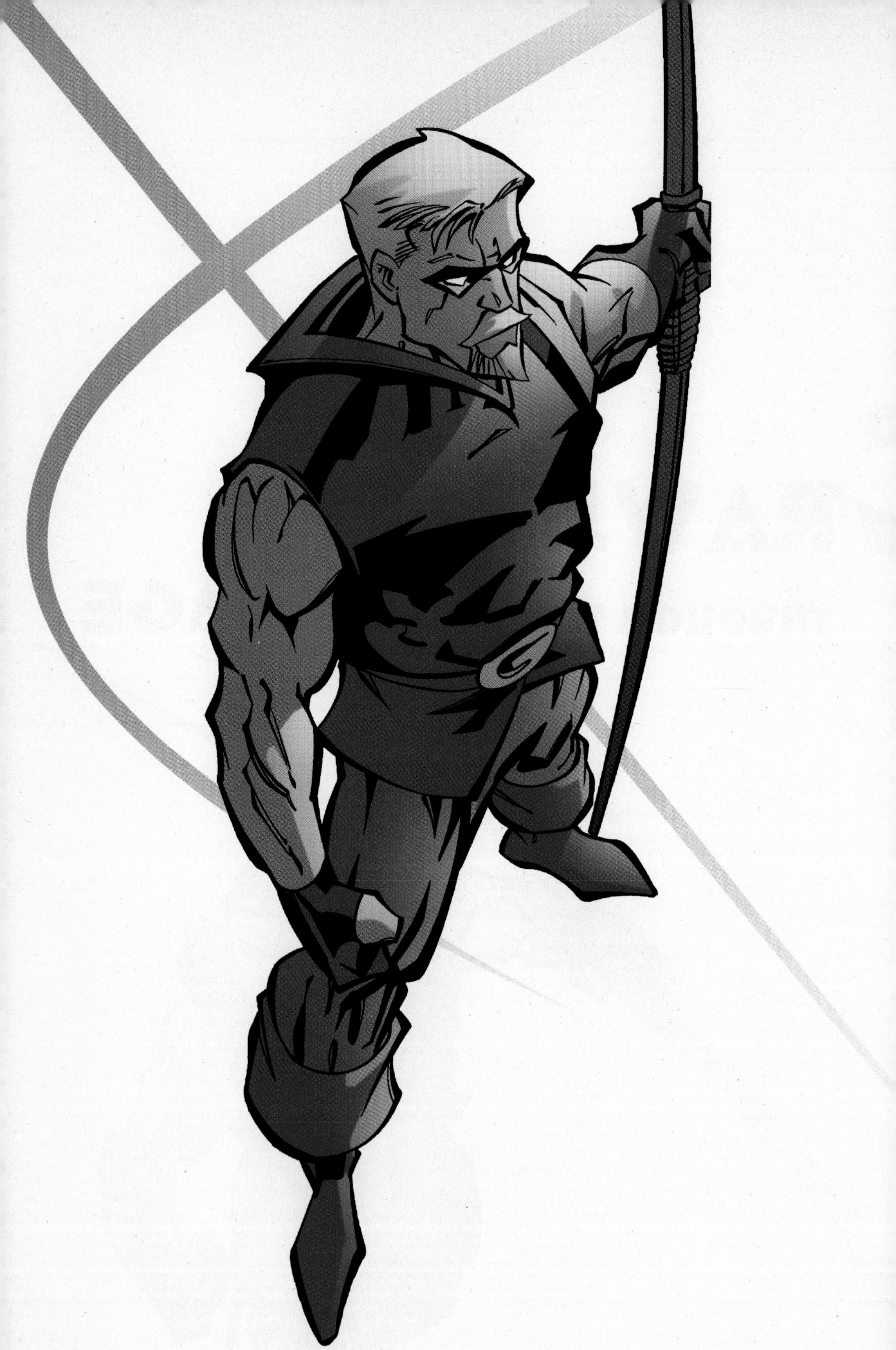

Judd Winick
Writer

Scott McDaniel
Penciller

Andy Owens
Inker

Guy Major
Colorist

Pat Brosseau
Letterer

Scott McDaniel
and Andy Owens
Original Series Covers

GREEN ARROW

CRAWLING
THROUGH THE WRECKAGE

DAN DIDIO
Senior VP-Executive Editor
MIKE CARLIN
Editor-original series
TOM PALMER, JR.
Associate Editor-original series
BOB HARRAS
Editor-collected edition
ROBBIN BROSTERMAN
Senior Art Director
PAUL LEVITZ
President & Publisher
GEORG BREWER
VP-Design & DC Direct Creative
RICHARD BRUNING
Senior VP-Creative Director
PATRICK CALDON
Executive VP-Finance & Operations
CHRIS CARAMALIS
VP-Finance
JOHN CUNNINGHAM
VP-Marketing
TERRI CUNNINGHAM
VP-Managing Editor

STEPHANIE FIERMAN
Senior VP-Sales & Marketing
ALISON GILL
VP-Manufacturing
HANK KANALZ
VP-General Manager, WildStorm
JIM LEE
Editorial Director-WildStorm
PAULA LOWITT
Senior VP-Business & Legal Affairs
MARYELLEN MCLAUGHLIN
VP-Advertising & Custom Publishing
JOHN NEE
VP-Business Development
GREGORY NOVECK
Senior VP-Creative Affairs
CHERYL RUBIN
Senior VP-Brand Management
JEFF TROJAN
VP-Business Development, DC Direct
BOB WAYNE
VP-Sales

Cover illustration by Scott McDaniel and Andy Owens.
Cover color by Guy Major.

GREEN ARROW:
CRAWLING THROUGH THE WRECKAGE

DC Comics does not read or accept
unsolicited submissions of ideas,
stories or artwork.
DC Comics, 1700 Broadway,
New York, NY 10019
A Warner Bros. Entertainment
Company
Printed in Canada. First Printing.

ISBN: 1-4012-1232-8
ISBN: 978-1-4012-1232-2

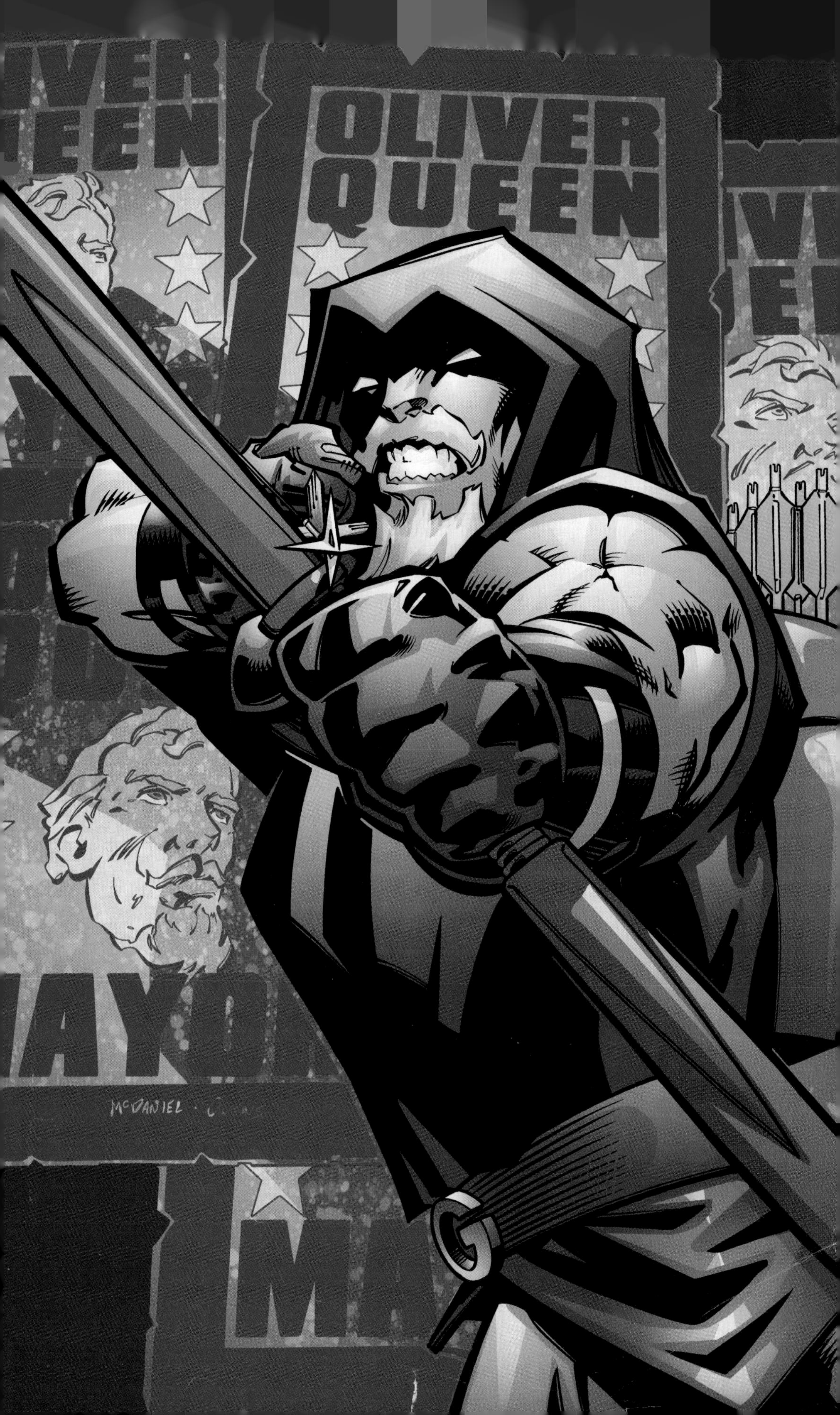
OLIVER
QUEEN

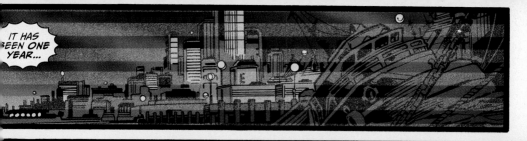

IT HAS BEEN *ONE YEAR*...

ONE YEAR EXACTLY, SINCE THE *AMSTERDAM DISASTER* HAD STRUCK STAR CITY.

AMSTERDAM

STAR CITY ACTION NEWS

FEW CAN FORGET THE DEVASTATION OF THAT NIGHT AS A PART OF THE CITY WAS LEVELED IN AN ATTACK...

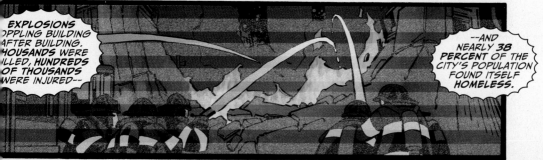

EXPLOSIONS TOPPLING BUILDING AFTER BUILDING. THOUSANDS WERE KILLED, HUNDREDS OF THOUSANDS WERE INJURED--

--AND NEARLY *38* PERCENT OF THE CITY'S POPULATION FOUND ITSELF *HOMELESS*.

ON TONIGHT'S PROGRAM WE LOOK BACK ON THE YEAR THAT HAS BEEN. HOW THE CITY HAS FOUGHT TO *HEAL* ITSELF...

AMSTERDAM

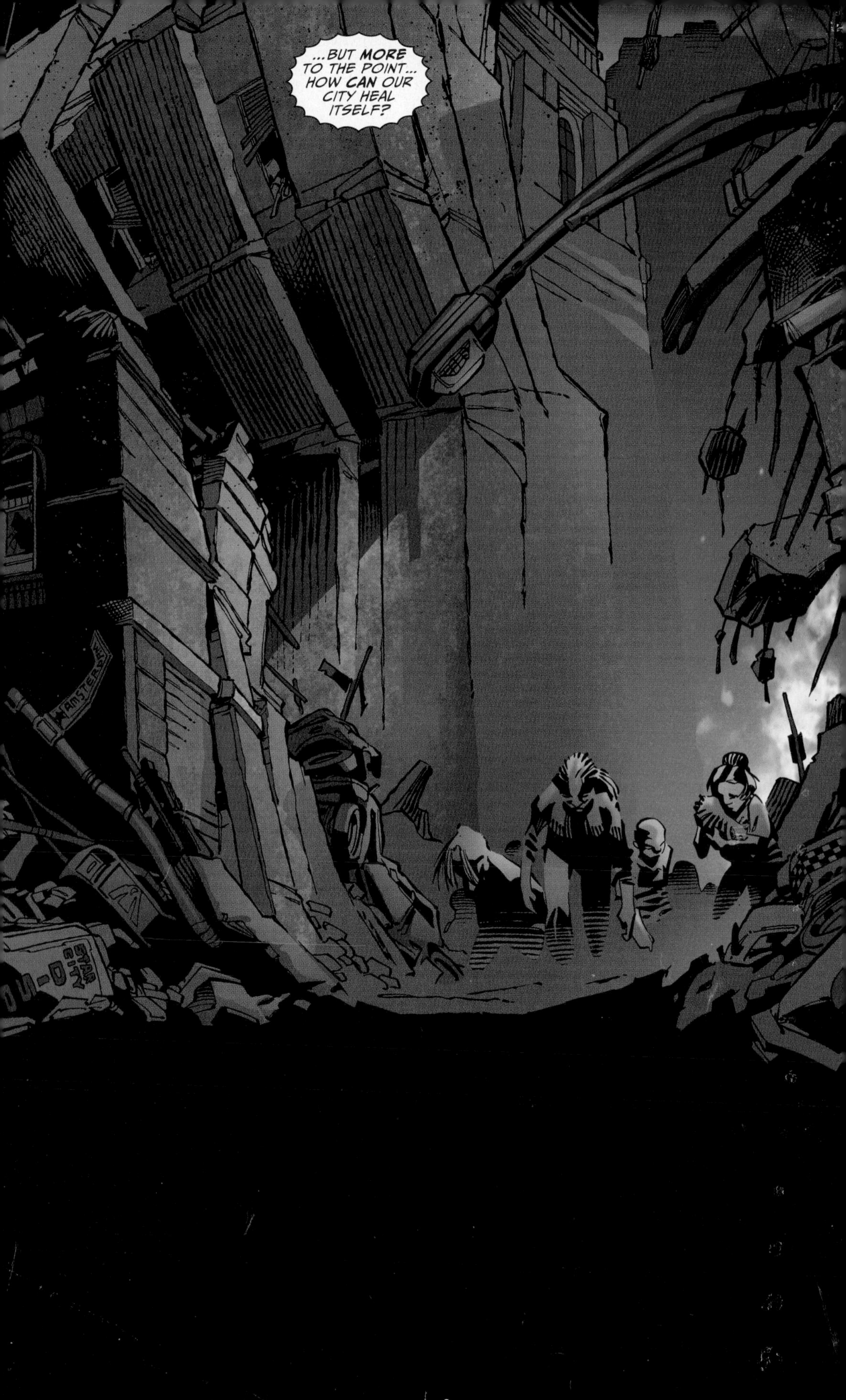
...BUT MORE TO THE POINT... HOW CAN OUR CITY HEAL ITSELF?

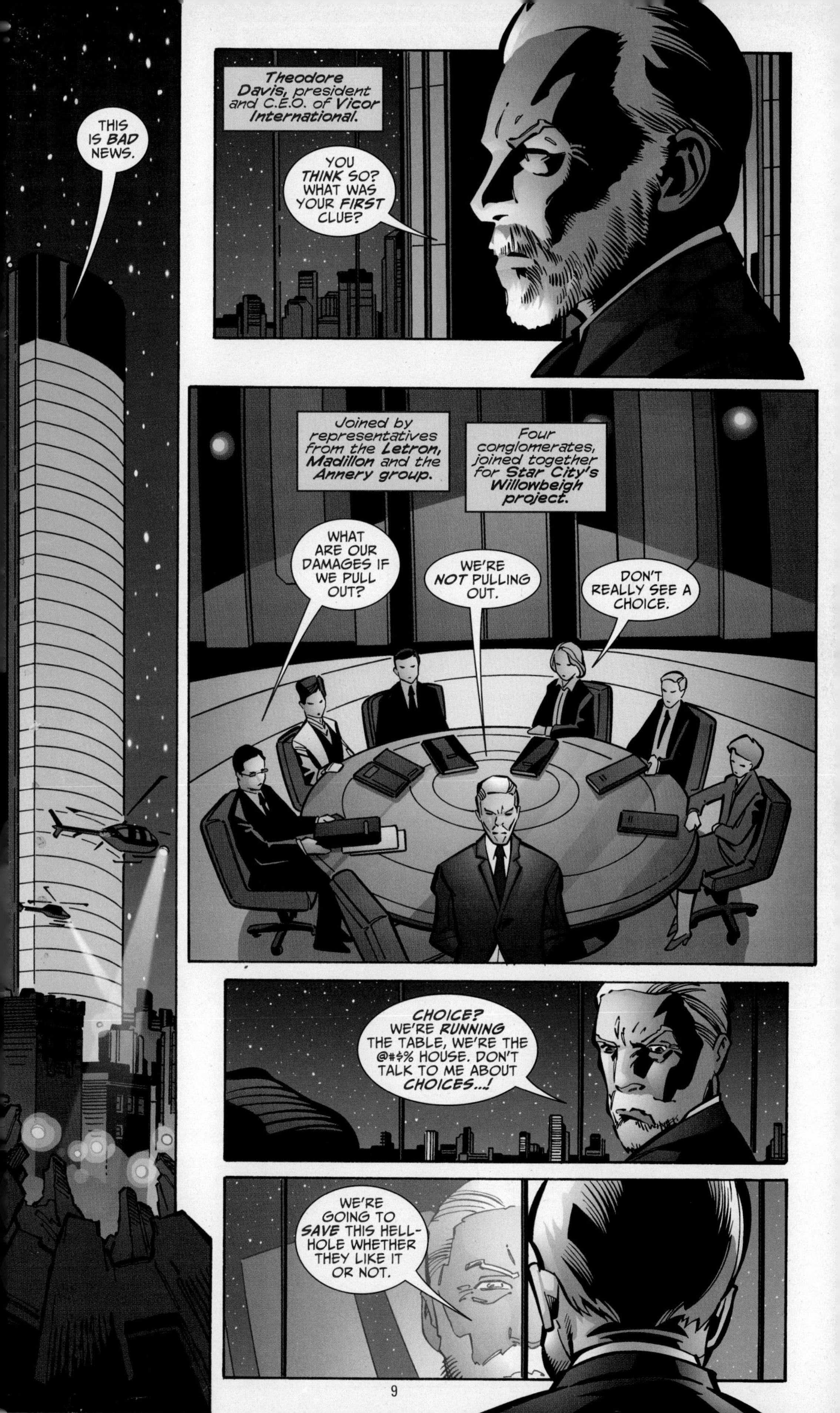
THIS IS BAD NEWS.
Theodore Davis, president and C.E.O. of Vicor International.
YOU THINK SO? WHAT WAS YOUR FIRST CLUE?
Joined by representatives from the Letron, Madillon and the Annery group.
Four conglomerates, joined together for Star City's Willowbeigh project.
WHAT ARE OUR DAMAGES IF WE PULL OUT?
WE'RE NOT PULLING OUT.
DON'T REALLY SEE A CHOICE.
CHOICE? WE'RE RUNNING THE TABLE, WE'RE THE @#$% HOUSE. DON'T TALK TO ME ABOUT CHOICES...!
WE'RE GOING TO SAVE THIS HELL-HOLE WHETHER THEY LIKE IT OR NOT.

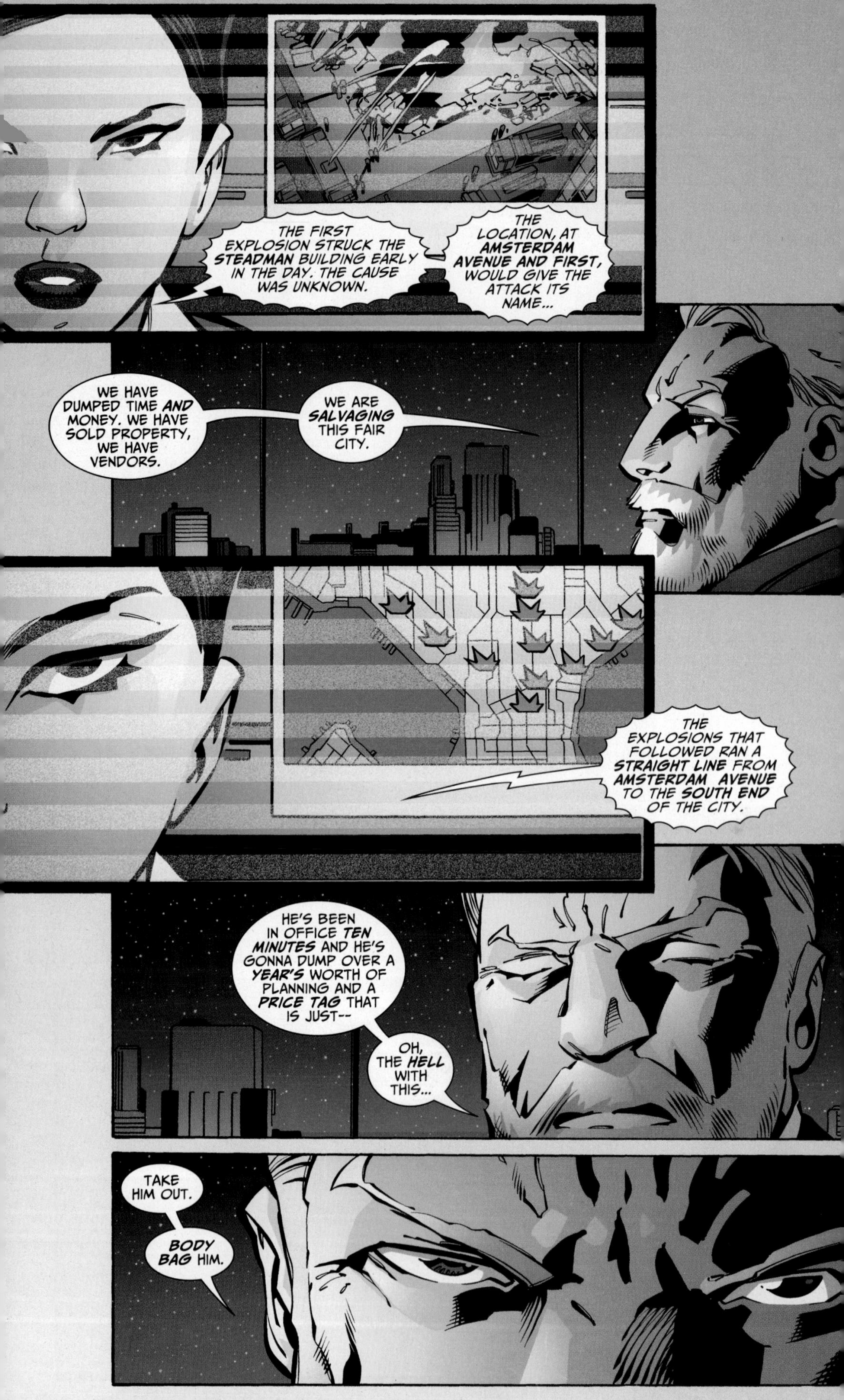
THE FIRST EXPLOSION STRUCK THE STEADMAN BUILDING EARLY IN THE DAY. THE CAUSE WAS UNKNOWN.
THE LOCATION, AT AMSTERDAM AVENUE AND FIRST, WOULD GIVE THE ATTACK ITS NAME...
WE HAVE DUMPED TIME AND MONEY. WE HAVE SOLD PROPERTY, WE HAVE VENDORS.
WE ARE SALVAGING THIS FAIR CITY.
THE EXPLOSIONS THAT FOLLOWED RAN A STRAIGHT LINE FROM AMSTERDAM AVENUE TO THE SOUTH END OF THE CITY.
HE'S BEEN IN OFFICE TEN MINUTES AND HE'S GONNA DUMP OVER A YEAR'S WORTH OF PLANNING AND A PRICE TAG THAT IS JUST--
OH, THE HELL WITH THIS...
TAKE HIM OUT.
BODY BAG HIM.

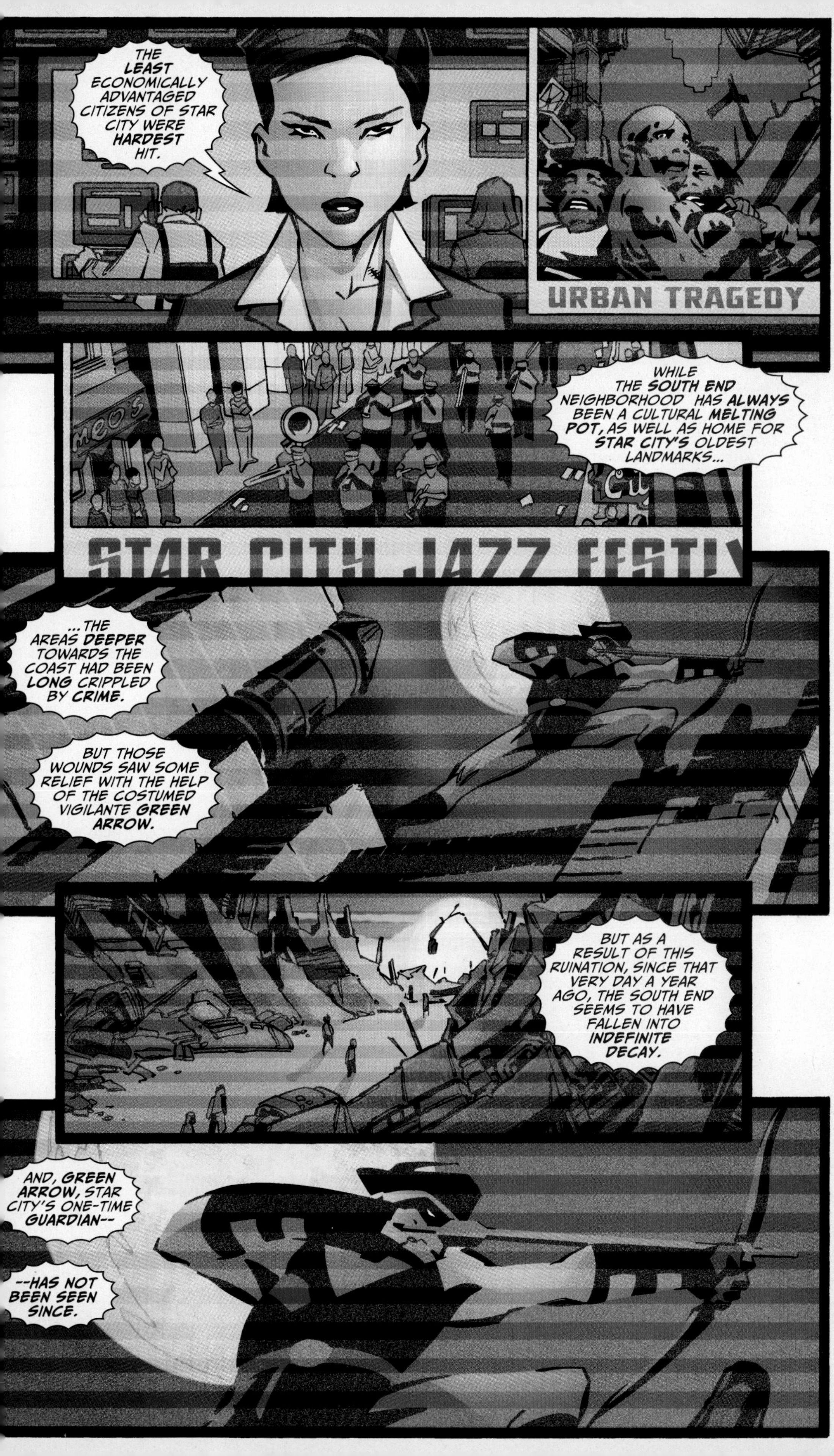
THE LEAST ECONOMICALLY ADVANTAGED CITIZENS OF STAR CITY WERE HARDEST HIT.
URBAN TRAGEDY
WHILE THE SOUTH END NEIGHBORHOOD HAS ALWAYS BEEN A CULTURAL MELTING POT, AS WELL AS HOME FOR STAR CITY'S OLDEST LANDMARKS...
STAR CITY JAZZ FESTI
...THE AREAS DEEPER TOWARDS THE COAST HAD BEEN LONG CRIPPLED BY CRIME.
BUT THOSE WOUNDS SAW SOME RELIEF WITH THE HELP OF THE COSTUMED VIGILANTE GREEN ARROW.
BUT AS A RESULT OF THIS RUINATION, SINCE THAT VERY DAY A YEAR AGO, THE SOUTH END SEEMS TO HAVE FALLEN INTO INDEFINITE DECAY.
AND, GREEN ARROW, STAR CITY'S ONE-TIME GUARDIAN--
--HAS NOT BEEN SEEN SINCE.

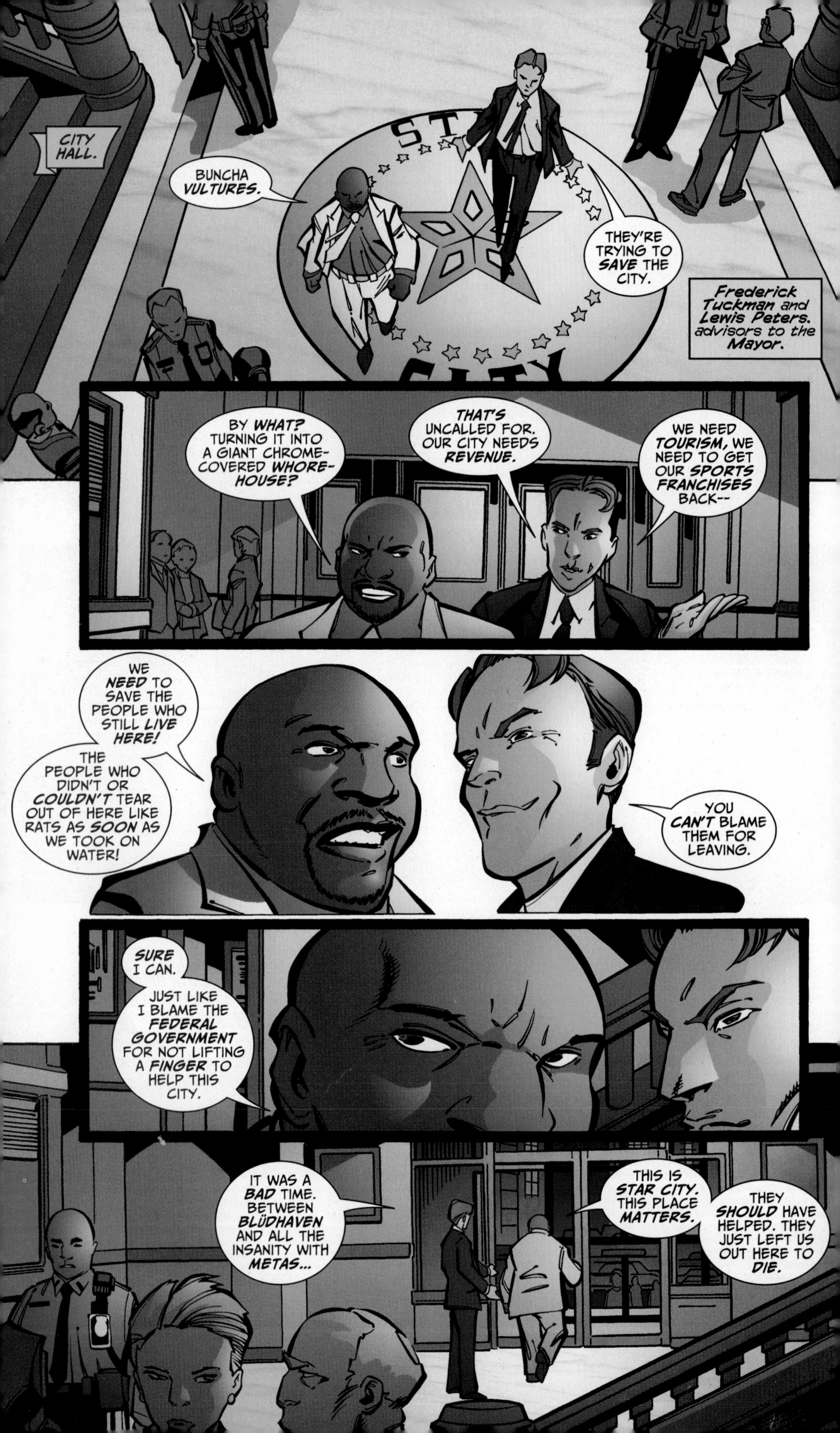

CITY HALL.
BUNCHA VULTURES.
THEY'RE TRYING TO SAVE THE CITY.
Frederick Tuckman and Lewis Peters. advisors to the Mayor.
BY WHAT? TURNING IT INTO A GIANT CHROME-COVERED WHORE-HOUSE?
THAT'S UNCALLED FOR. OUR CITY NEEDS REVENUE.
WE NEED TOURISM, WE NEED TO GET OUR SPORTS FRANCHISES BACK--
WE NEED TO SAVE THE PEOPLE WHO STILL LIVE HERE!
THE PEOPLE WHO DIDN'T OR COULDN'T TEAR OUT OF HERE LIKE RATS AS SOON AS WE TOOK ON WATER!
YOU CAN'T BLAME THEM FOR LEAVING.
SURE I CAN.
JUST LIKE I BLAME THE FEDERAL GOVERNMENT FOR NOT LIFTING A FINGER TO HELP THIS CITY.
IT WAS A BAD TIME. BETWEEN BLÜDHAVEN AND ALL THE INSANITY WITH METAS...
THIS IS STAR CITY. THIS PLACE MATTERS.
THEY SHOULD HAVE HELPED. THEY JUST LEFT US OUT HERE TO DIE.

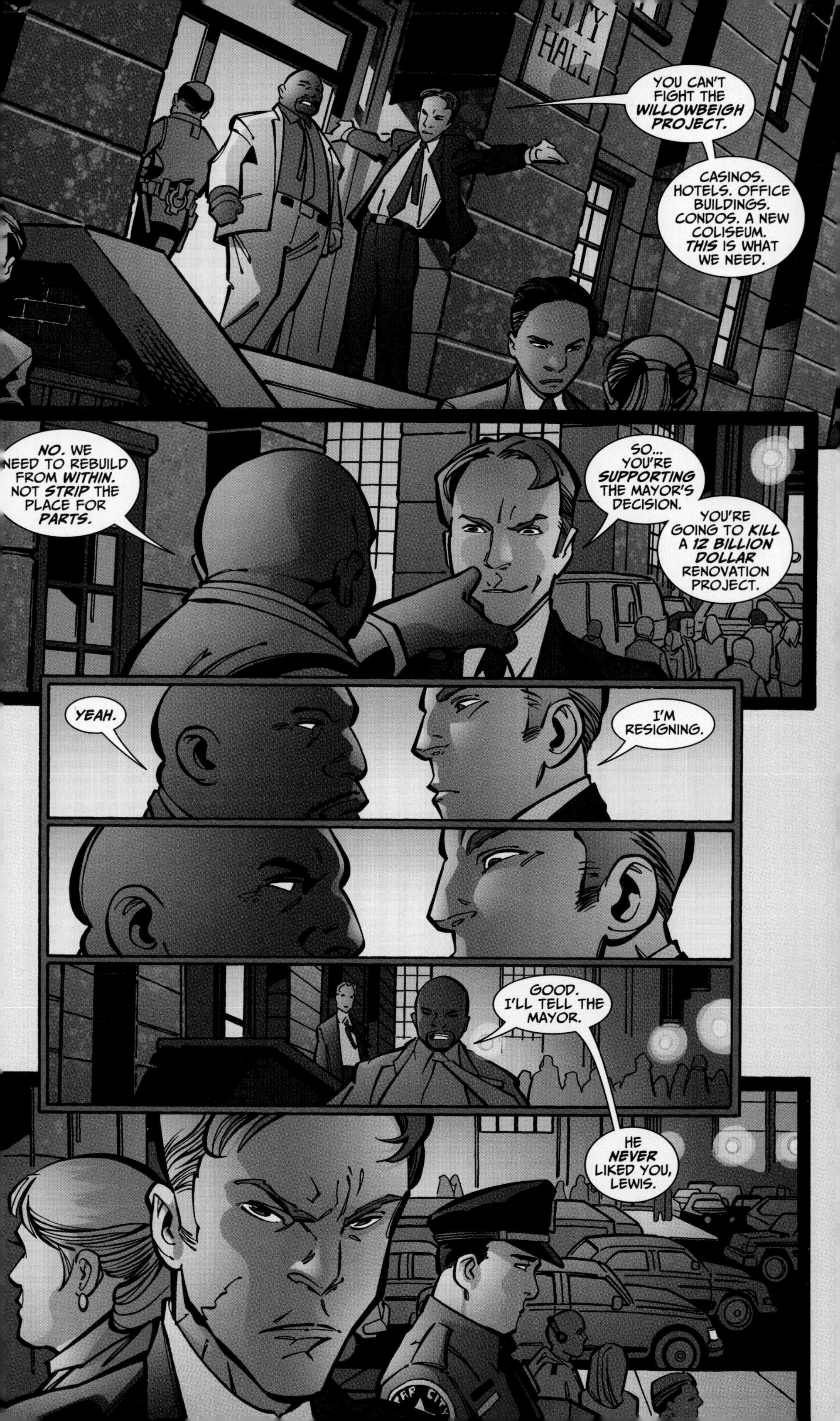
CITY HALL
YOU CAN'T FIGHT THE WILLOWBEIGH PROJECT.
CASINOS. HOTELS. OFFICE BUILDINGS. CONDOS. A NEW COLISEUM. THIS IS WHAT WE NEED.
NO. WE NEED TO REBUILD FROM WITHIN. NOT STRIP THE PLACE FOR PARTS.
SO... YOU'RE SUPPORTING THE MAYOR'S DECISION.
YOU'RE GOING TO KILL A 12 BILLION DOLLAR RENOVATION PROJECT.
YEAH.
I'M RESIGNING.
GOOD. I'LL TELL THE MAYOR.
HE NEVER LIKED YOU, LEWIS.

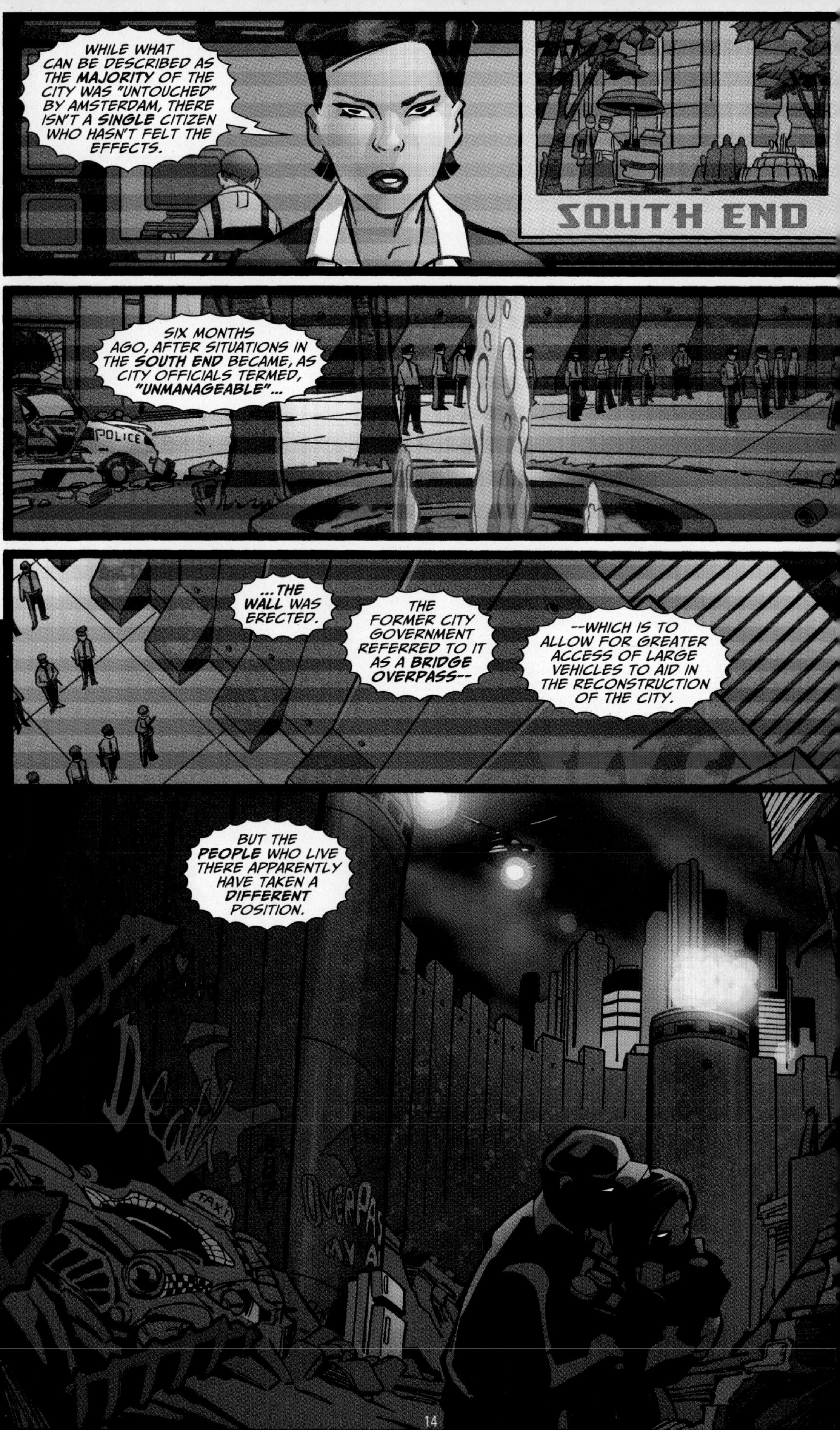

WHILE WHAT CAN BE DESCRIBED AS THE MAJORITY OF THE CITY WAS "UNTOUCHED" BY AMSTERDAM, THERE ISN'T A SINGLE CITIZEN WHO HASN'T FELT THE EFFECTS.
SOUTH END
SIX MONTHS AGO, AFTER SITUATIONS IN THE SOUTH END BECAME, AS CITY OFFICIALS TERMED, "UNMANAGEABLE"...
POLICE
...THE WALL WAS ERECTED.
THE FORMER CITY GOVERNMENT REFERRED TO IT AS A BRIDGE OVERPASS--
--WHICH IS TO ALLOW FOR GREATER ACCESS OF LARGE VEHICLES TO AID IN THE RECONSTRUCTION OF THE CITY.
BUT THE PEOPLE WHO LIVE THERE APPARENTLY HAVE TAKEN A DIFFERENT POSITION.
TAXI

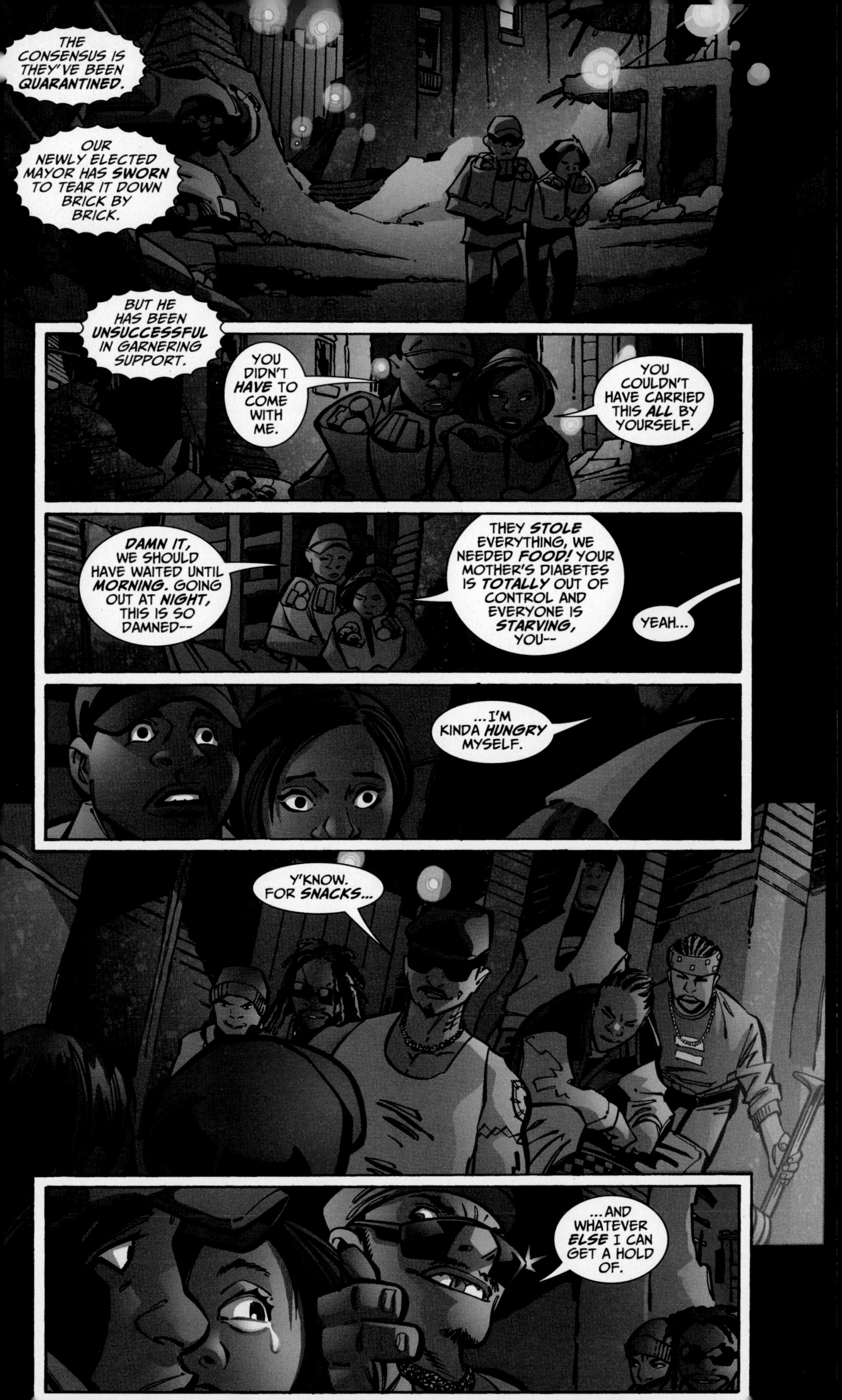
THE CONSENSUS IS THEY'VE BEEN QUARANTINED.
OUR NEWLY ELECTED MAYOR HAS SWORN TO TEAR IT DOWN BRICK BY BRICK.
BUT HE HAS BEEN UNSUCCESSFUL IN GARNERING SUPPORT.
YOU DIDN'T HAVE TO COME WITH ME.
YOU COULDN'T HAVE CARRIED THIS ALL BY YOURSELF.
DAMN IT, WE SHOULD HAVE WAITED UNTIL MORNING. GOING OUT AT NIGHT, THIS IS SO DAMNED--
THEY STOLE EVERYTHING, WE NEEDED FOOD! YOUR MOTHER'S DIABETES IS TOTALLY OUT OF CONTROL AND EVERYONE IS STARVING, YOU--
YEAH...
...I'M KINDA HUNGRY MYSELF.
Y'KNOW. FOR SNACKS...
...AND WHATEVER ELSE I CAN GET A HOLD OF.

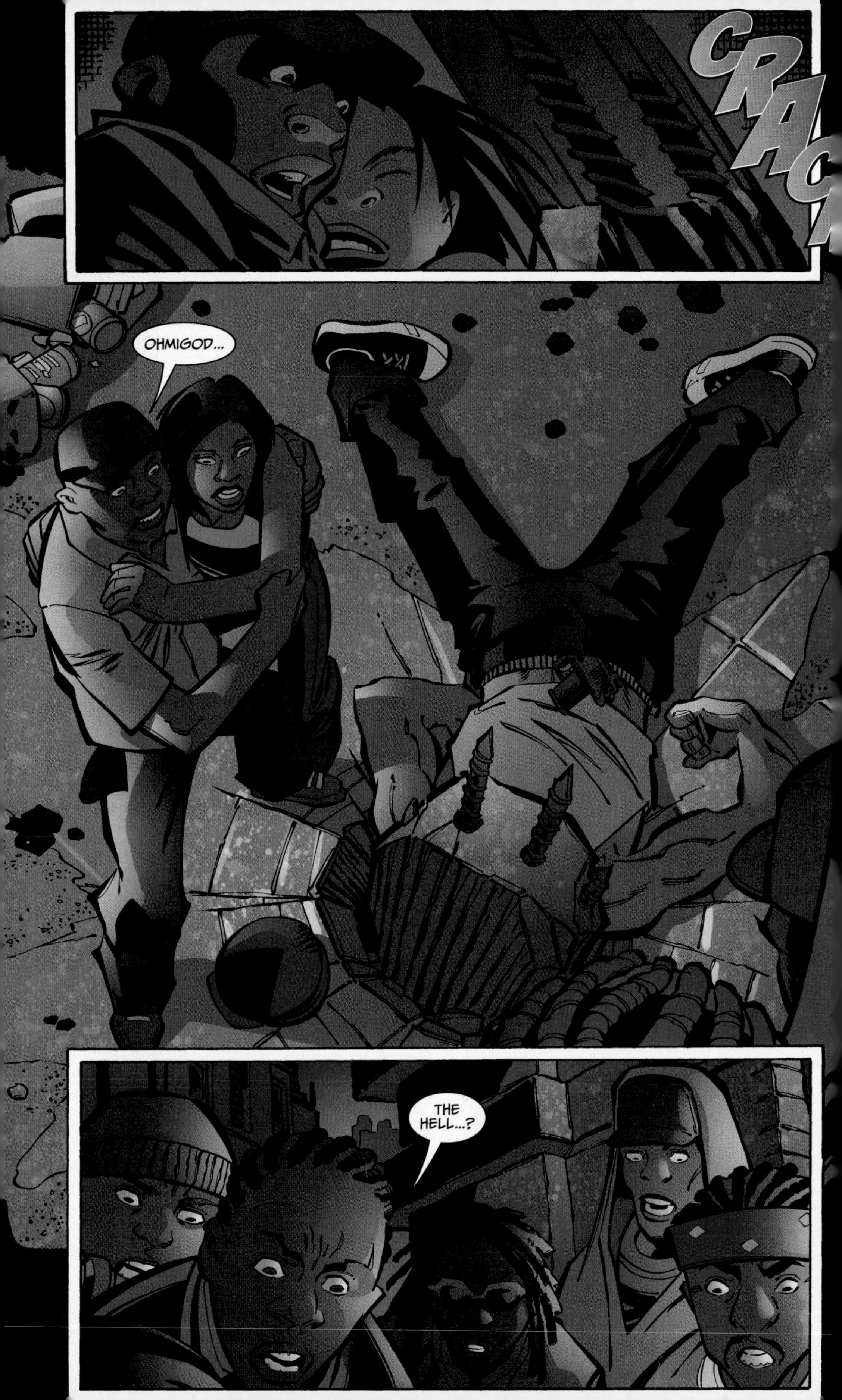
CRACK
OHMIGOD...
THE HELL...?

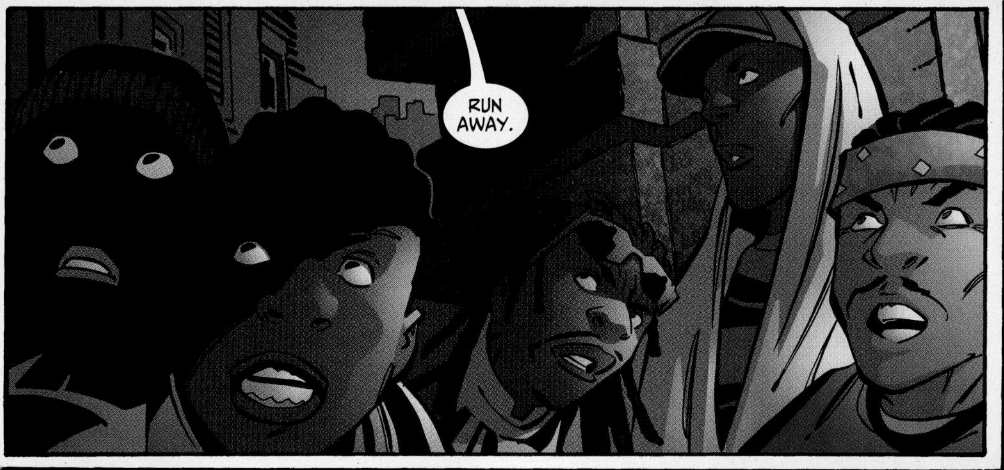
RUN AWAY.

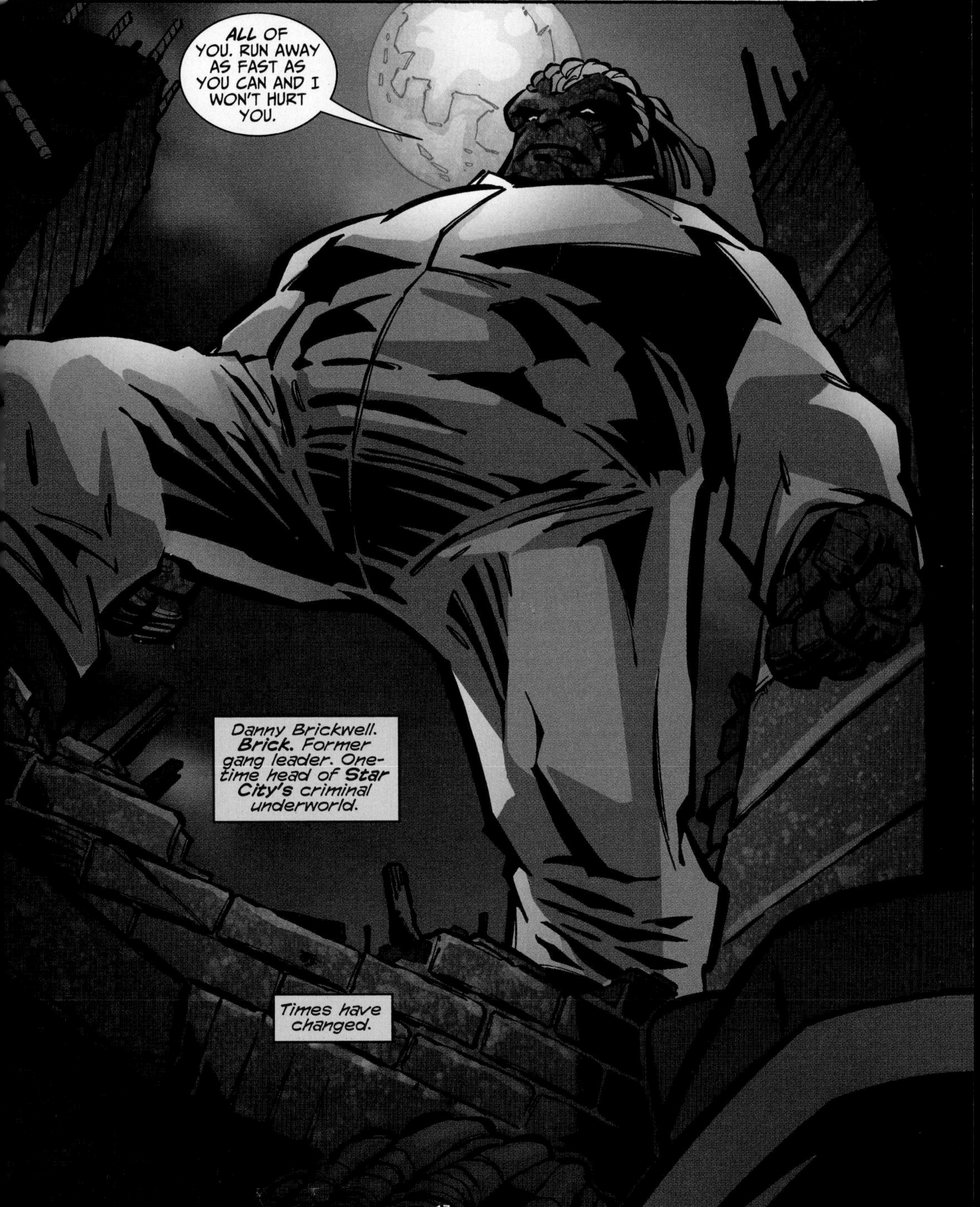
ALL OF YOU. RUN AWAY AS FAST AS YOU CAN AND I WON'T HURT YOU.
Danny Brickwell. Brick. Former gang leader. One-time head of Star City's criminal underworld.
Times have changed.

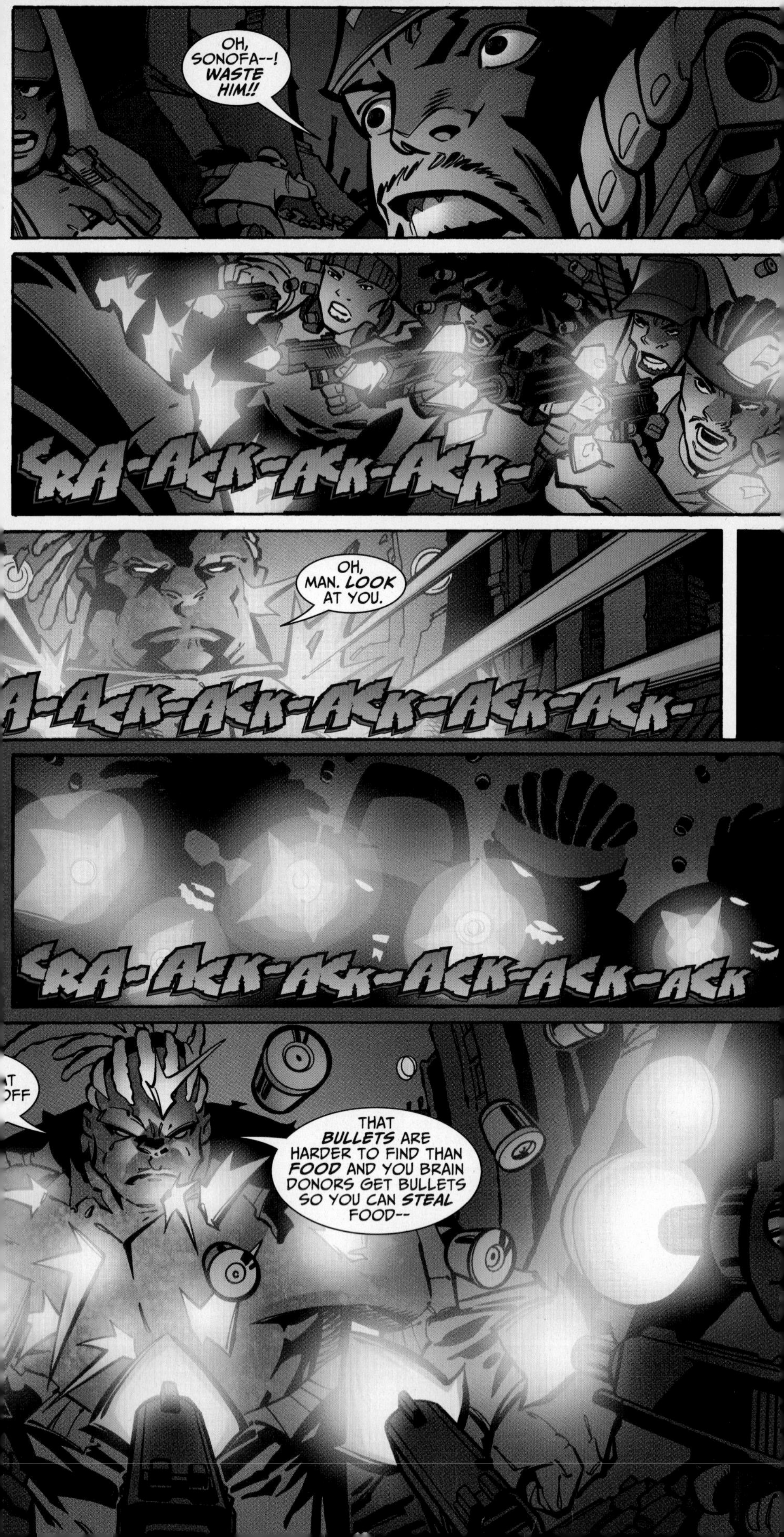
OH, SONOFA--! WASTE HIM!!
CRA-ACK-ACK-ACK-
OH, MAN. LOOK AT YOU.
A-ACK-ACK-ACK-ACK-ACK-
CRA-ACK-ACK-ACK-ACK-ACK
THAT BULLETS ARE HARDER TO FIND THAN FOOD AND YOU BRAIN DONORS GET BULLETS SO YOU CAN STEAL FOOD--

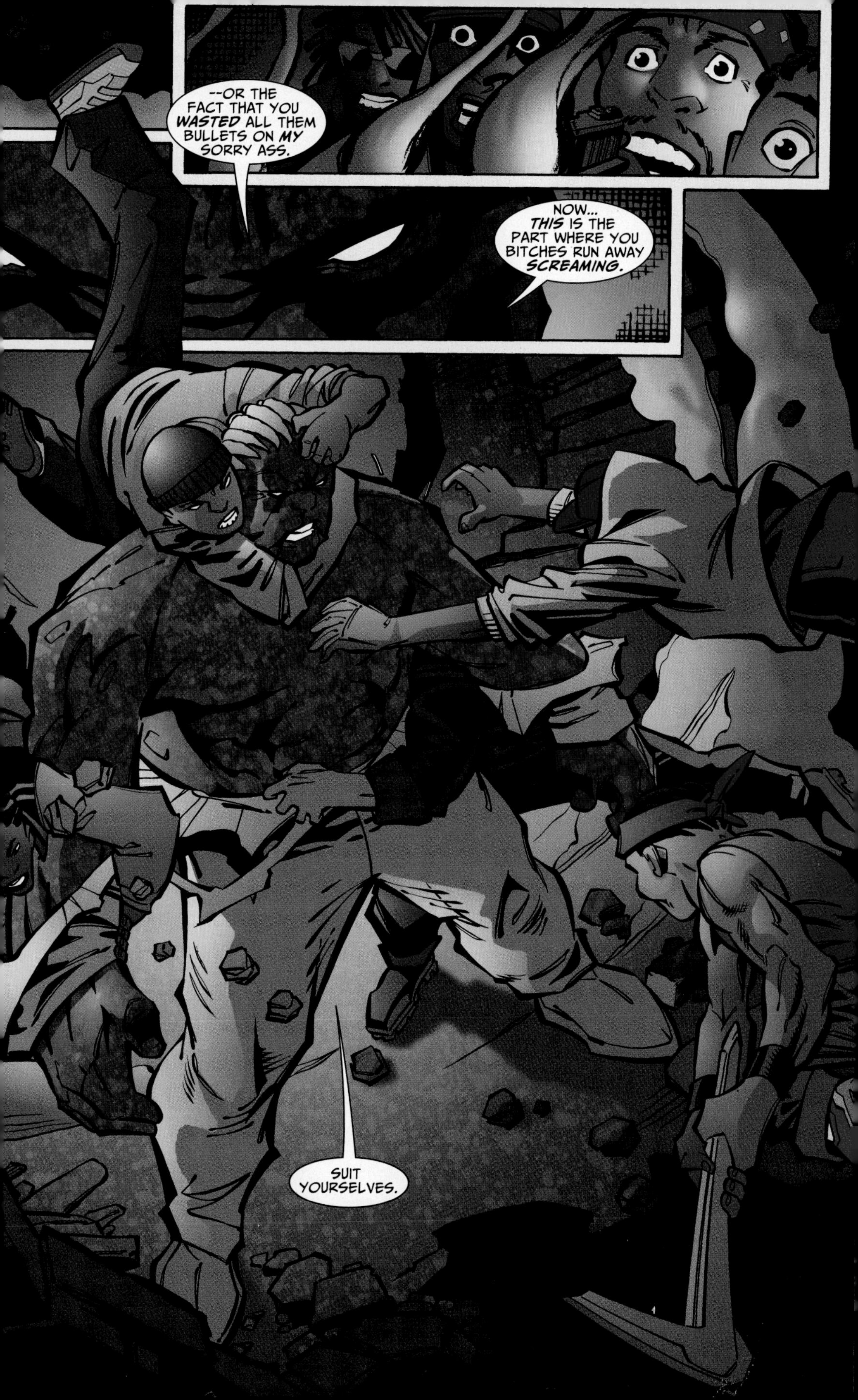
--OR THE FACT THAT YOU WASTED ALL THEM BULLETS ON MY SORRY ASS.
NOW... THIS IS THE PART WHERE YOU BITCHES RUN AWAY SCREAMING.
SUIT YOURSELVES.

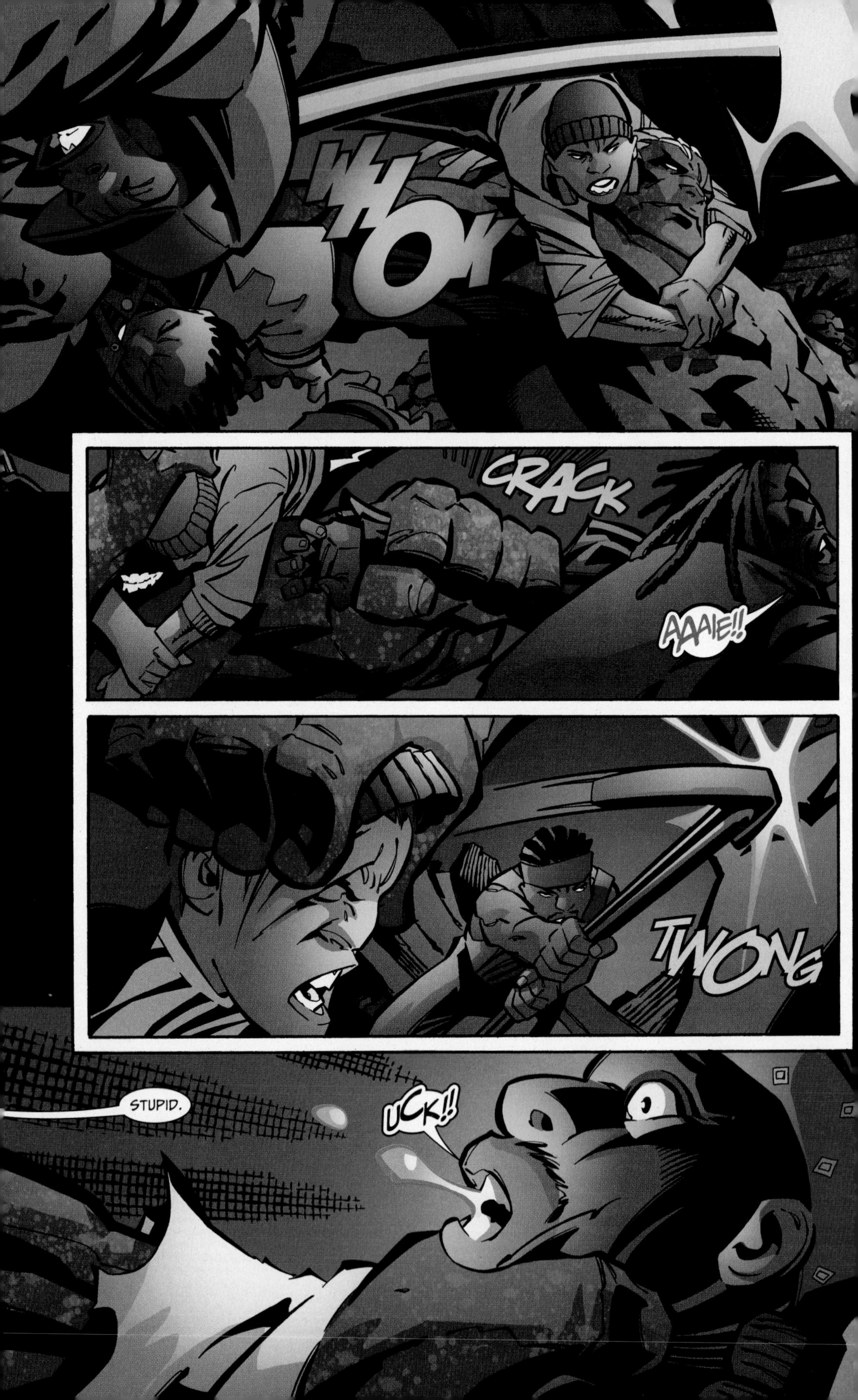
WHOK
CRACK
AAAIE!!
TWONG
STUPID.
UCK!!

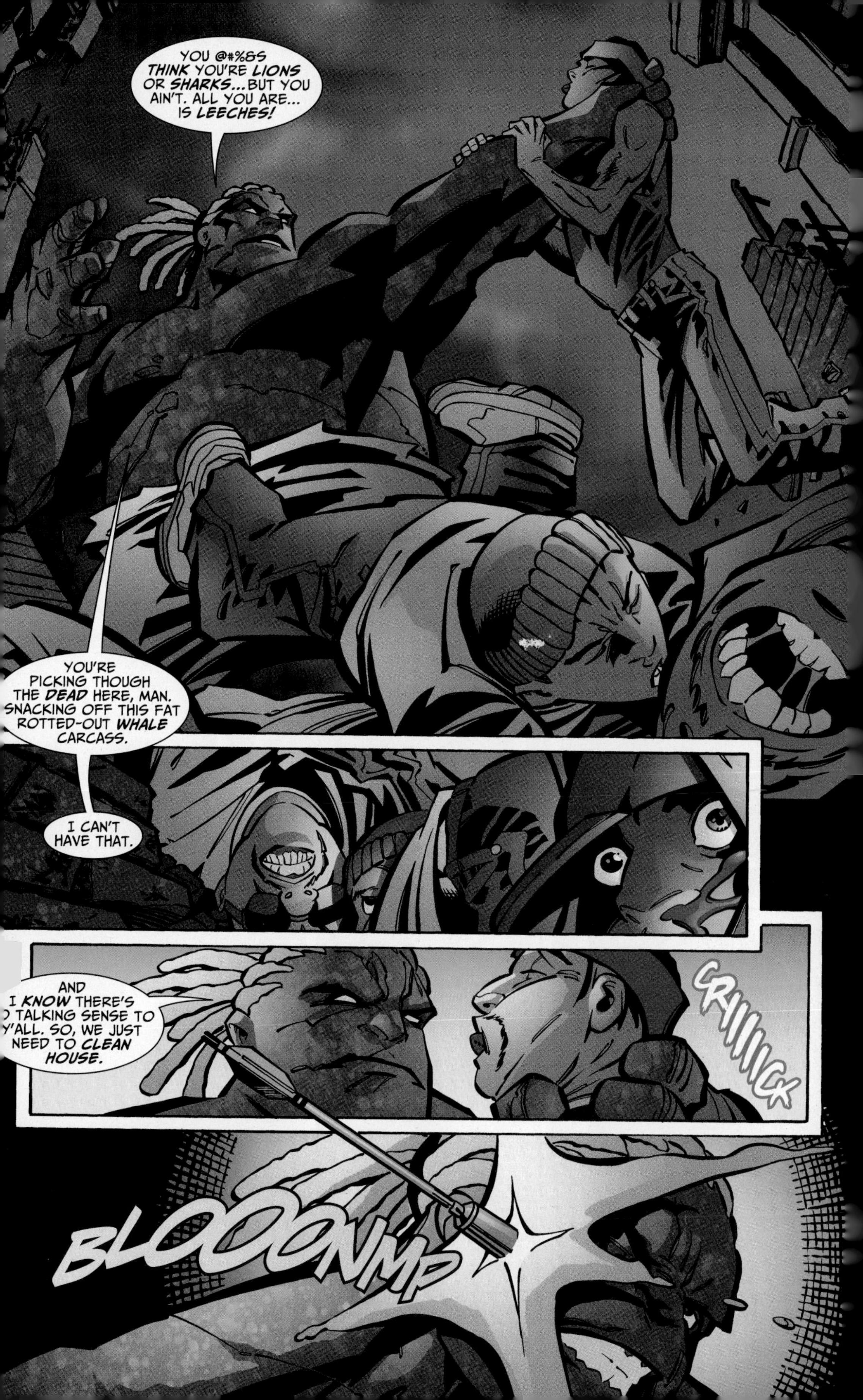

YOU @#%&S THINK YOU'RE LIONS OR SHARKS... BUT YOU AIN'T. ALL YOU ARE... IS LEECHES!
YOU'RE PICKING THOUGH THE DEAD HERE, MAN. SNACKING OFF THIS FAT ROTTED-OUT WHALE CARCASS.
I CAN'T HAVE THAT.
AND I KNOW THERE'S TALKING SENSE TO Y'ALL. SO, WE JUST NEED TO CLEAN HOUSE.
CRIIIIICK
BLOOOONMP

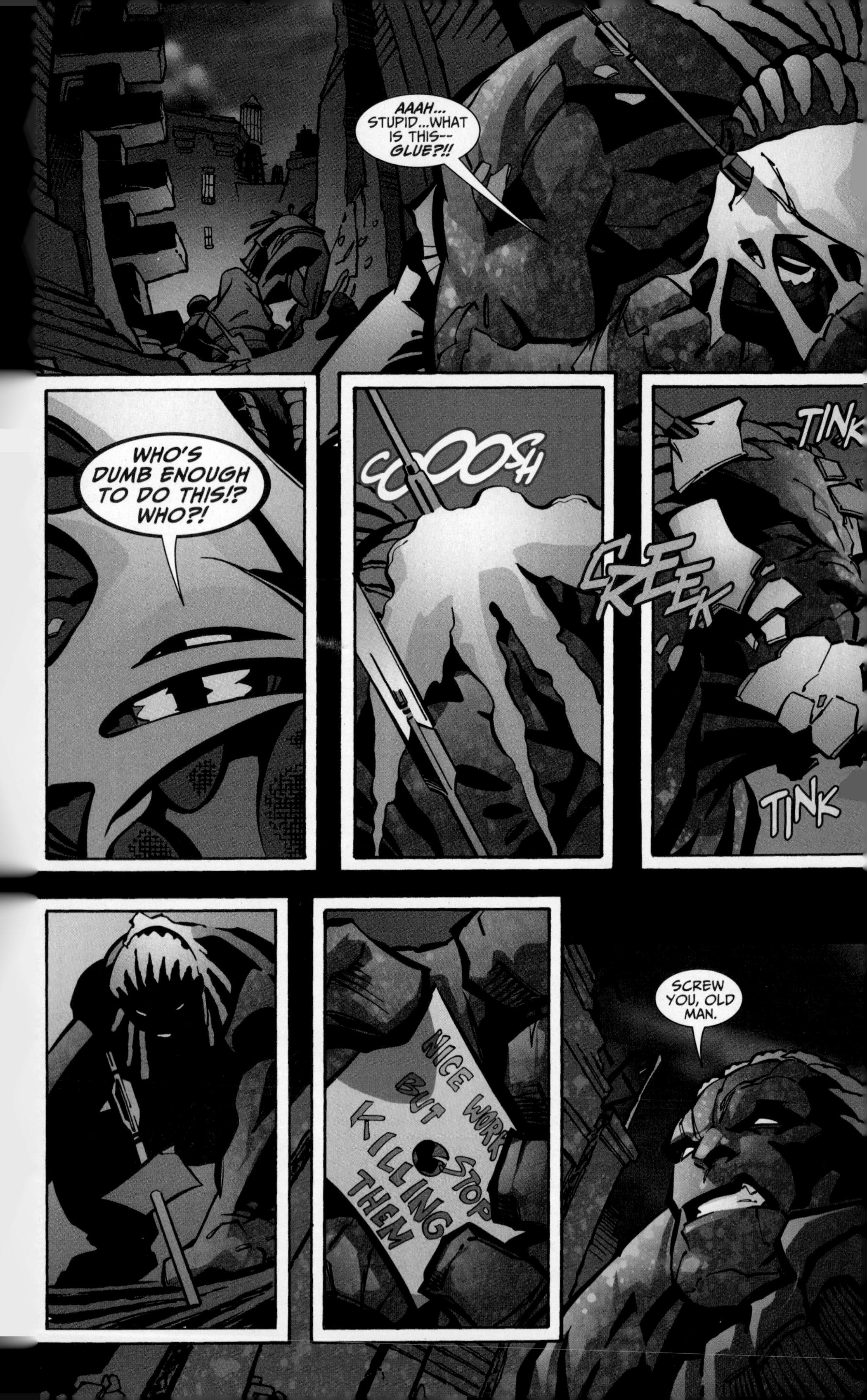
AAAH... STUPID...WHAT IS THIS-- GLUE?!!
WHO'S DUMB ENOUGH TO DO THIS!? WHO?!
COOOOSH
TINK
CREEK
TINK
NICE WORK BUT STOP KILLING THEM
SCREW YOU, OLD MAN.

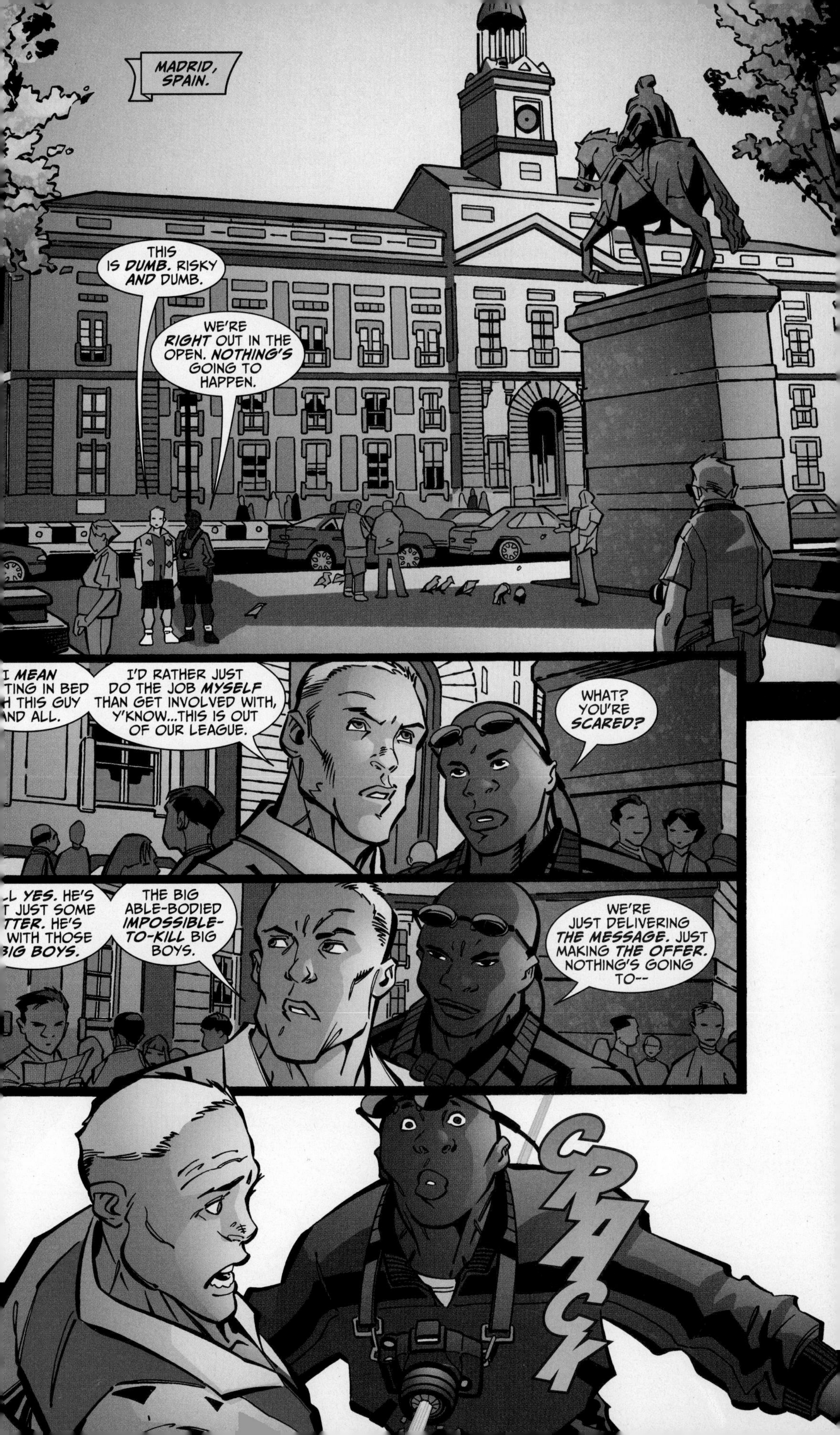
MADRID, SPAIN.
THIS IS DUMB. RISKY AND DUMB.
WE'RE RIGHT OUT IN THE OPEN. NOTHING'S GOING TO HAPPEN.
I MEAN
TING IN BED
H THIS GUY
AND ALL.
I'D RATHER JUST DO THE JOB MYSELF THAN GET INVOLVED WITH, Y'KNOW...THIS IS OUT OF OUR LEAGUE.
WHAT? YOU'RE SCARED?
L YES. HE'S
T JUST SOME
TTER. HE'S
WITH THOSE
BIG BOYS.
THE BIG ABLE-BODIED IMPOSSIBLE-TO-KILL BIG BOYS.
WE'RE JUST DELIVERING THE MESSAGE. JUST MAKING THE OFFER. NOTHING'S GOING TO--
CRACK

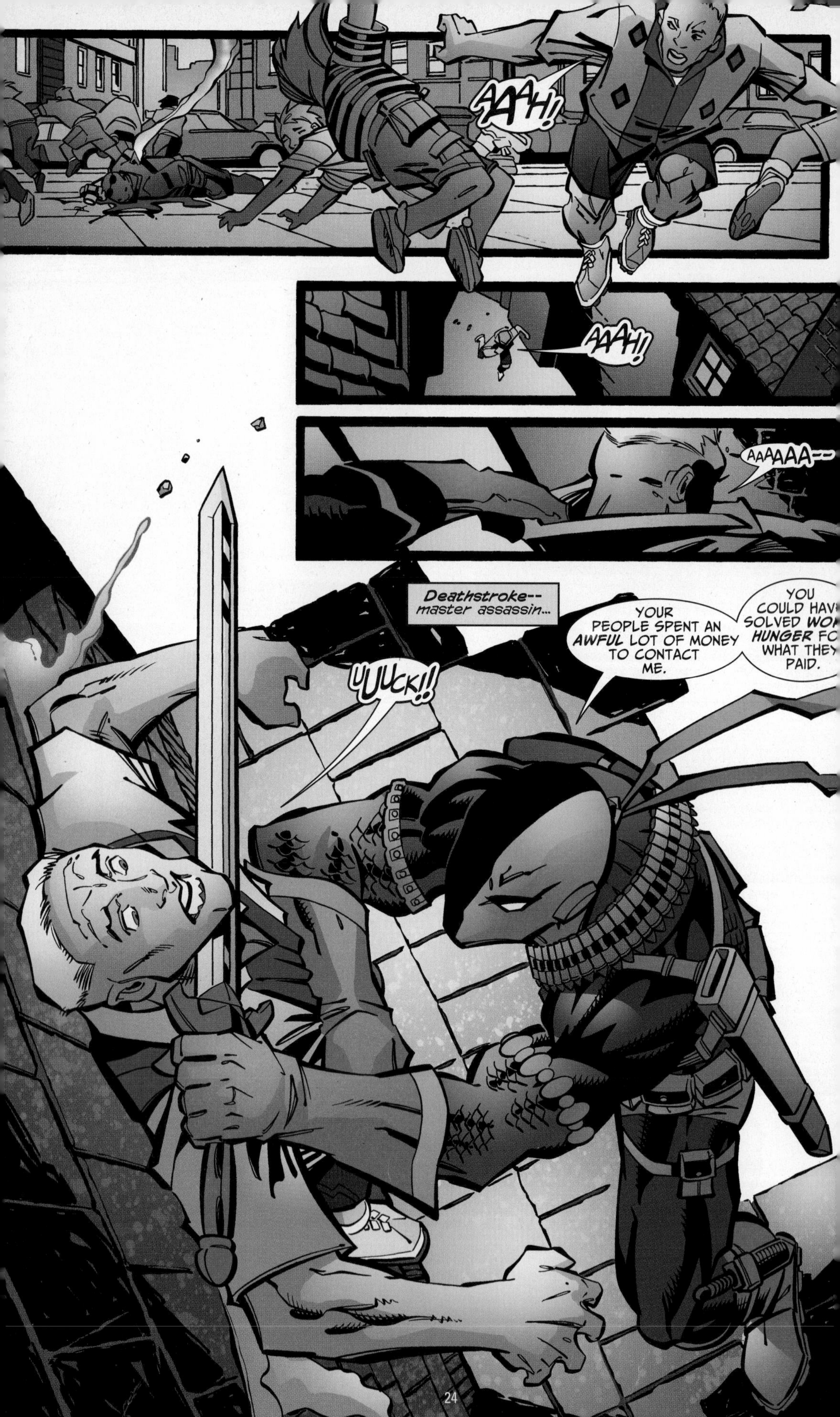
AAAH!
AAAH!
AAAAAA--
Deathstroke--
master assassin...
UUUCK!!
YOUR PEOPLE SPENT AN AWFUL LOT OF MONEY TO CONTACT ME.
YOU COULD HAV SOLVED WO HUNGER FO WHAT THEY PAID.

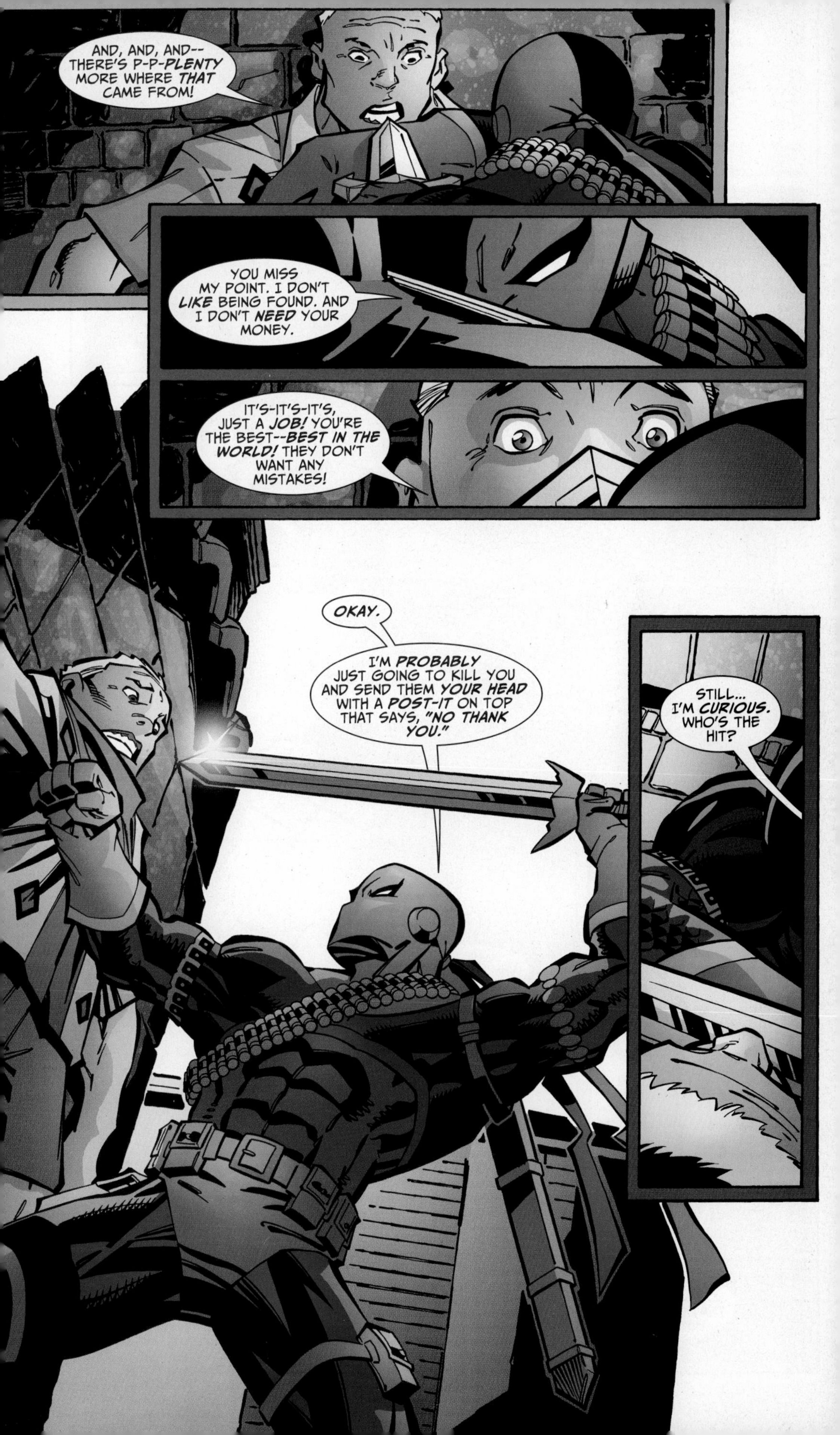
AND, AND, AND-- THERE'S P-P-PLENTY MORE WHERE THAT CAME FROM!
YOU MISS MY POINT. I DON'T LIKE BEING FOUND. AND I DON'T NEED YOUR MONEY.
IT'S-IT'S-IT'S, JUST A JOB! YOU'RE THE BEST--BEST IN THE WORLD! THEY DON'T WANT ANY MISTAKES!
OKAY.
I'M PROBABLY JUST GOING TO KILL YOU AND SEND THEM YOUR HEAD WITH A POST-IT ON TOP THAT SAYS, "NO THANK YOU."
STILL... I'M CURIOUS. WHO'S THE HIT?

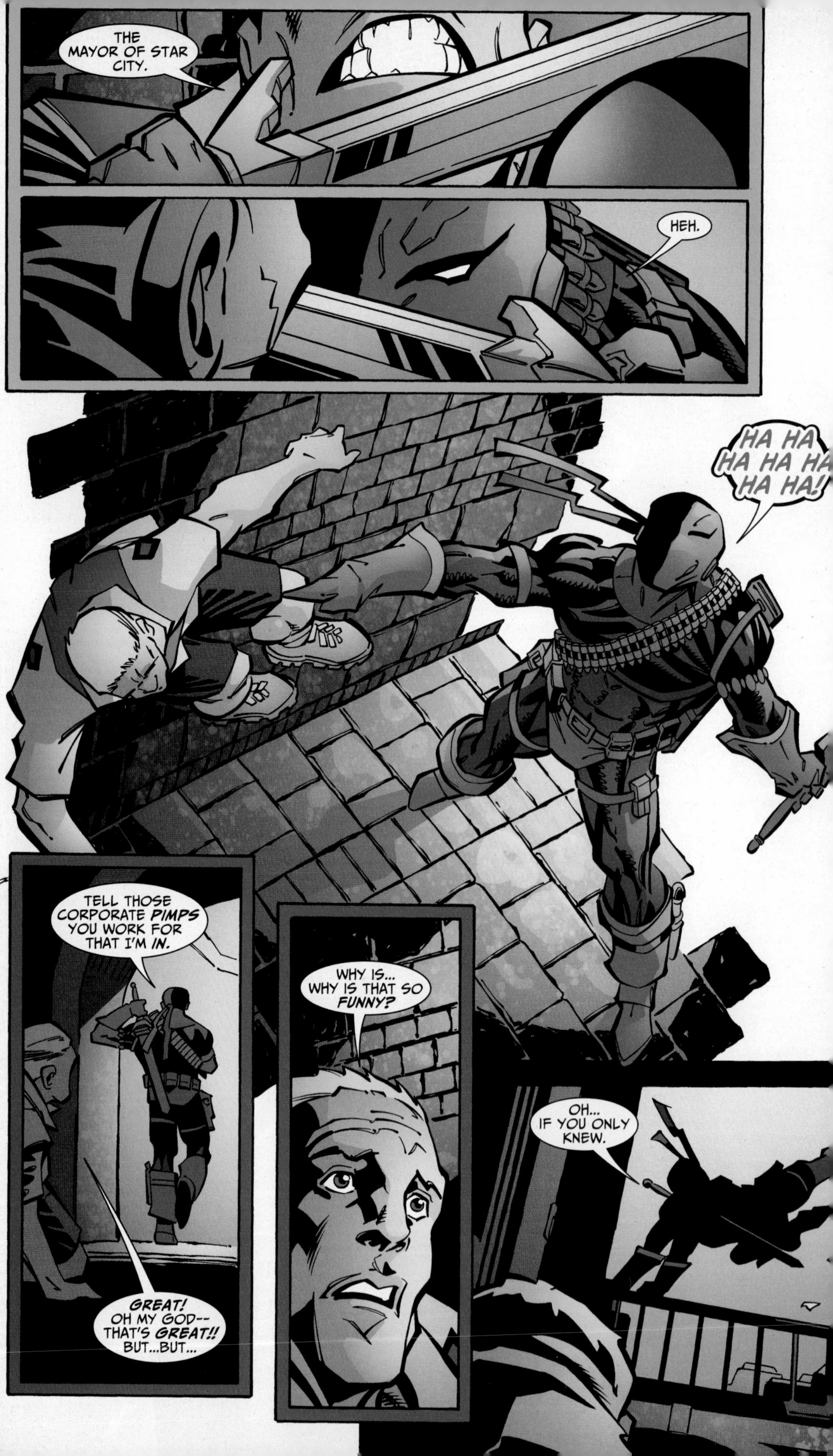
THE MAYOR OF STAR CITY.
HEH.
HA HA HA HA HA HA HA!
TELL THOSE CORPORATE PIMPS YOU WORK FOR THAT I'M IN.
GREAT! OH MY GOD-- THAT'S GREAT!! BUT...BUT...
WHY IS... WHY IS THAT SO FUNNY?
OH... IF YOU ONLY KNEW.

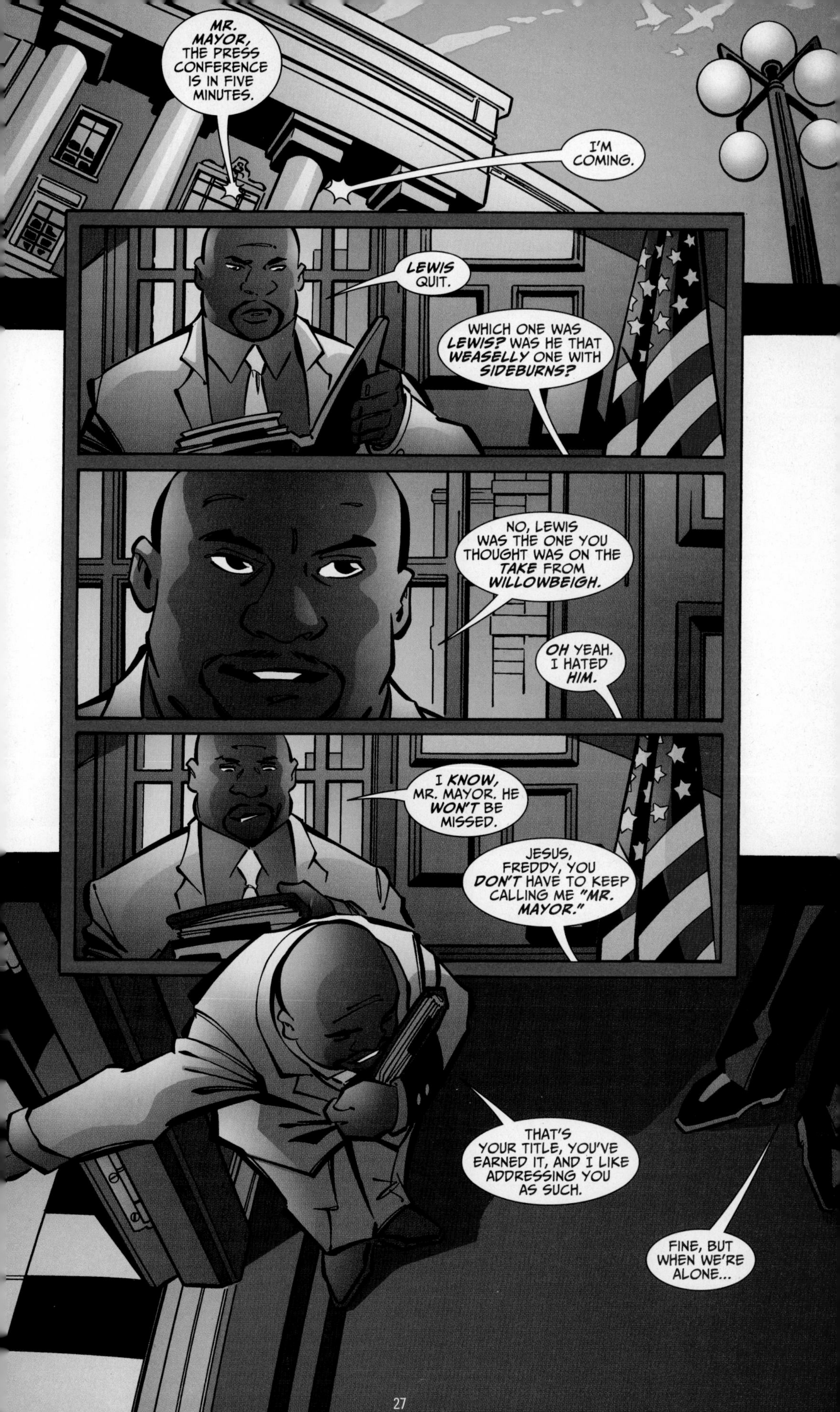
MR. MAYOR, THE PRESS CONFERENCE IS IN FIVE MINUTES.
I'M COMING.
LEWIS QUIT.
WHICH ONE WAS LEWIS? WAS HE THAT WEASELLY ONE WITH SIDEBURNS?
NO, LEWIS WAS THE ONE YOU THOUGHT WAS ON THE TAKE FROM WILLOWBEIGH.
OH YEAH. I HATED HIM.
I KNOW, MR. MAYOR. HE WON'T BE MISSED.
JESUS, FREDDY, YOU DON'T HAVE TO KEEP CALLING ME "MR. MAYOR."
THAT'S YOUR TITLE, YOU'VE EARNED IT, AND I LIKE ADDRESSING YOU AS SUCH.
FINE, BUT WHEN WE'RE ALONE...

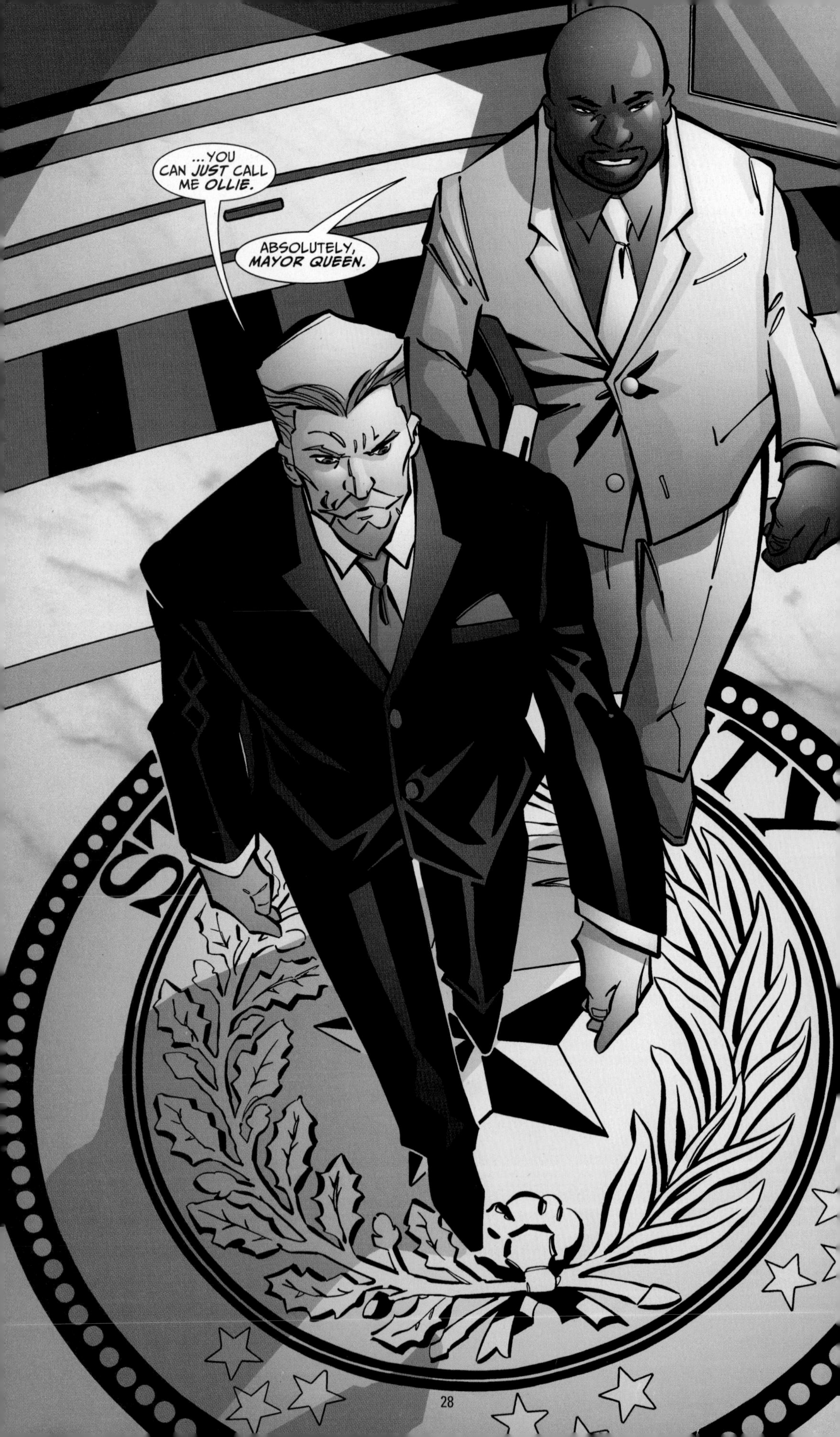
...YOU CAN JUST CALL ME OLLIE.
ABSOLUTELY, MAYOR QUEEN.

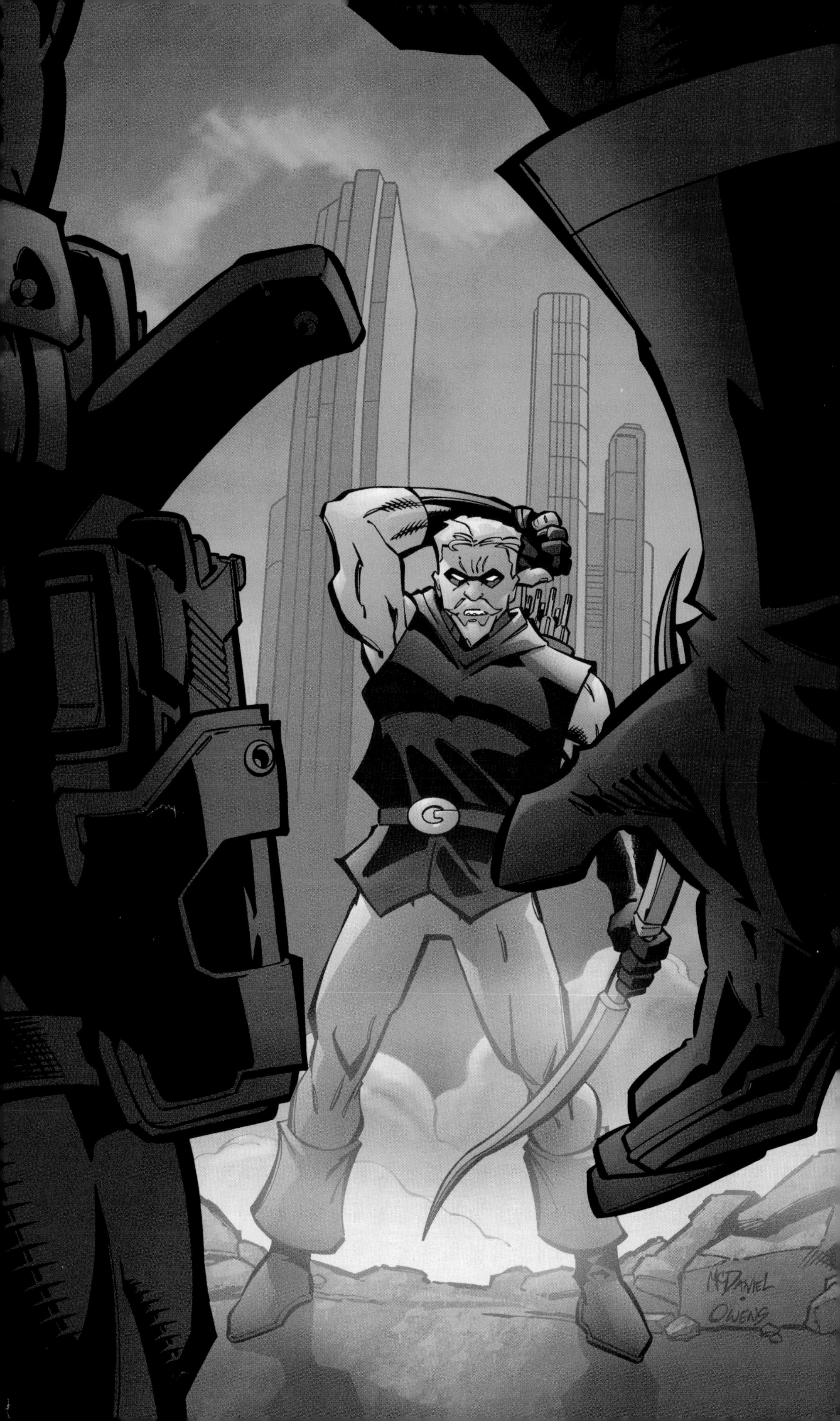
McDANIEL
OWENS

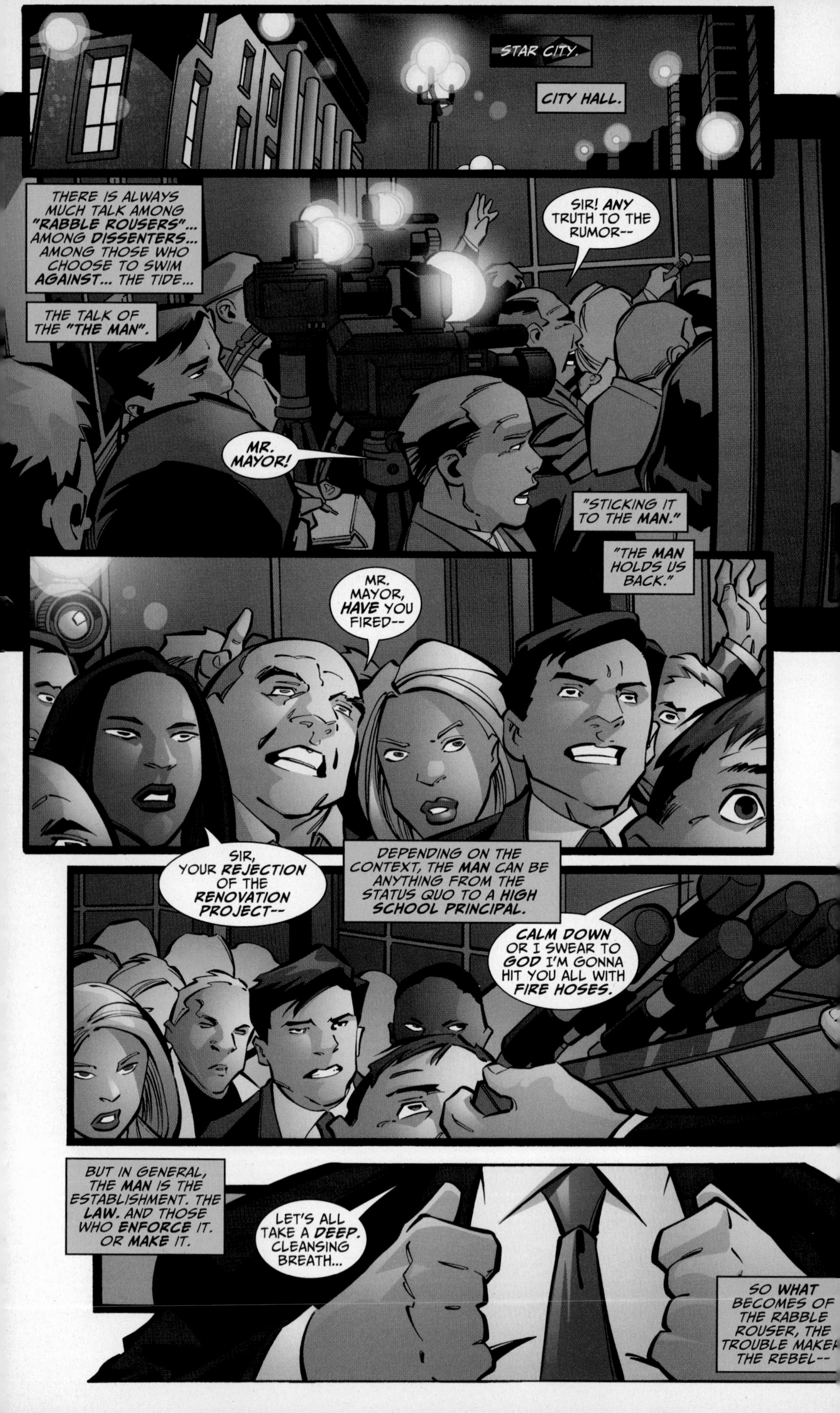

STAR CITY.
CITY HALL.
THERE IS ALWAYS MUCH TALK AMONG "RABBLE ROUSERS"... AMONG DISSENTERS... AMONG THOSE WHO CHOOSE TO SWIM AGAINST... THE TIDE...
THE TALK OF THE "THE MAN".
SIR! ANY TRUTH TO THE RUMOR--
MR. MAYOR!
"STICKING IT TO THE MAN."
"THE MAN HOLDS US BACK."
MR. MAYOR, HAVE YOU FIRED--
SIR, YOUR REJECTION OF THE RENOVATION PROJECT--
DEPENDING ON THE CONTEXT, THE MAN CAN BE ANYTHING FROM THE STATUS QUO TO A HIGH SCHOOL PRINCIPAL.
CALM DOWN OR I SWEAR TO GOD I'M GONNA HIT YOU ALL WITH FIRE HOSES.
BUT IN GENERAL, THE MAN IS THE ESTABLISHMENT. THE LAW. AND THOSE WHO ENFORCE IT. OR MAKE IT.
LET'S ALL TAKE A DEEP, CLEANSING BREATH...
SO WHAT BECOMES OF THE RABBLE ROUSER, THE TROUBLE MAKE THE REBEL--

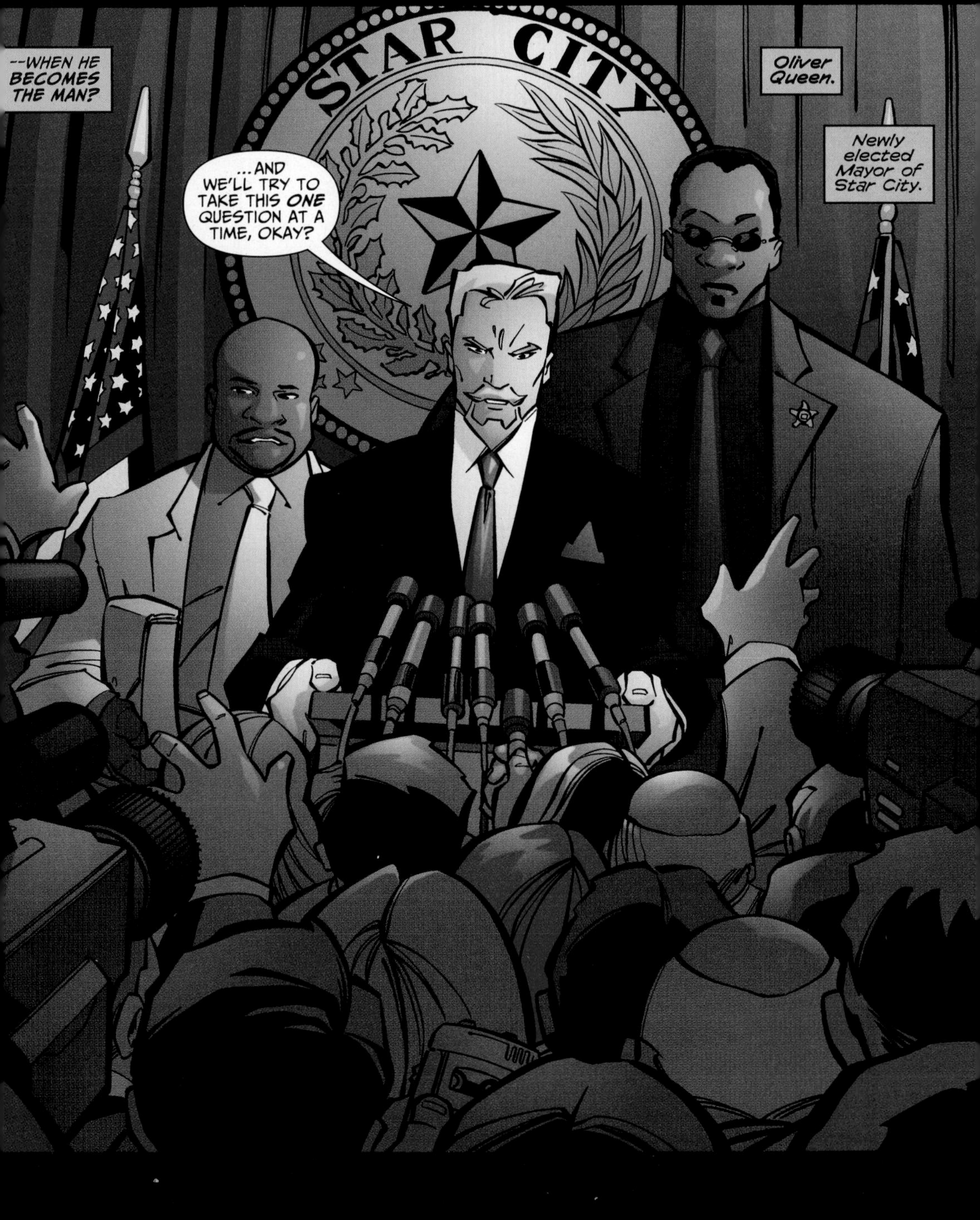
--WHEN HE BECOMES THE MAN?
STAR CITY
...AND WE'LL TRY TO TAKE THIS ONE QUESTION AT A TIME, OKAY?
Oliver Queen.
Newly elected Mayor of Star City.

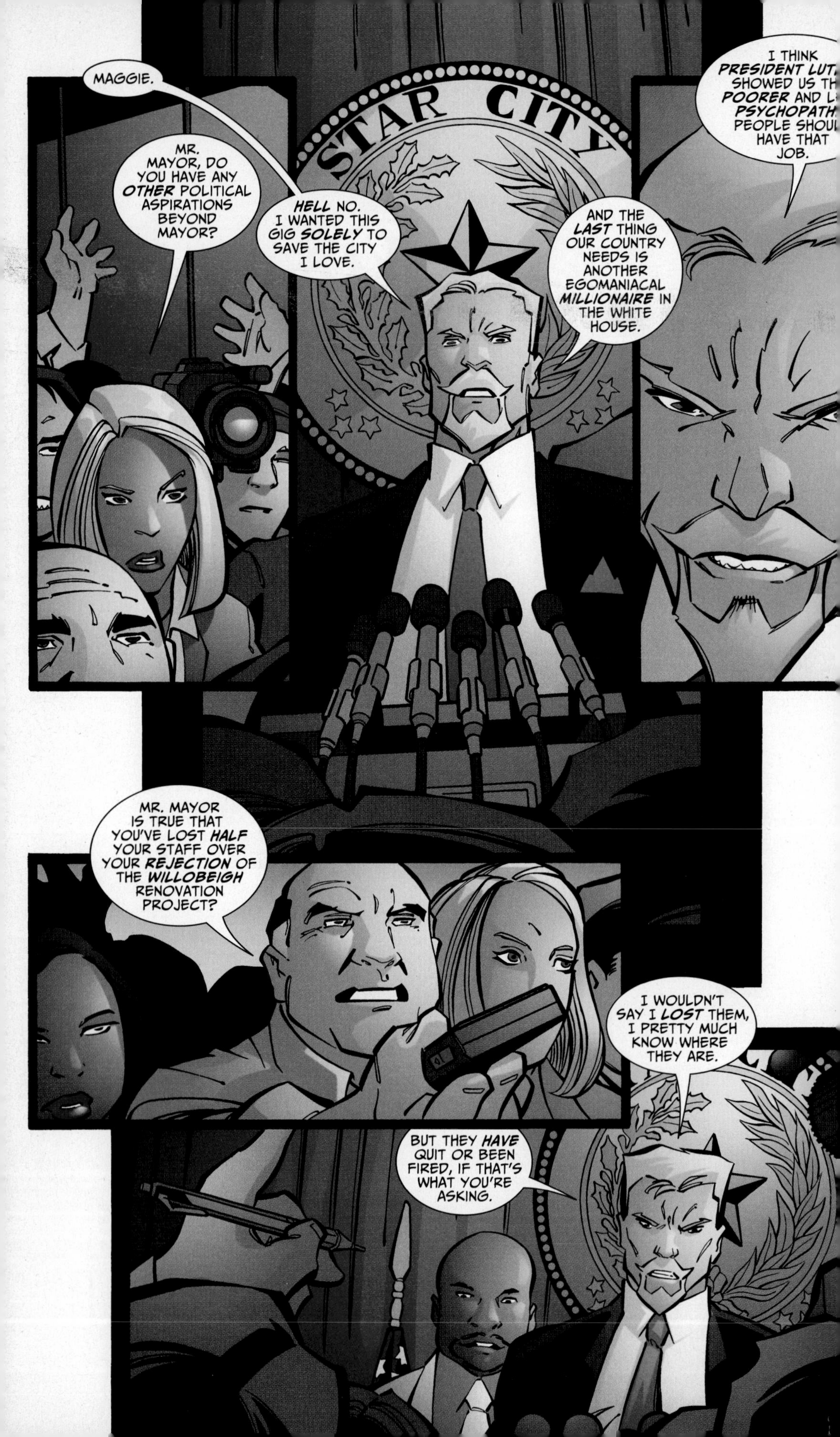
MAGGIE.
MR. MAYOR, DO YOU HAVE ANY OTHER POLITICAL ASPIRATIONS BEYOND MAYOR?
HELL NO. I WANTED THIS GIG SOLELY TO SAVE THE CITY I LOVE.
AND THE LAST THING OUR COUNTRY NEEDS IS ANOTHER EGOMANIACAL MILLIONAIRE IN THE WHITE HOUSE.
STAR CITY
MR. MAYOR IS TRUE THAT YOU'VE LOST HALF YOUR STAFF OVER YOUR REJECTION OF THE WILLOBEIGH RENOVATION PROJECT?
I WOULDN'T SAY I LOST THEM, I PRETTY MUCH KNOW WHERE THEY ARE.
BUT THEY HAVE QUIT OR BEEN FIRED, IF THAT'S WHAT YOU'RE ASKING.

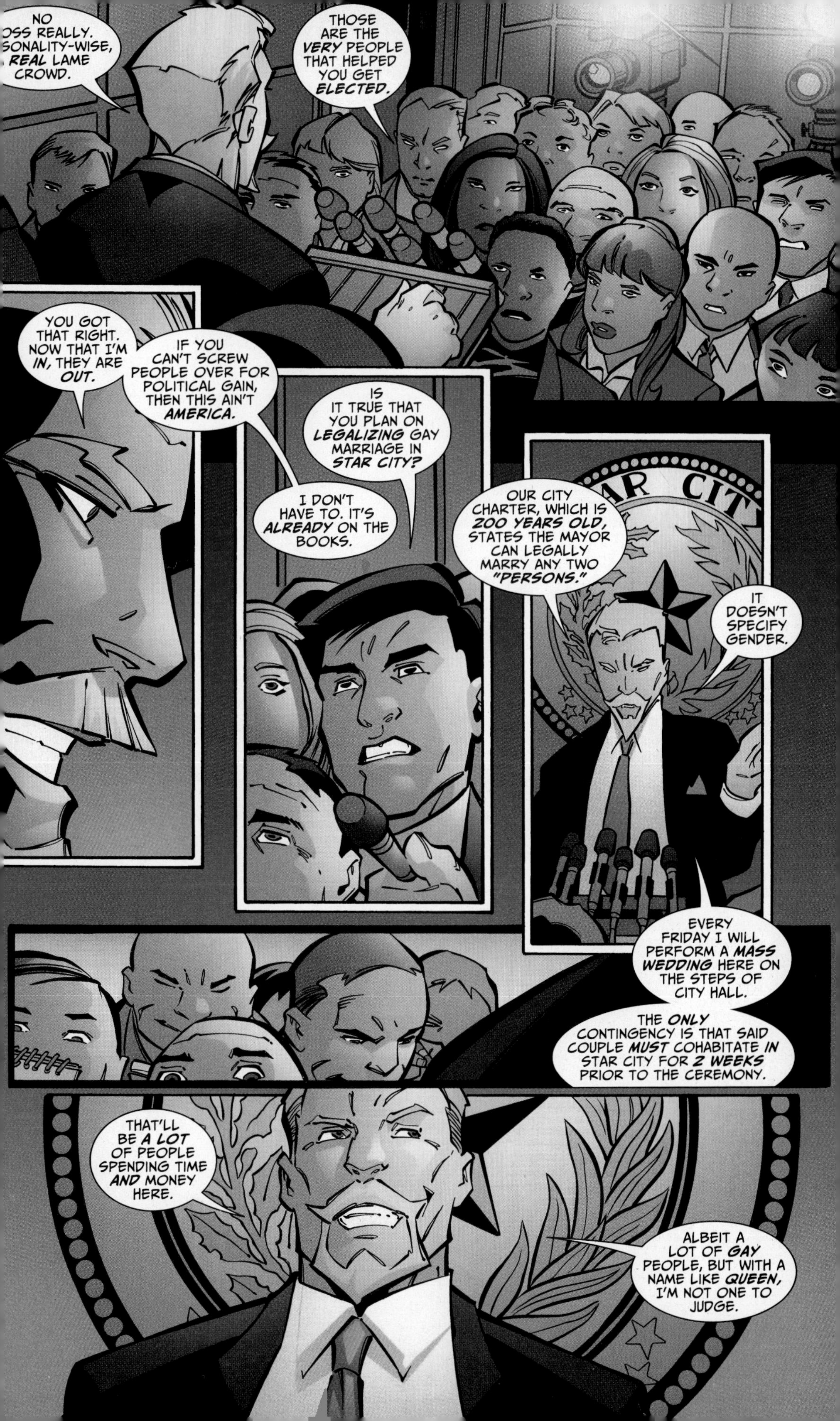

NO [L]OSS REALLY. [PER]SONALITY-WISE, *REAL* LAME CROWD.
THOSE ARE THE *VERY* PEOPLE THAT HELPED YOU GET *ELECTED*.
YOU GOT THAT RIGHT. NOW THAT I'M *IN*, THEY ARE *OUT*.
IF YOU CAN'T SCREW PEOPLE OVER FOR POLITICAL GAIN, THEN THIS AIN'T *AMERICA*.
IS IT TRUE THAT YOU PLAN ON *LEGALIZING* GAY MARRIAGE IN *STAR CITY?*
I DON'T HAVE TO. IT'S *ALREADY* ON THE BOOKS.
OUR CITY CHARTER, WHICH IS *200 YEARS OLD*, STATES THE MAYOR CAN LEGALLY MARRY ANY TWO *"PERSONS."*
IT DOESN'T SPECIFY GENDER.
EVERY FRIDAY I WILL PERFORM A *MASS WEDDING* HERE ON THE STEPS OF CITY HALL.
THE *ONLY* CONTINGENCY IS THAT SAID COUPLE *MUST* COHABITATE *IN* STAR CITY FOR *2 WEEKS* PRIOR TO THE CEREMONY.
THAT'LL BE *A LOT* OF PEOPLE SPENDING TIME *AND* MONEY HERE.
ALBEIT A LOT OF *GAY* PEOPLE, BUT WITH A NAME LIKE *QUEEN*, I'M NOT ONE TO JUDGE.

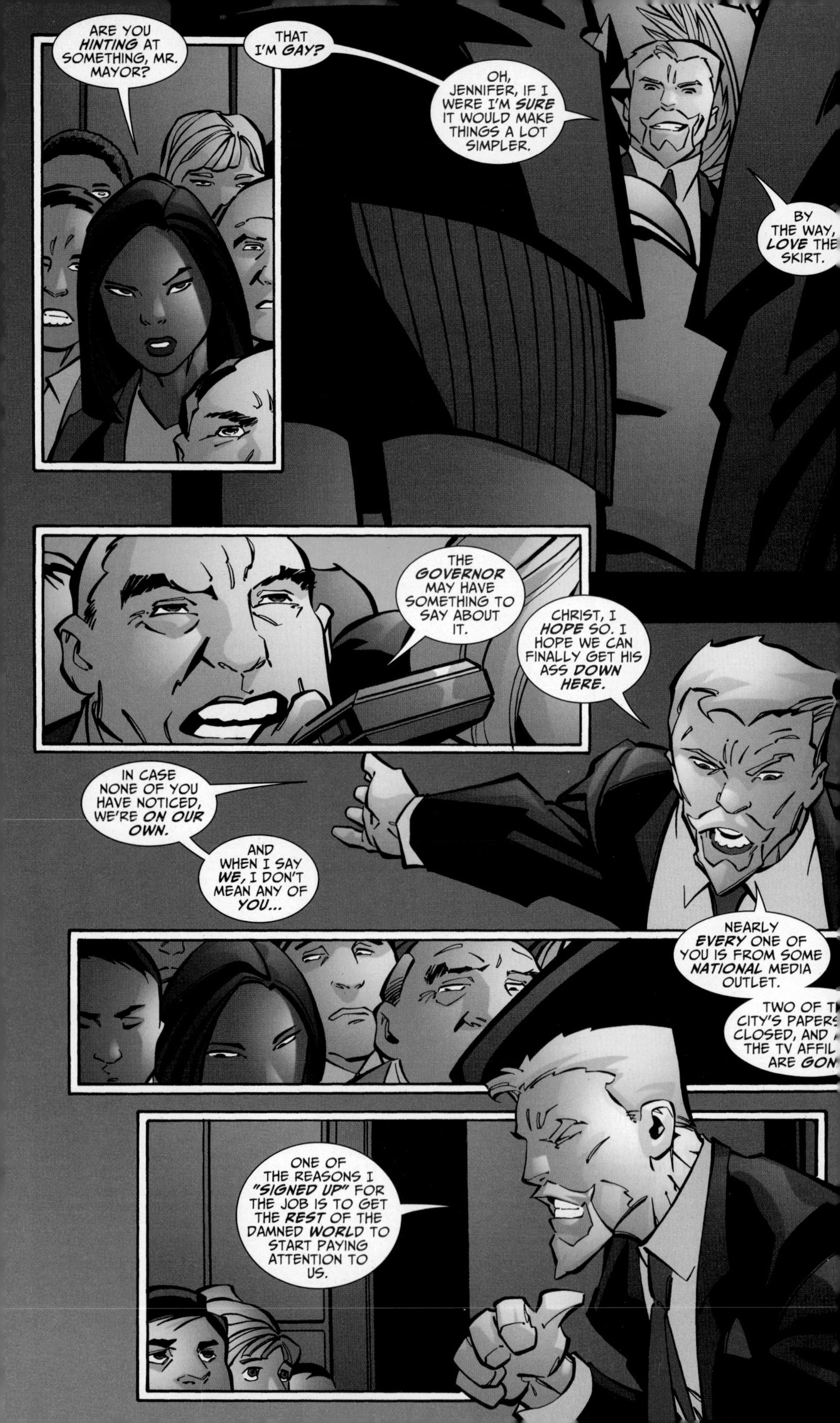
ARE YOU HINTING AT SOMETHING, MR. MAYOR?
THAT I'M GAY?
OH, JENNIFER, IF I WERE I'M SURE IT WOULD MAKE THINGS A LOT SIMPLER.
BY THE WAY, LOVE THE SKIRT.
THE GOVERNOR MAY HAVE SOMETHING TO SAY ABOUT IT.
CHRIST, I HOPE SO. I HOPE WE CAN FINALLY GET HIS ASS DOWN HERE.
IN CASE NONE OF YOU HAVE NOTICED, WE'RE ON OUR OWN.
AND WHEN I SAY WE, I DON'T MEAN ANY OF YOU...
NEARLY EVERY ONE OF YOU IS FROM SOME NATIONAL MEDIA OUTLET.
TWO OF T
CITY'S PAPERS
CLOSED, AND
THE TV AFFIL
ARE GON
ONE OF THE REASONS I "SIGNED UP" FOR THE JOB IS TO GET THE REST OF THE DAMNED WORLD TO START PAYING ATTENTION TO US.

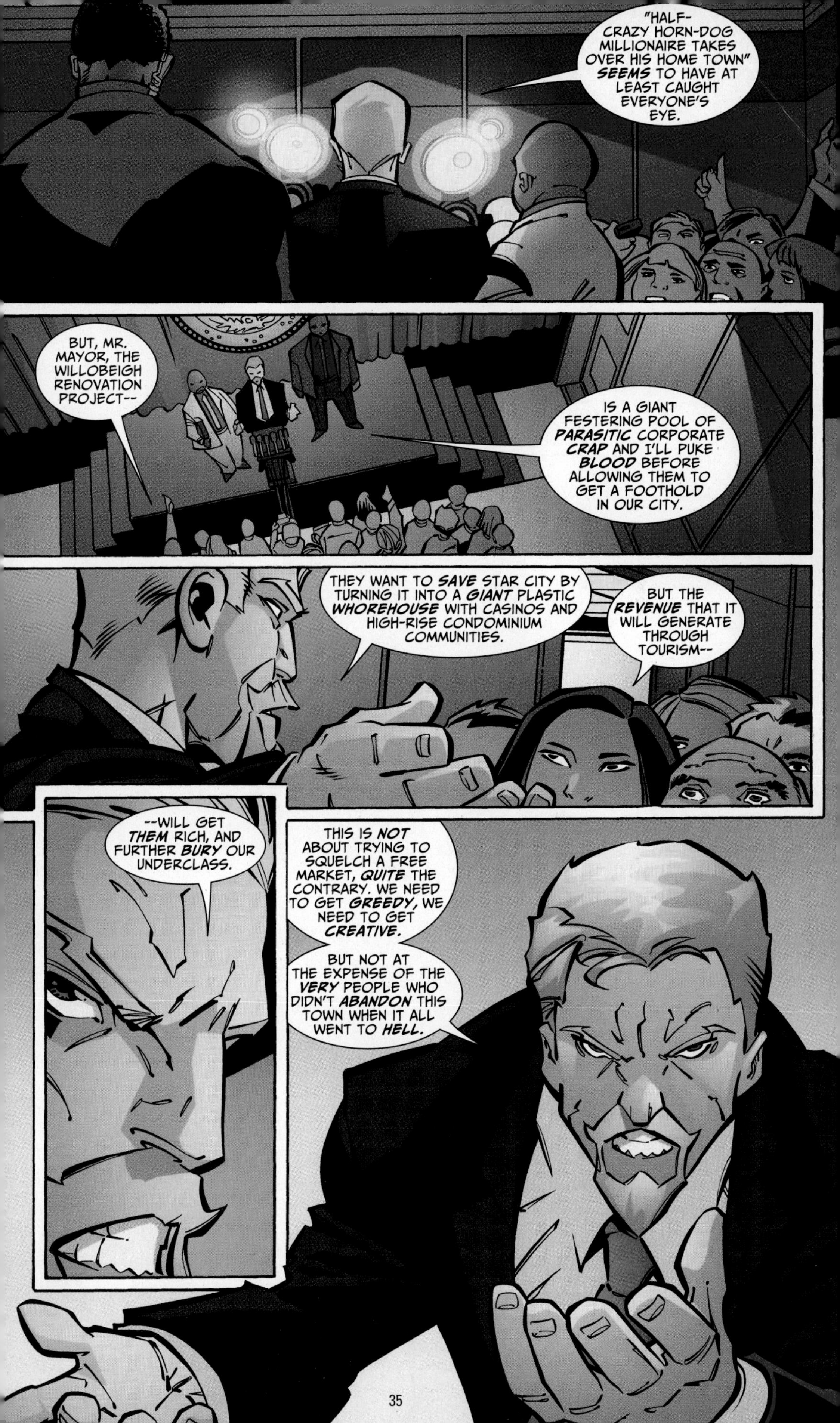
"HALF-CRAZY HORN-DOG MILLIONAIRE TAKES OVER HIS HOME TOWN" SEEMS TO HAVE AT LEAST CAUGHT EVERYONE'S EYE.
BUT, MR. MAYOR, THE WILLOBEIGH RENOVATION PROJECT--
IS A GIANT FESTERING POOL OF PARASITIC CORPORATE CRAP AND I'LL PUKE BLOOD BEFORE ALLOWING THEM TO GET A FOOTHOLD IN OUR CITY.
THEY WANT TO SAVE STAR CITY BY TURNING IT INTO A GIANT PLASTIC WHOREHOUSE WITH CASINOS AND HIGH-RISE CONDOMINIUM COMMUNITIES.
BUT THE REVENUE THAT IT WILL GENERATE THROUGH TOURISM--
--WILL GET THEM RICH, AND FURTHER BURY OUR UNDERCLASS.
THIS IS NOT ABOUT TRYING TO SQUELCH A FREE MARKET, QUITE THE CONTRARY. WE NEED TO GET GREEDY, WE NEED TO GET CREATIVE.
BUT NOT AT THE EXPENSE OF THE VERY PEOPLE WHO DIDN'T ABANDON THIS TOWN WHEN IT ALL WENT TO HELL.

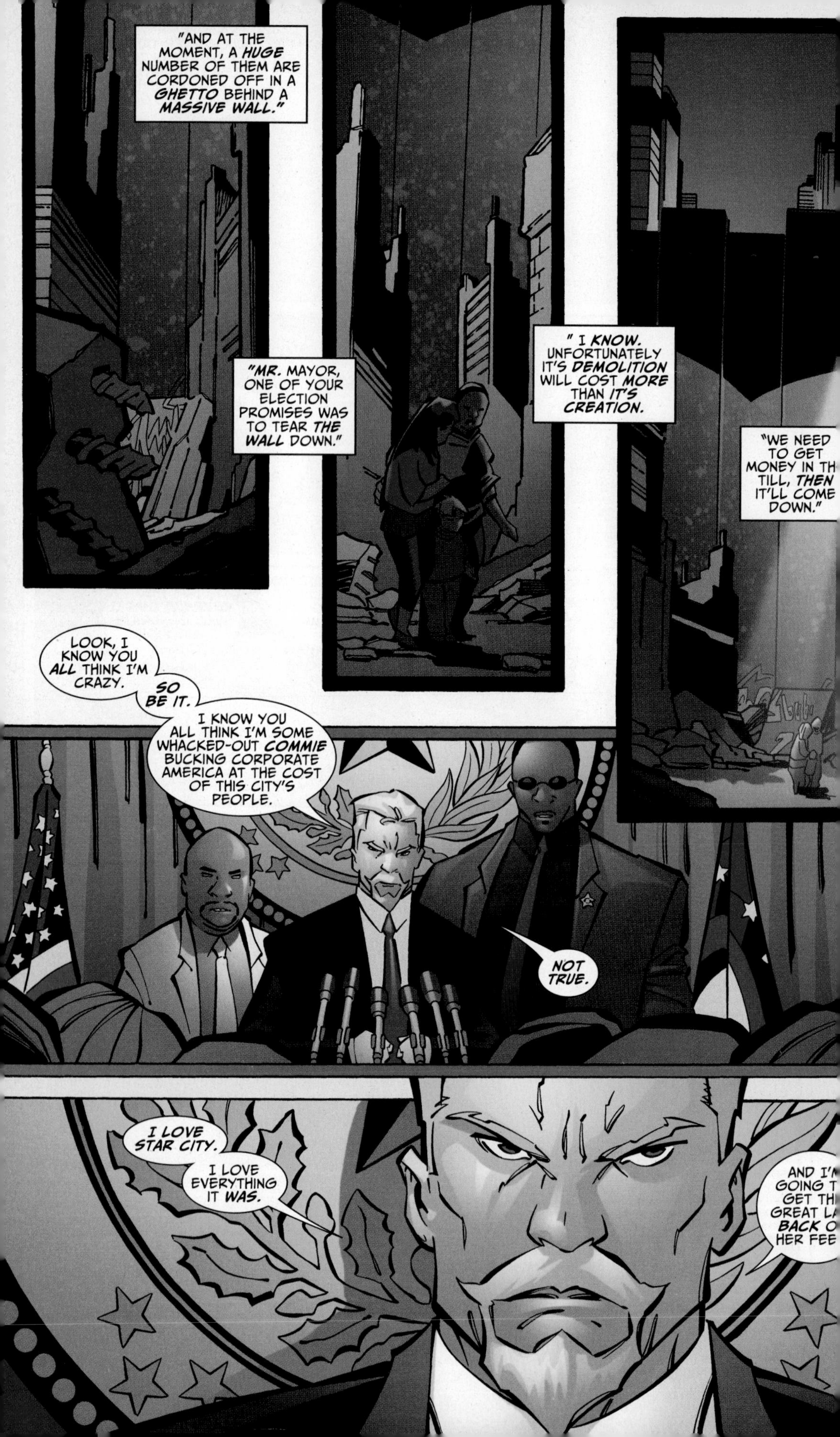
"AND AT THE MOMENT, A HUGE NUMBER OF THEM ARE CORDONED OFF IN A GHETTO BEHIND A MASSIVE WALL."
"MR. MAYOR, ONE OF YOUR ELECTION PROMISES WAS TO TEAR THE WALL DOWN."
" I KNOW. UNFORTUNATELY IT'S DEMOLITION WILL COST MORE THAN IT'S CREATION.
"WE NEED TO GET MONEY IN TH TILL, THEN IT'LL COME DOWN."
LOOK, I KNOW YOU ALL THINK I'M CRAZY.
SO BE IT.
I KNOW YOU ALL THINK I'M SOME WHACKED-OUT COMMIE BUCKING CORPORATE AMERICA AT THE COST OF THIS CITY'S PEOPLE.
NOT TRUE.
I LOVE STAR CITY.
I LOVE EVERYTHING IT WAS.
AND I'M GOING T GET TH GREAT LA BACK O HER FEE

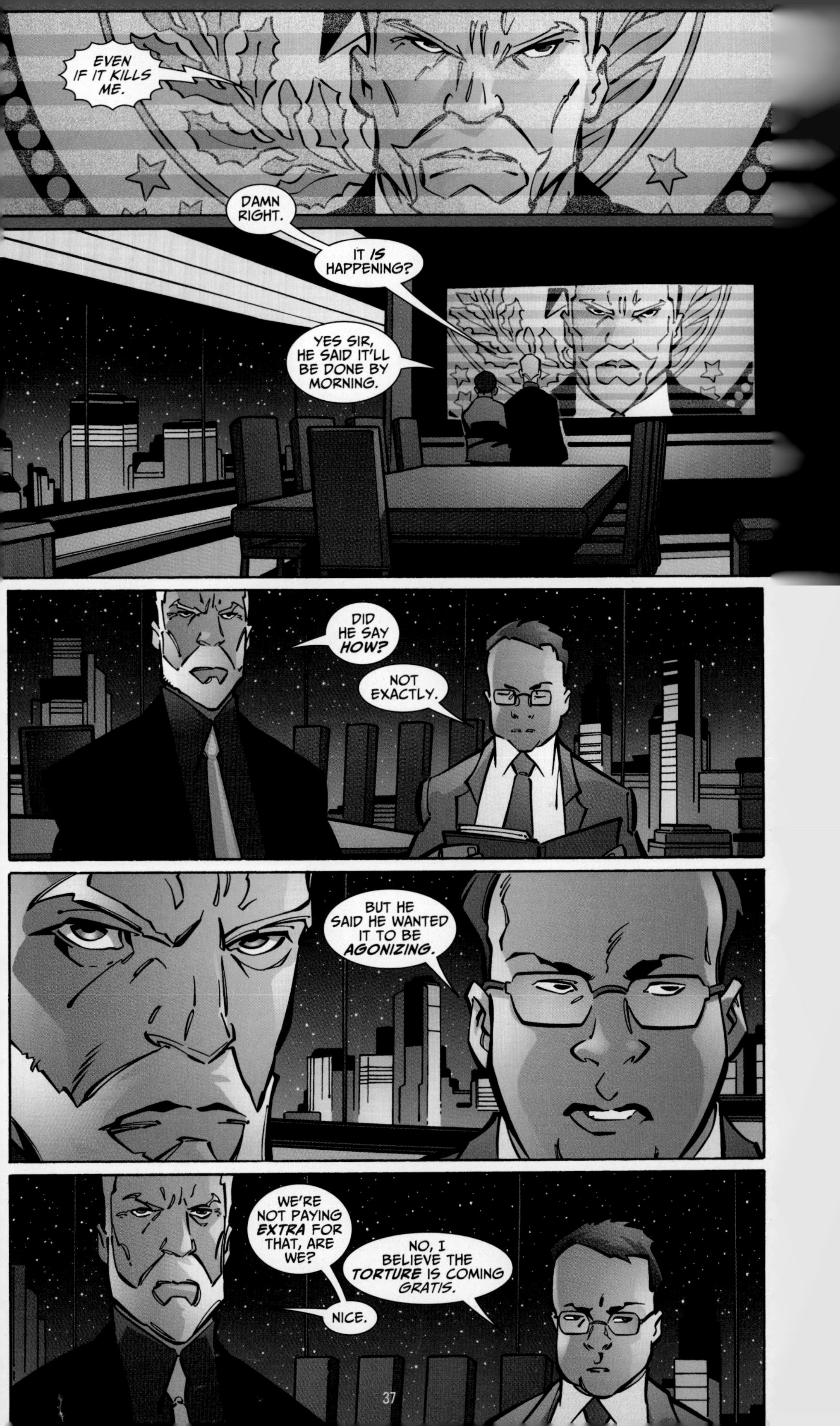

EVEN IF IT KILLS ME.
DAMN RIGHT.
IT IS HAPPENING?
YES SIR, HE SAID IT'LL BE DONE BY MORNING.
DID HE SAY HOW?
NOT EXACTLY.
BUT HE SAID HE WANTED IT TO BE AGONIZING.
WE'RE NOT PAYING EXTRA FOR THAT, ARE WE?
NO, I BELIEVE THE TORTURE IS COMING GRATIS.
NICE.

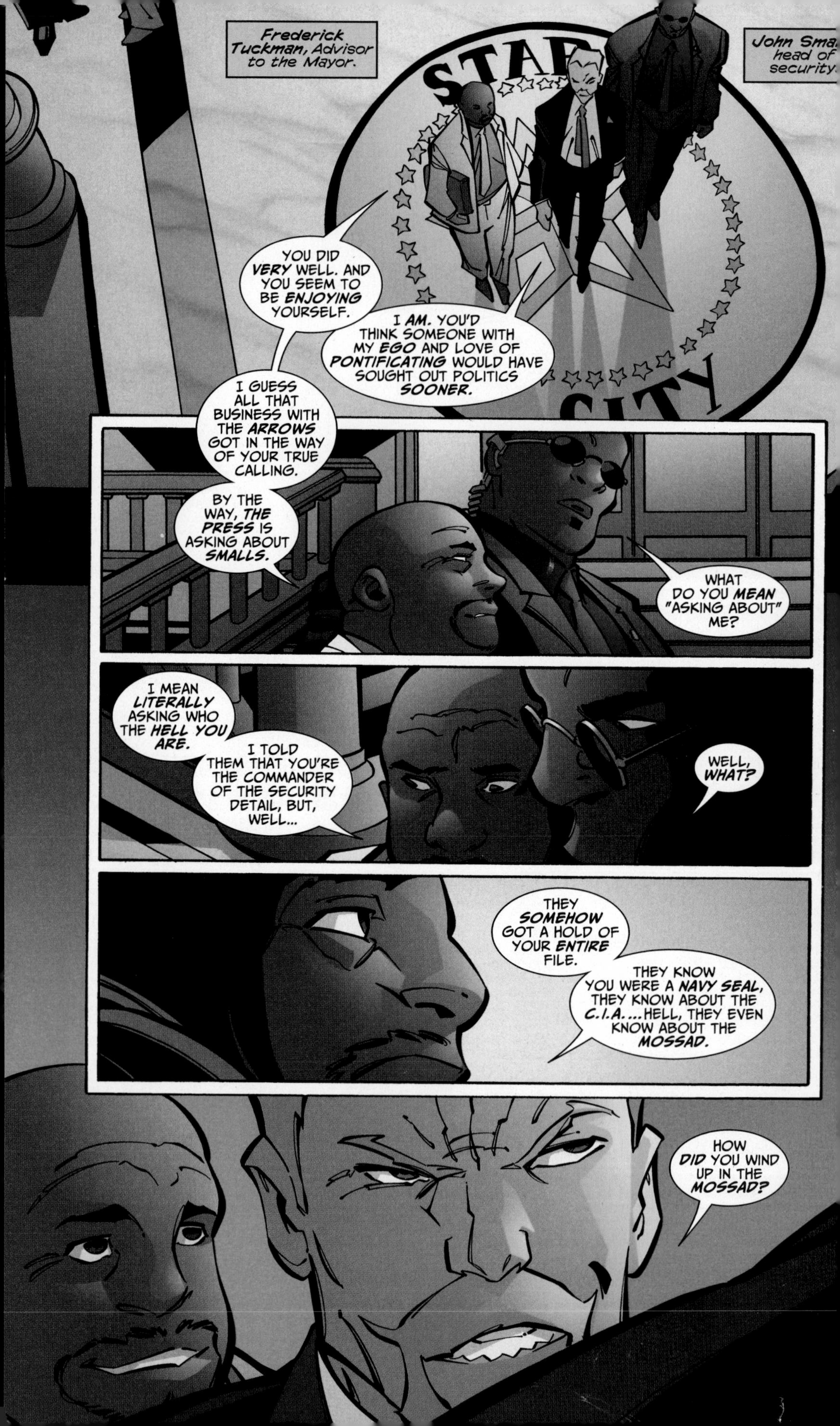

Frederick Tuckman, Advisor to the Mayor.
John Sma head of security.
STAR CITY
YOU DID VERY WELL. AND YOU SEEM TO BE ENJOYING YOURSELF.
I AM. YOU'D THINK SOMEONE WITH MY EGO AND LOVE OF PONTIFICATING WOULD HAVE SOUGHT OUT POLITICS SOONER.
I GUESS ALL THAT BUSINESS WITH THE ARROWS GOT IN THE WAY OF YOUR TRUE CALLING.
BY THE WAY, THE PRESS IS ASKING ABOUT SMALLS.
WHAT DO YOU MEAN "ASKING ABOUT" ME?
I MEAN LITERALLY ASKING WHO THE HELL YOU ARE.
I TOLD THEM THAT YOU'RE THE COMMANDER OF THE SECURITY DETAIL, BUT, WELL...
WELL, WHAT?
THEY SOMEHOW GOT A HOLD OF YOUR ENTIRE FILE.
THEY KNOW YOU WERE A NAVY SEAL, THEY KNOW ABOUT THE C.I.A.... HELL, THEY EVEN KNOW ABOUT THE MOSSAD.
HOW DID YOU WIND UP IN THE MOSSAD?

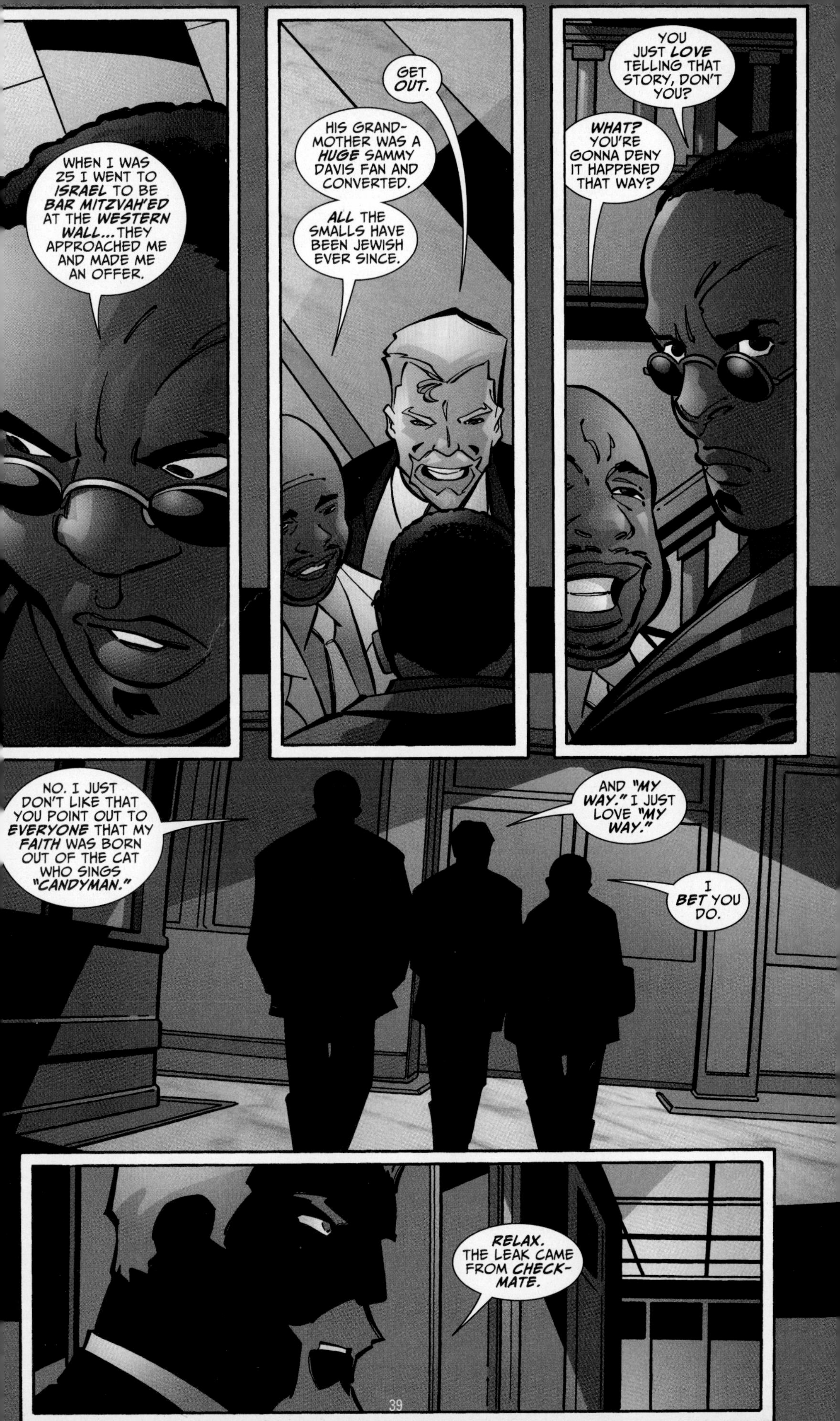
WHEN I WAS 25 I WENT TO ISRAEL TO BE BAR MITZVAH'ED AT THE WESTERN WALL... THEY APPROACHED ME AND MADE ME AN OFFER.
GET OUT.
HIS GRAND-MOTHER WAS A HUGE SAMMY DAVIS FAN AND CONVERTED.
ALL THE SMALLS HAVE BEEN JEWISH EVER SINCE.
YOU JUST LOVE TELLING THAT STORY, DON'T YOU?
WHAT? YOU'RE GONNA DENY IT HAPPENED THAT WAY?
NO. I JUST DON'T LIKE THAT YOU POINT OUT TO EVERYONE THAT MY FAITH WAS BORN OUT OF THE CAT WHO SINGS "CANDYMAN."
AND "MY WAY." I JUST LOVE "MY WAY."
I BET YOU DO.
RELAX. THE LEAK CAME FROM CHECK-MATE.

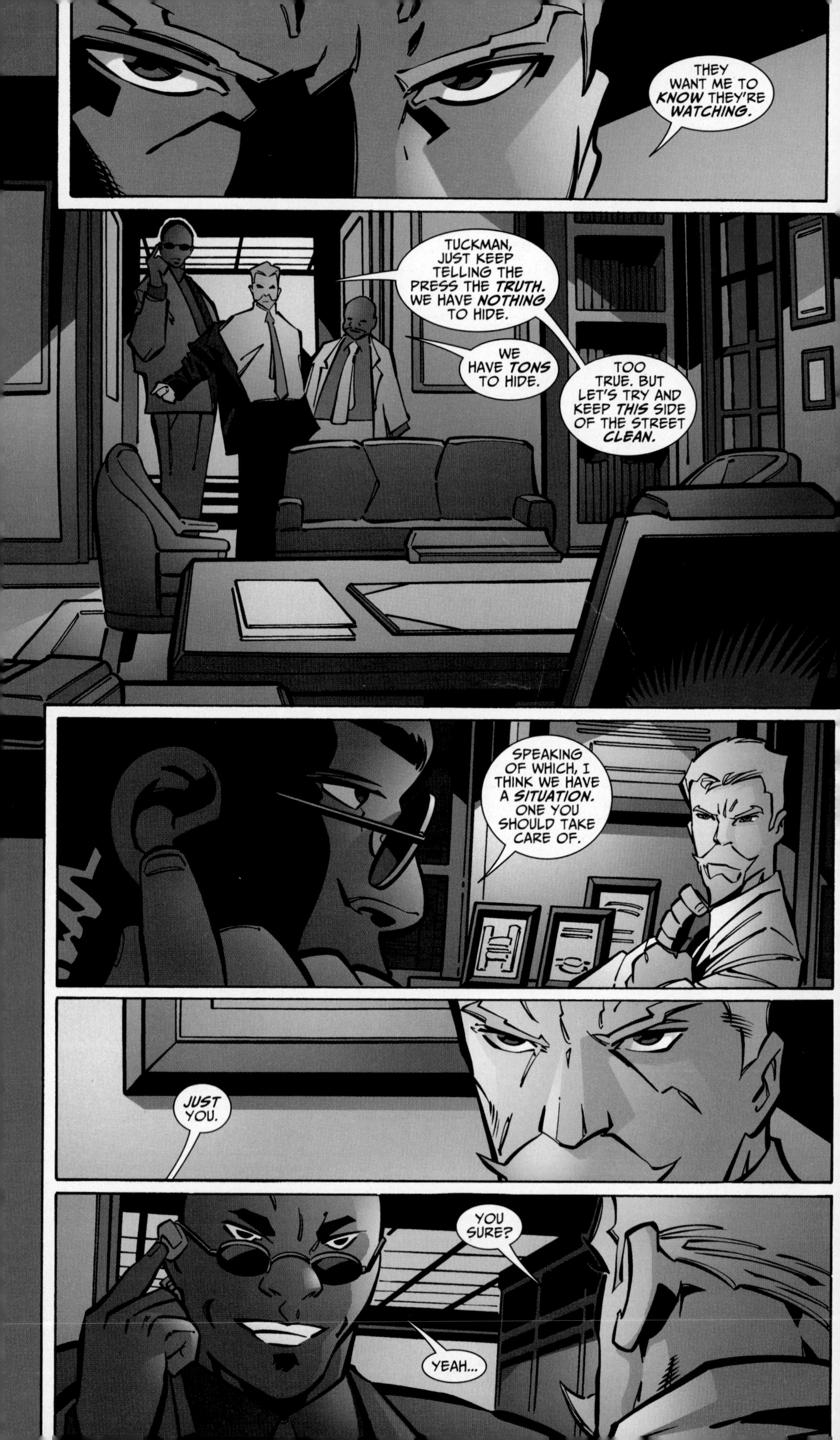
THEY WANT ME TO KNOW THEY'RE WATCHING.
TUCKMAN, JUST KEEP TELLING THE PRESS THE TRUTH. WE HAVE NOTHING TO HIDE.
WE HAVE TONS TO HIDE.
TOO TRUE. BUT LET'S TRY AND KEEP THIS SIDE OF THE STREET CLEAN.
SPEAKING OF WHICH, I THINK WE HAVE A SITUATION. ONE YOU SHOULD TAKE CARE OF.
JUST YOU.
YOU SURE?
YEAH...

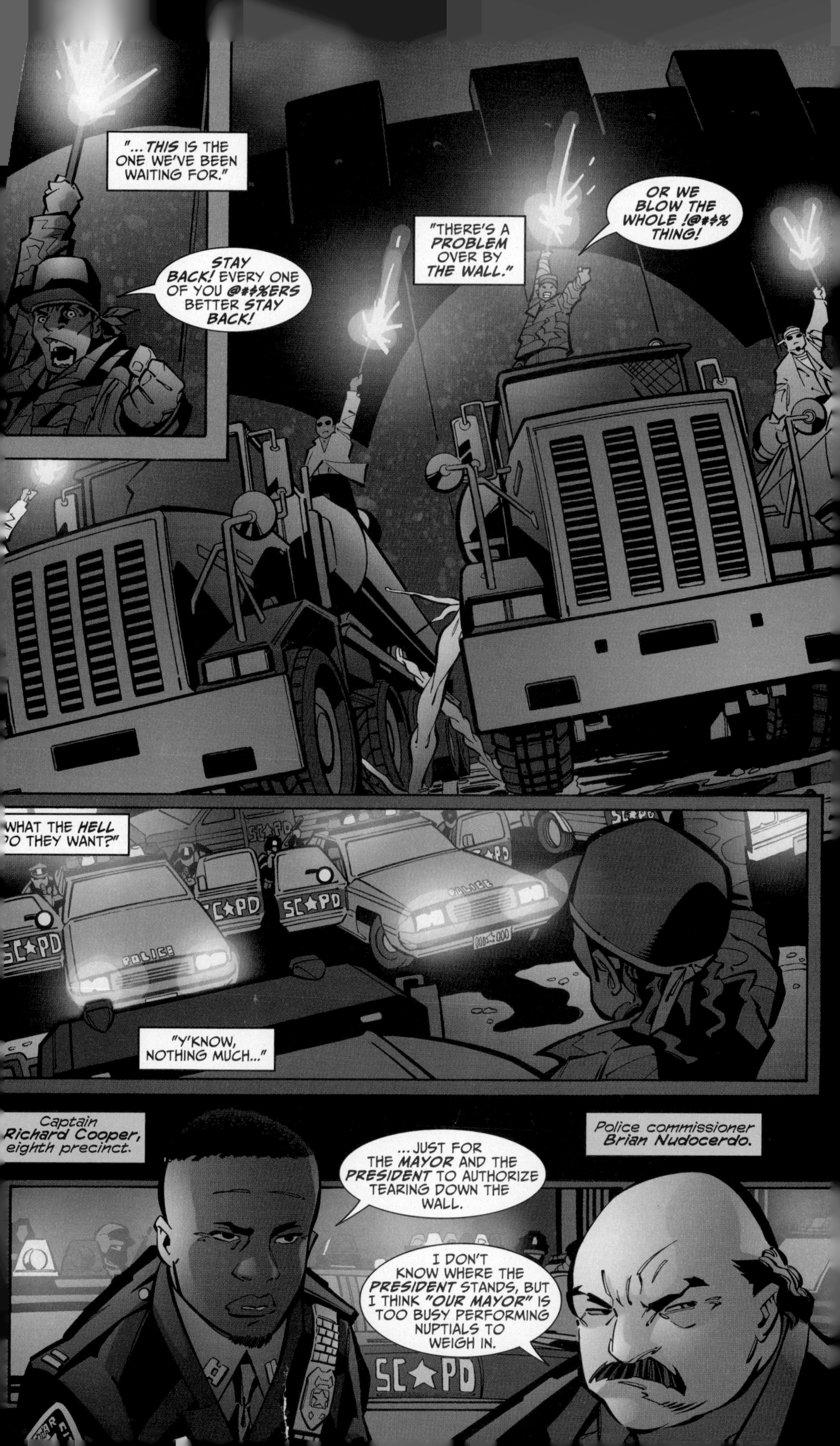
"...THIS IS THE ONE WE'VE BEEN WAITING FOR."
STAY BACK! EVERY ONE OF YOU @#$%ERS BETTER STAY BACK!
"THERE'S A PROBLEM OVER BY THE WALL."
OR WE BLOW THE WHOLE !@#$% THING!
WHAT THE HELL DO THEY WANT?"
"Y'KNOW, NOTHING MUCH..."
Captain Richard Cooper, eighth precinct.
Police commissioner Brian Nudocerdo.
...JUST FOR THE MAYOR AND THE PRESIDENT TO AUTHORIZE TEARING DOWN THE WALL.
I DON'T KNOW WHERE THE PRESIDENT STANDS, BUT I THINK "OUR MAYOR" IS TOO BUSY PERFORMING NUPTIALS TO WEIGH IN.

WHAT ARE OUR *OPTIONS*, COOPER?

WE'VE GOT A *NEGOTIATOR* MAKING SOME HEADWAY, BUT--

PLEASE. WE'VE GOT A FEW *TONS* OF GASOLINE THERE.

POOCH THIS AND THE *ENTIRE* CITY BLOCK'LL GO UP. WE'RE NOT *CHATTING* THESE WHACK JOBS UP.

CAN WE TAKE THEM OUT FROM THE *ROOFTOPS?*

NO. WE HIT THEM, THEY *DROP* THE FLARES.

WE COVERED THE STREETS WITH *FOAM,* BUT THEY DUMPED SO MUCH GAS *BEFORE* WE GOT HERE...

JESUS. HAVE WE I.D.ED THESE %@#$?

TWO OF THEM.

FINE. ROUND UP WHATEVER *FAMILY* THEY HAVE AND DRAG THEM *DOWN HERE.*

I THOUGHT YOU DIDN'T *WANT* TO *NEGOTIATE.*

WE'RE *NOT.* WE'RE GOING TO SIT THEIR *MOTHERS,* AND *BROTHERS,* AND *WIVE*... AND *KIDS RIGHT DOW*... IN FRONT OF THE *TRUCKS.*

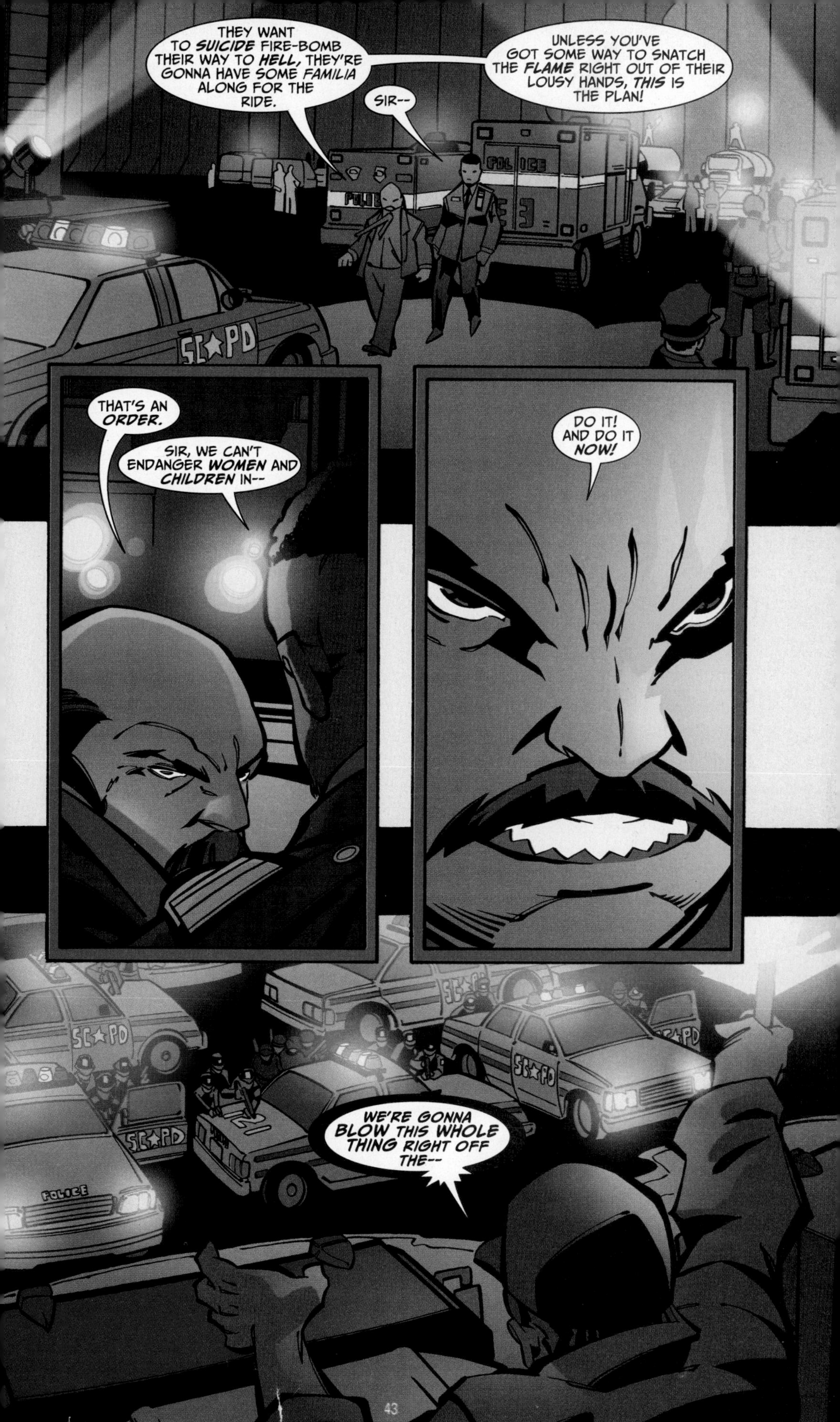
THEY WANT TO SUICIDE FIRE-BOMB THEIR WAY TO HELL, THEY'RE GONNA HAVE SOME FAMILIA ALONG FOR THE RIDE.
SIR--
UNLESS YOU'VE GOT SOME WAY TO SNATCH THE FLAME RIGHT OUT OF THEIR LOUSY HANDS, THIS IS THE PLAN!
THAT'S AN ORDER.
SIR, WE CAN'T ENDANGER WOMEN AND CHILDREN IN--
DO IT! AND DO IT NOW!
WE'RE GONNA BLOW THIS WHOLE THING RIGHT OFF THE--

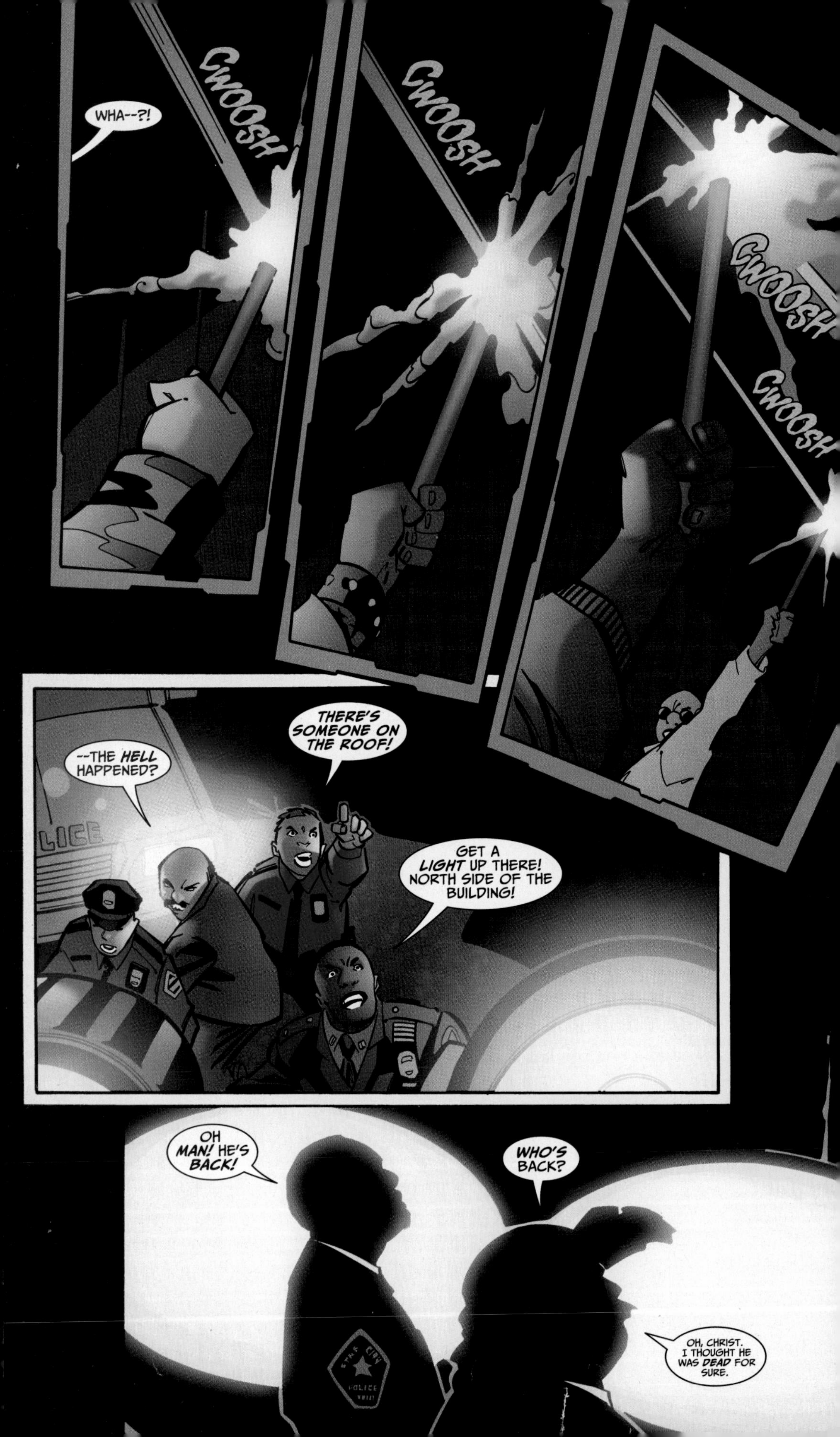

WHA--?!
GWOOSH
GWOOSH
GWOOSH
GWOOSH
--THE HELL HAPPENED?
THERE'S SOMEONE ON THE ROOF!
GET A LIGHT UP THERE! NORTH SIDE OF THE BUILDING!
OH MAN! HE'S BACK!
WHO'S BACK?
OH, CHRIST. I THOUGHT HE WAS DEAD FOR SURE.

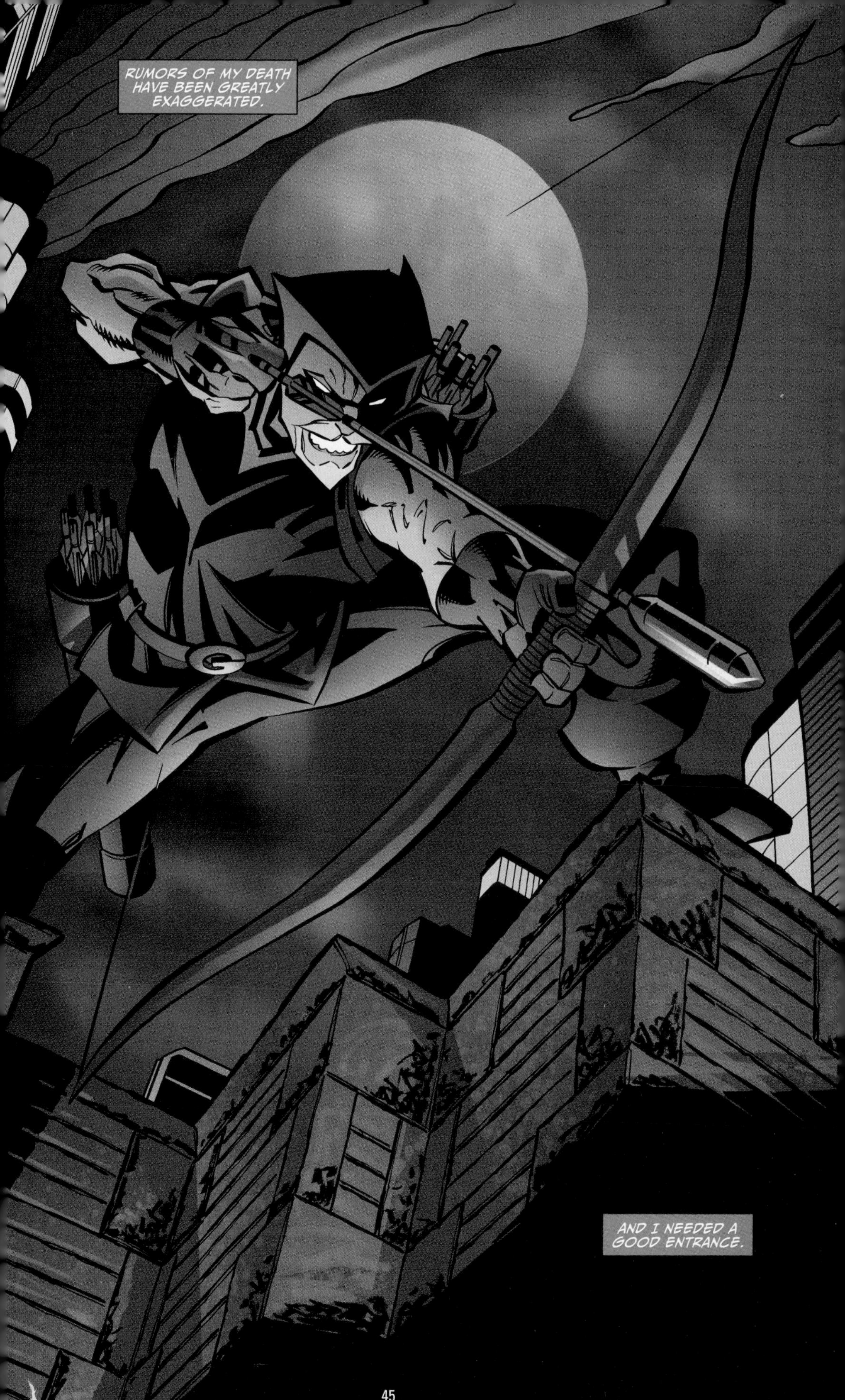
RUMORS OF MY DEATH HAVE BEEN GREATLY EXAGGERATED.
AND I NEEDED A GOOD ENTRANCE.

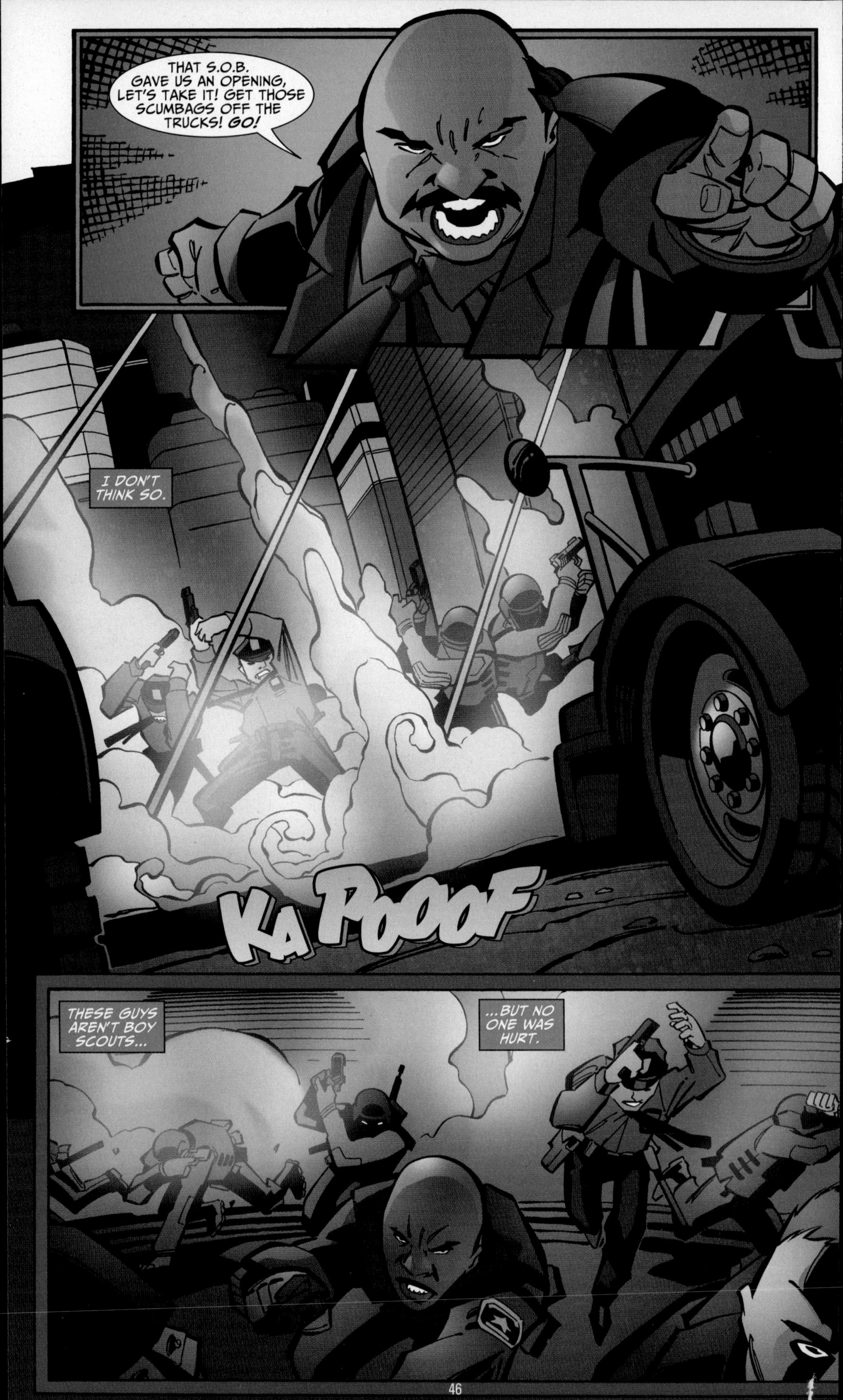
THAT S.O.B. GAVE US AN OPENING, LET'S TAKE IT! GET THOSE SCUMBAGS OFF THE TRUCKS! GO!
I DON'T THINK SO.
KA POOOF
THESE GUYS AREN'T BOY SCOUTS...
...BUT NO ONE WAS HURT.

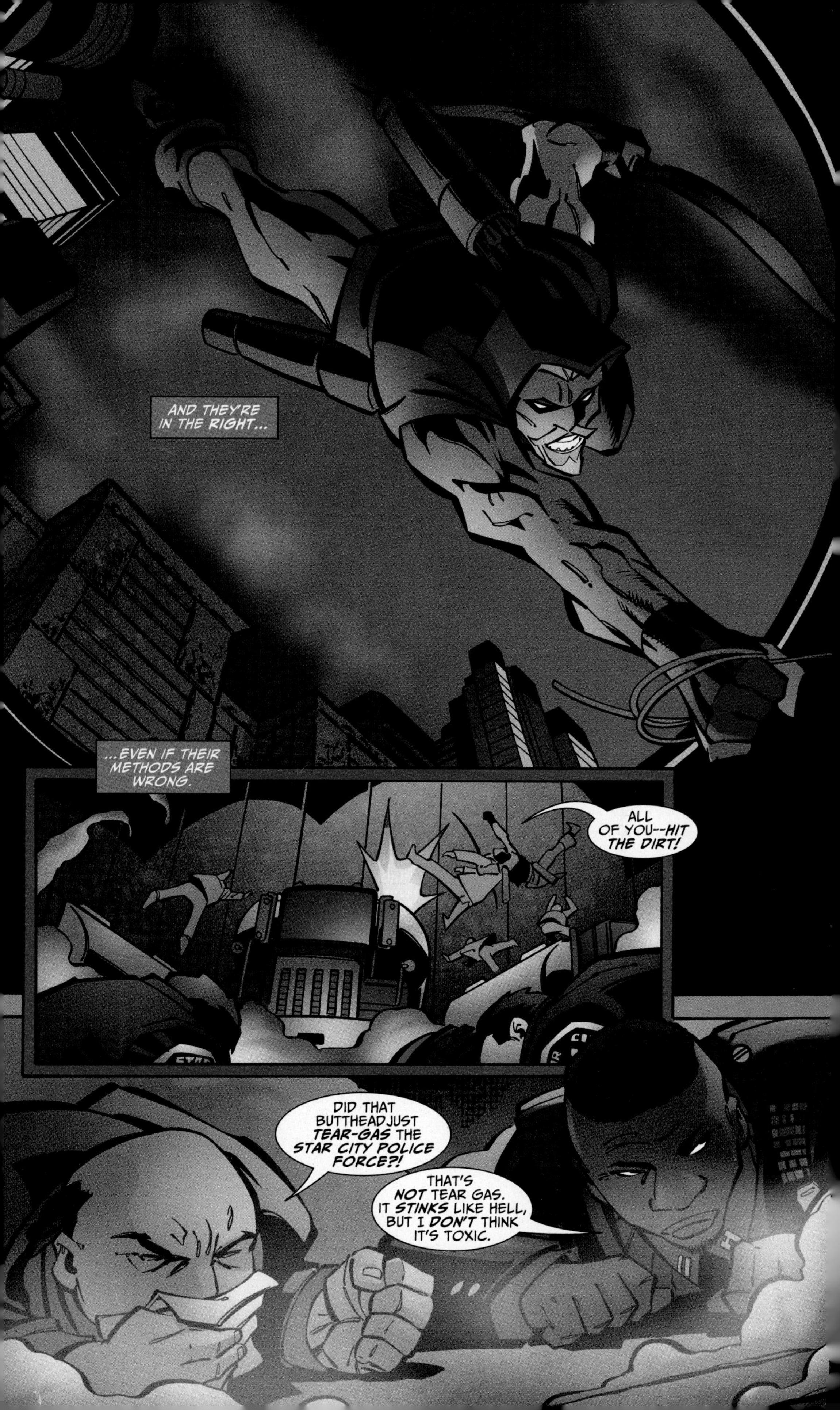

AND THEY'RE IN THE RIGHT...
...EVEN IF THEIR METHODS ARE WRONG.
ALL OF YOU--HIT THE DIRT!
DID THAT BUTTHEADJUST TEAR-GAS THE STAR CITY POLICE FORCE?!
THAT'S NOT TEAR GAS. IT STINKS LIKE HELL, BUT I DON'T THINK IT'S TOXIC.

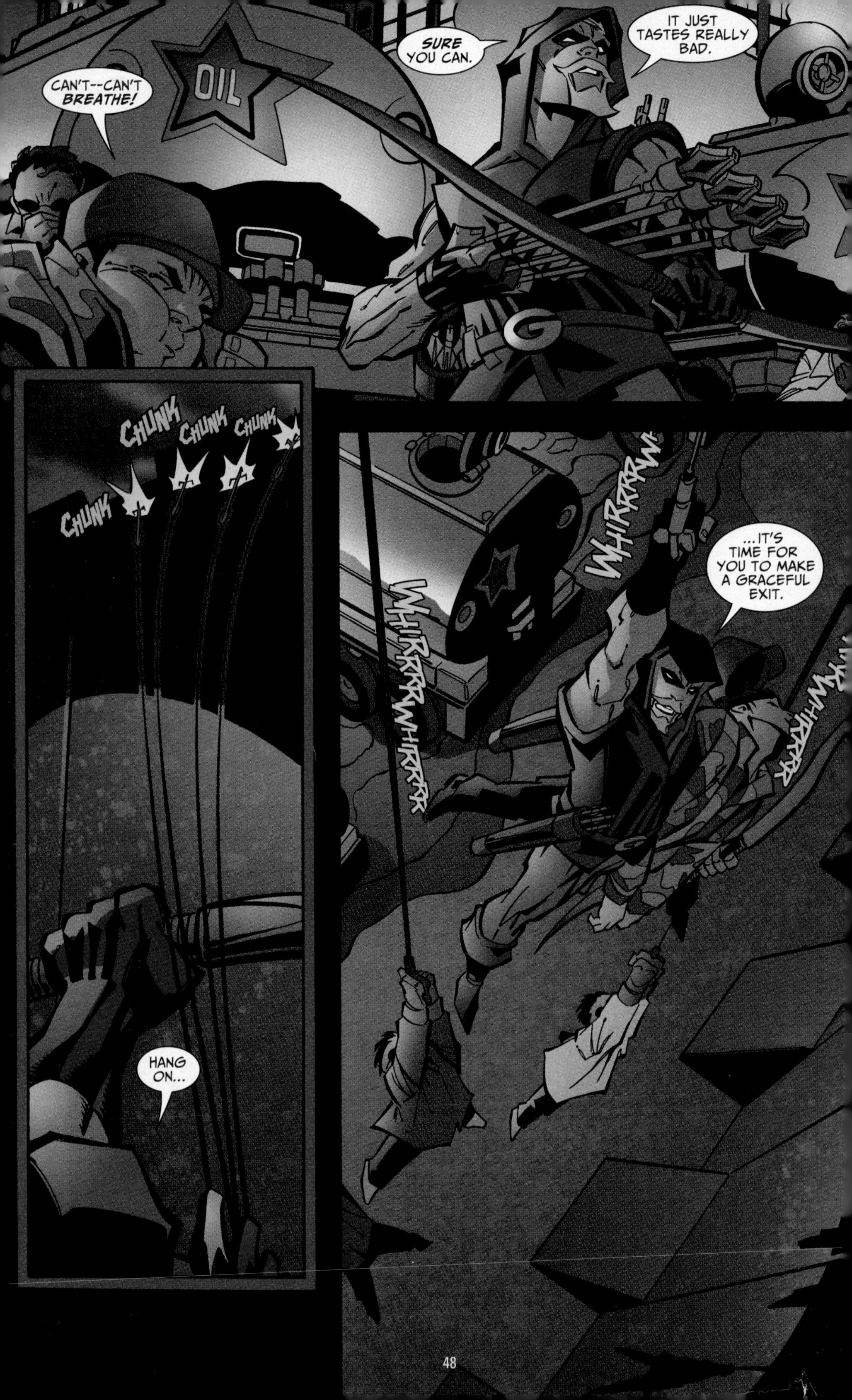
CAN'T--CAN'T BREATHE!
SURE YOU CAN.
IT JUST TASTES REALLY BAD.
CHUNK
CHUNK
CHUNK
CHUNK
HANG ON...
...IT'S TIME FOR YOU TO MAKE A GRACEFUL EXIT.

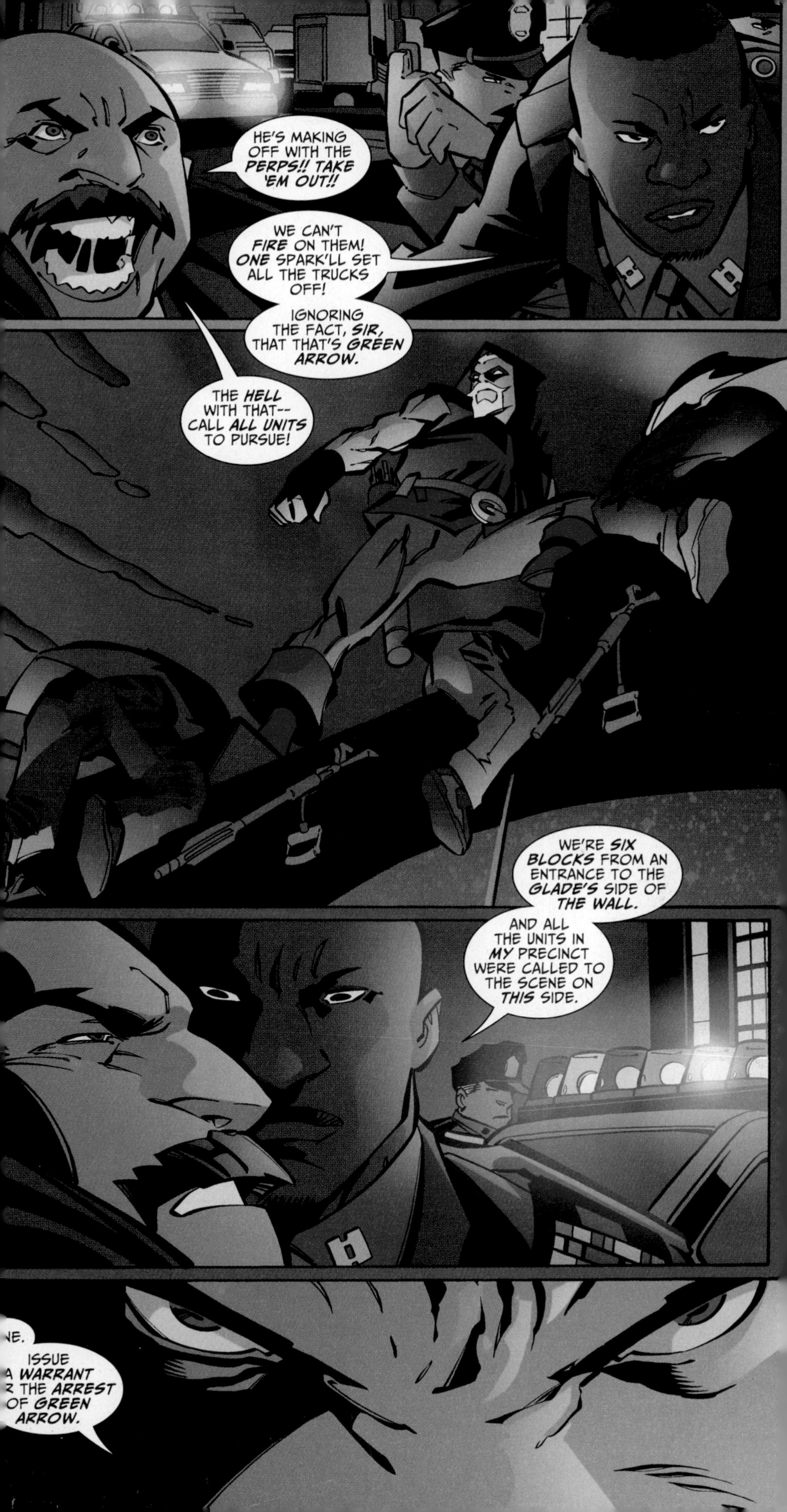
HE'S MAKING OFF WITH THE PERPS!! TAKE 'EM OUT!!
WE CAN'T FIRE ON THEM! ONE SPARK'LL SET ALL THE TRUCKS OFF!
IGNORING THE FACT, SIR, THAT THAT'S GREEN ARROW.
THE HELL WITH THAT-- CALL ALL UNITS TO PURSUE!
WE'RE SIX BLOCKS FROM AN ENTRANCE TO THE GLADE'S SIDE OF THE WALL.
AND ALL THE UNITS IN MY PRECINCT WERE CALLED TO THE SCENE ON THIS SIDE.
ISSUE A WARRANT THE ARREST OF GREEN ARROW.

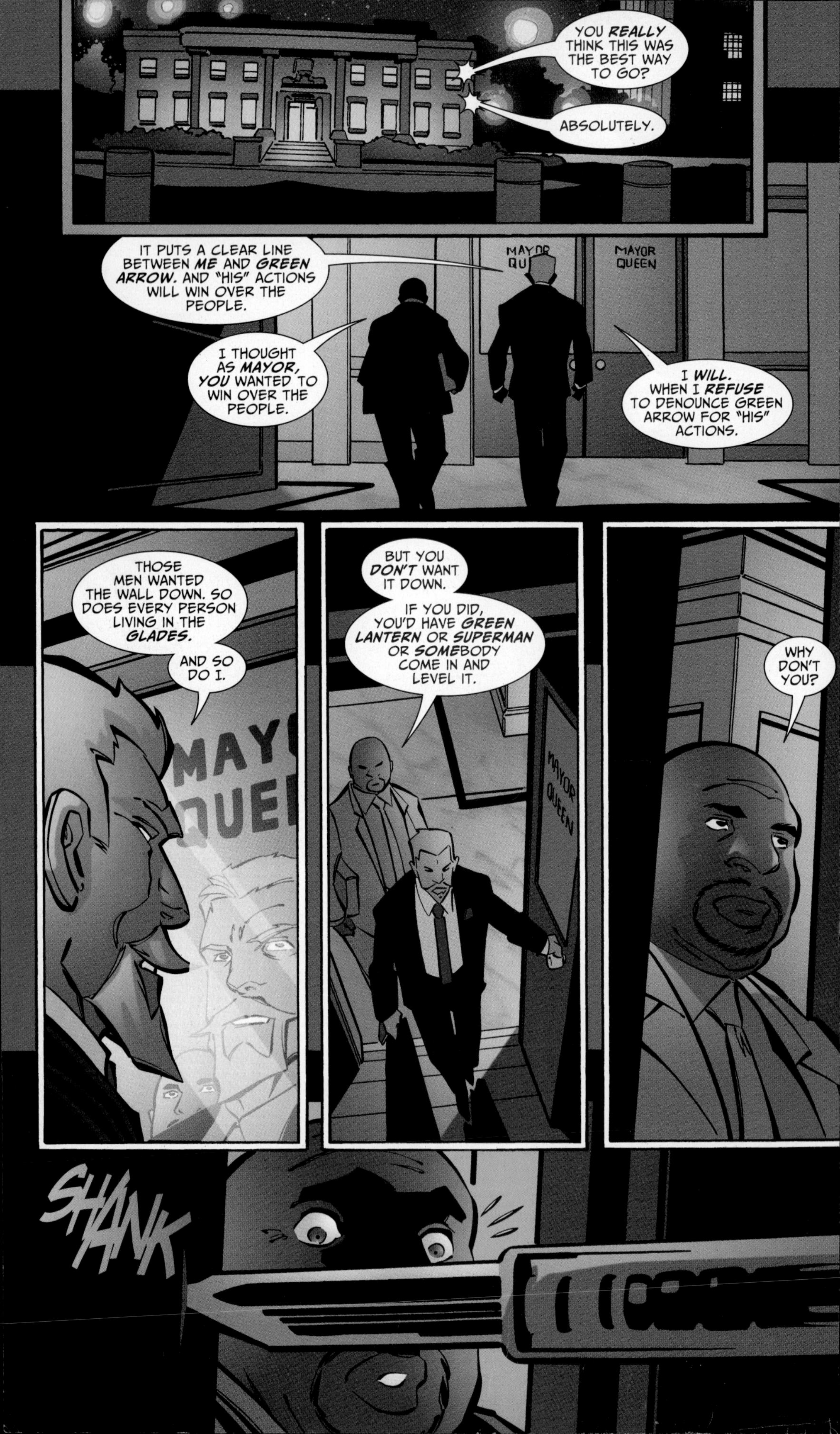
YOU **REALLY** THINK THIS WAS THE BEST WAY TO GO?
ABSOLUTELY.
IT PUTS A CLEAR LINE BETWEEN **ME** AND **GREEN ARROW.** AND "HIS" ACTIONS WILL WIN OVER THE PEOPLE.
MAYOR QU
MAYOR QUEEN
I THOUGHT AS **MAYOR, YOU** WANTED TO WIN OVER THE PEOPLE.
I **WILL.** WHEN I **REFUSE** TO DENOUNCE GREEN ARROW FOR "HIS" ACTIONS.
THOSE MEN WANTED THE WALL DOWN. SO DOES EVERY PERSON LIVING IN THE **GLADES.**
AND SO DO I.
MAYO QUE
BUT YOU **DON'T** WANT IT DOWN.
IF YOU DID, YOU'D HAVE **GREEN LANTERN** OR **SUPERMAN** OR **SOME**BODY COME IN AND LEVEL IT.
MAYOR QUEEN
WHY DON'T YOU?
SHANK

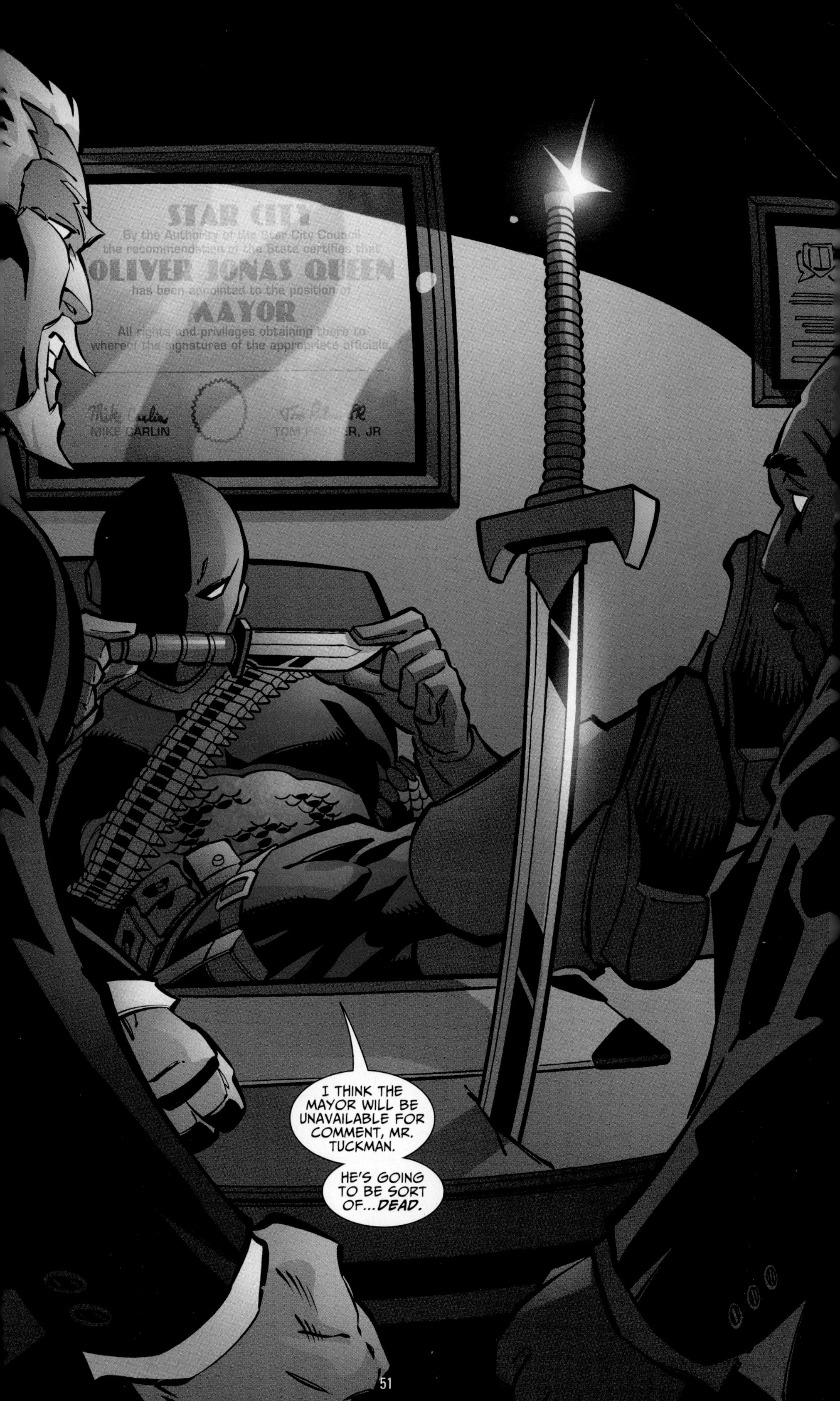
STAR CITY
By the Authority of the Star City Council
the recommendation of the State certifies that
OLIVER JONAS QUEEN
has been appointed to the position of
MAYOR
All rights and privileges obtaining there to
whereof the signatures of the appropriate officials.
MIKE CARLIN
TOM PALMER, JR
I THINK THE MAYOR WILL BE UNAVAILABLE FOR COMMENT, MR. TUCKMAN.
HE'S GOING TO BE SORT OF... **DEAD.**

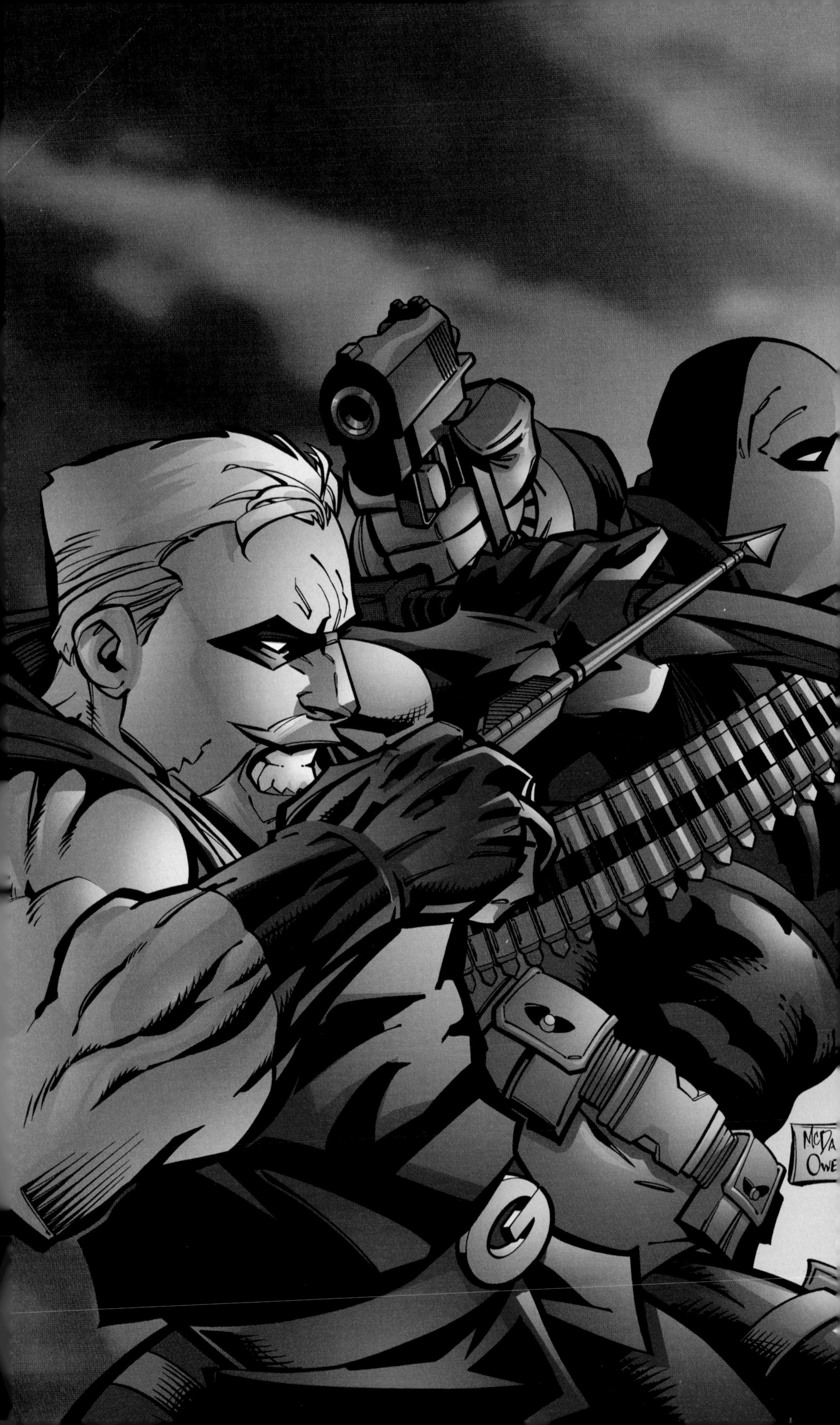

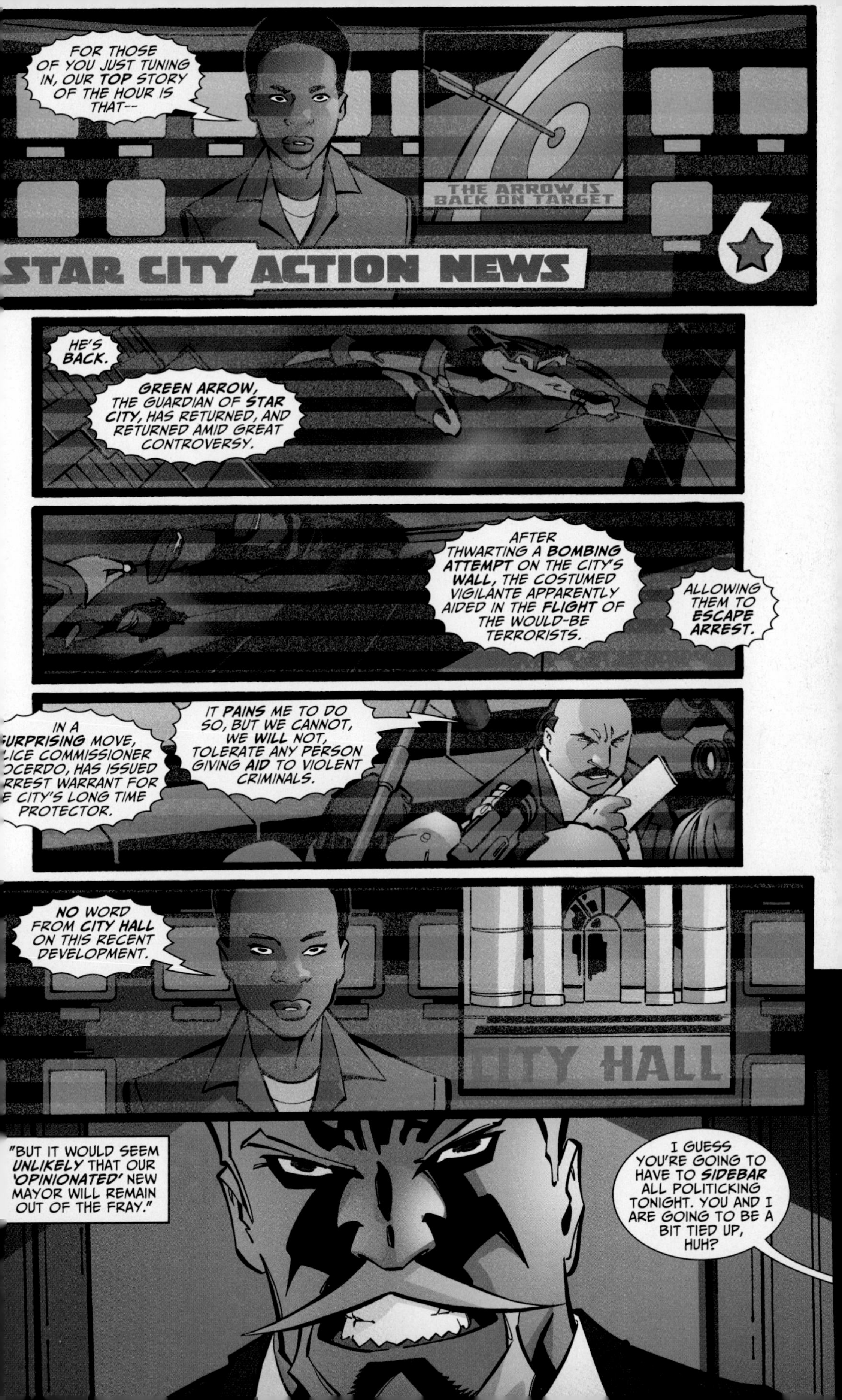

FOR THOSE OF YOU JUST TUNING IN, OUR TOP STORY OF THE HOUR IS THAT--
THE ARROW IS BACK ON TARGET
STAR CITY ACTION NEWS
HE'S BACK.
GREEN ARROW, THE GUARDIAN OF STAR CITY, HAS RETURNED, AND RETURNED AMID GREAT CONTROVERSY.
AFTER THWARTING A BOMBING ATTEMPT ON THE CITY'S WALL, THE COSTUMED VIGILANTE APPARENTLY AIDED IN THE FLIGHT OF THE WOULD-BE TERRORISTS.
ALLOWING THEM TO ESCAPE ARREST.
IN A SURPRISING MOVE, LICE COMMISSIONER OCERDO, HAS ISSUED RREST WARRANT FOR E CITY'S LONG TIME PROTECTOR.
IT PAINS ME TO DO SO, BUT WE CANNOT, WE WILL NOT, TOLERATE ANY PERSON GIVING AID TO VIOLENT CRIMINALS.
NO WORD FROM CITY HALL ON THIS RECENT DEVELOPMENT.
CITY HALL
"BUT IT WOULD SEEM UNLIKELY THAT OUR 'OPINIONATED' NEW MAYOR WILL REMAIN OUT OF THE FRAY."
I GUESS YOU'RE GOING TO HAVE TO SIDEBAR ALL POLITICKING TONIGHT. YOU AND I ARE GOING TO BE A BIT TIED UP, HUH?

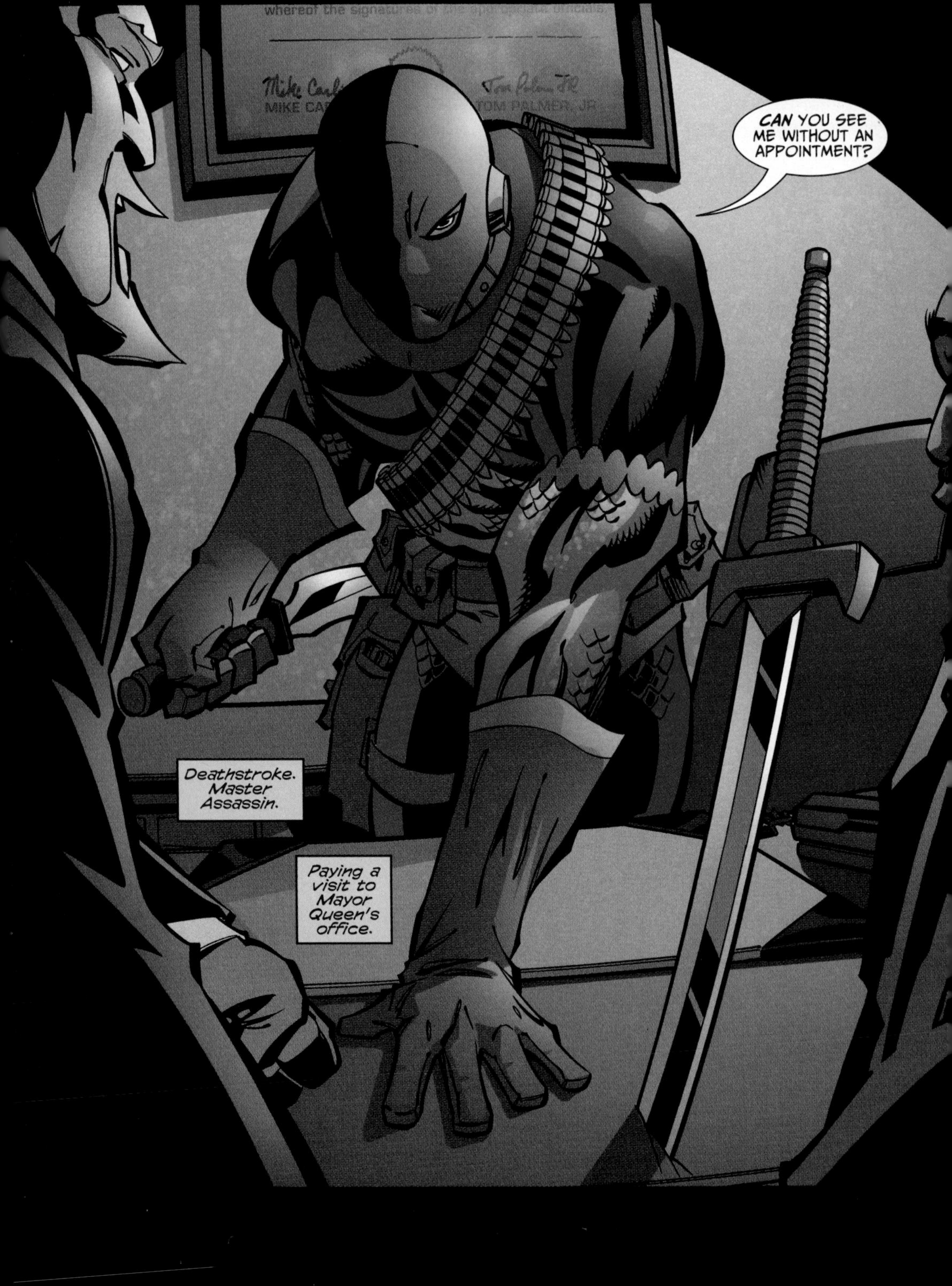
CAN YOU SEE ME WITHOUT AN APPOINTMENT?
Deathstroke. Master Assassin.
Paying a visit to Mayor Queen's office.

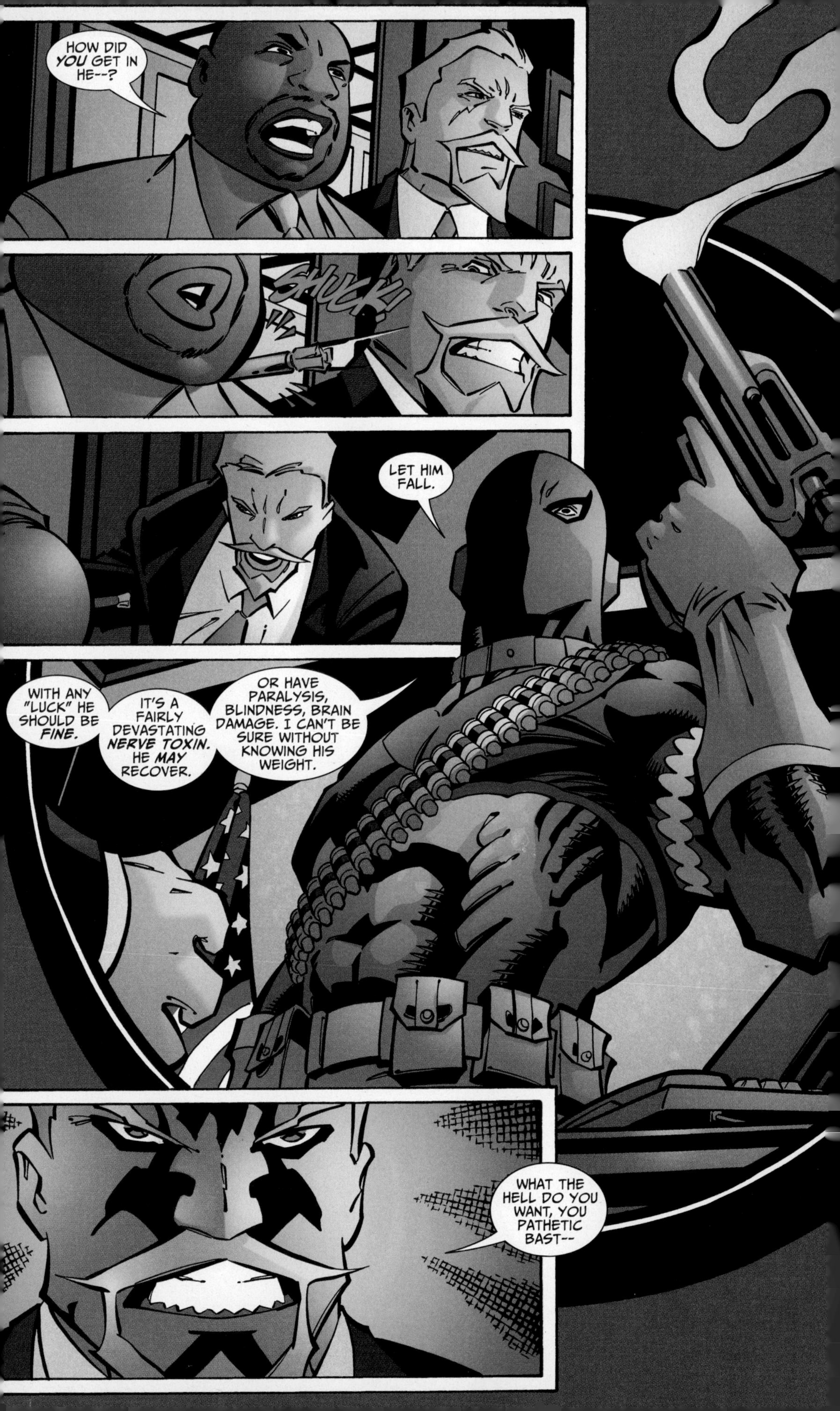
HOW DID YOU GET IN HE--?
SHUCK!
LET HIM FALL.
WITH ANY "LUCK" HE SHOULD BE FINE.
IT'S A FAIRLY DEVASTATING NERVE TOXIN. HE MAY RECOVER.
OR HAVE PARALYSIS, BLINDNESS, BRAIN DAMAGE. I CAN'T BE SURE WITHOUT KNOWING HIS WEIGHT.
WHAT THE HELL DO YOU WANT, YOU PATHETIC BAST--

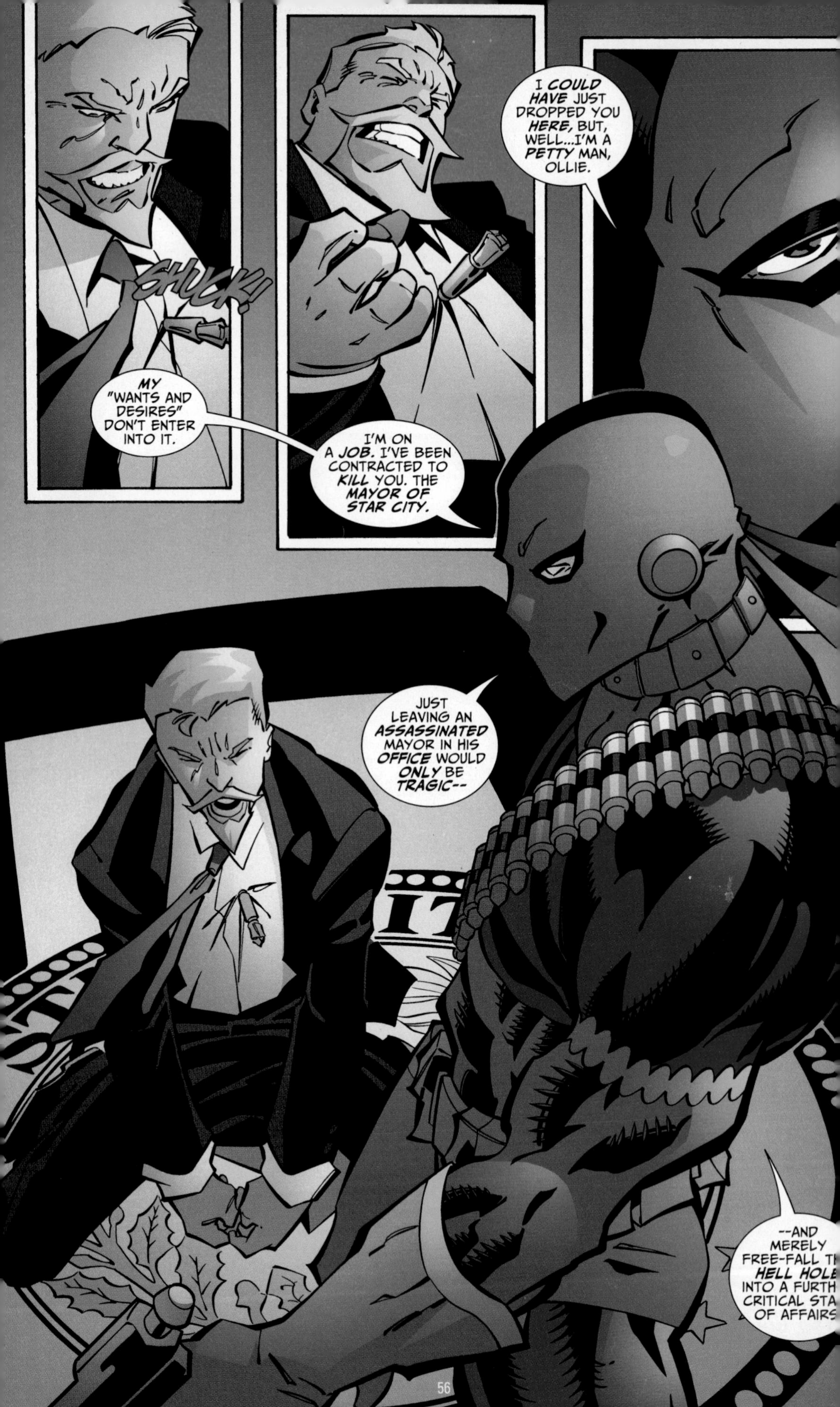
SHUCK!!
MY "WANTS AND DESIRES" DON'T ENTER INTO IT.
I'M ON A JOB. I'VE BEEN CONTRACTED TO KILL YOU. THE MAYOR OF STAR CITY.
I COULD HAVE JUST DROPPED YOU HERE, BUT, WELL...I'M A PETTY MAN, OLLIE.
JUST LEAVING AN ASSASSINATED MAYOR IN HIS OFFICE WOULD ONLY BE TRAGIC--
--AND MERELY FREE-FALL T
HELL HOLE
INTO A FURTH
CRITICAL STA
OF AFFAIRS

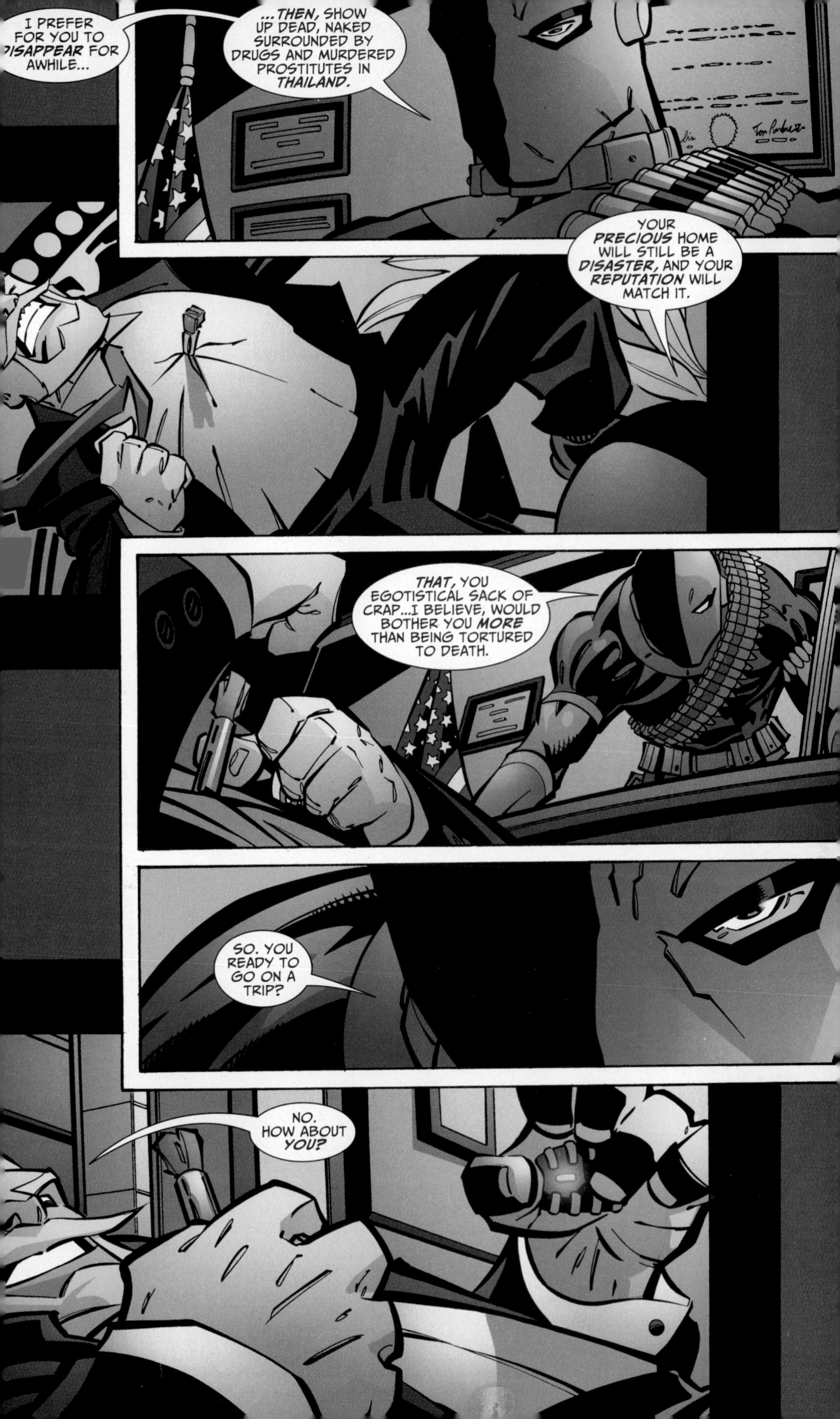
I PREFER FOR YOU TO DISAPPEAR FOR AWHILE...
...THEN, SHOW UP DEAD, NAKED SURROUNDED BY DRUGS AND MURDERED PROSTITUTES IN THAILAND.
YOUR PRECIOUS HOME WILL STILL BE A DISASTER, AND YOUR REPUTATION WILL MATCH IT.
THAT, YOU EGOTISTICAL SACK OF CRAP...I BELIEVE, WOULD BOTHER YOU MORE THAN BEING TORTURED TO DEATH.
SO. YOU READY TO GO ON A TRIP?
NO. HOW ABOUT YOU?

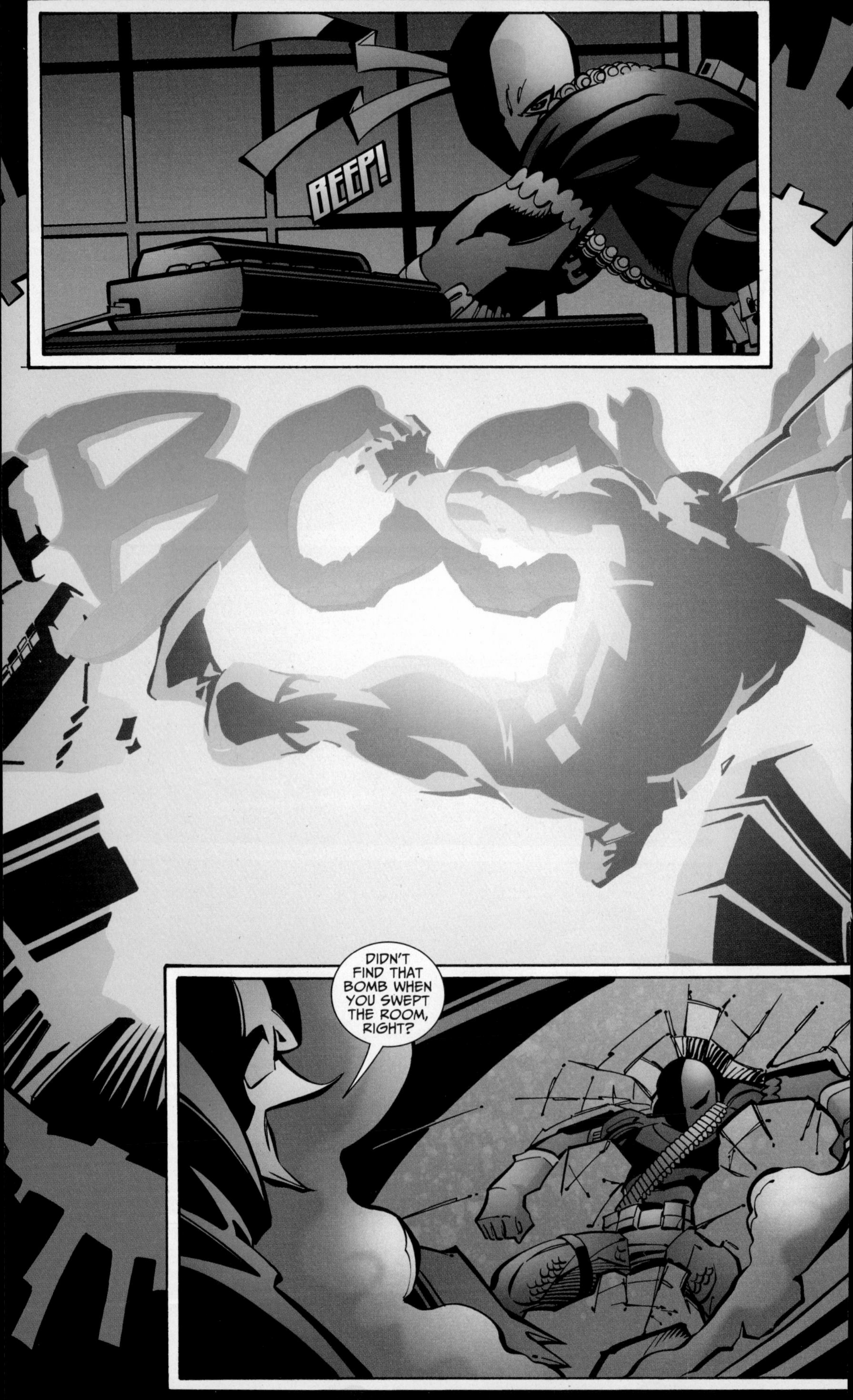
BEEP!
DIDN'T FIND THAT BOMB WHEN YOU SWEPT THE ROOM, RIGHT?

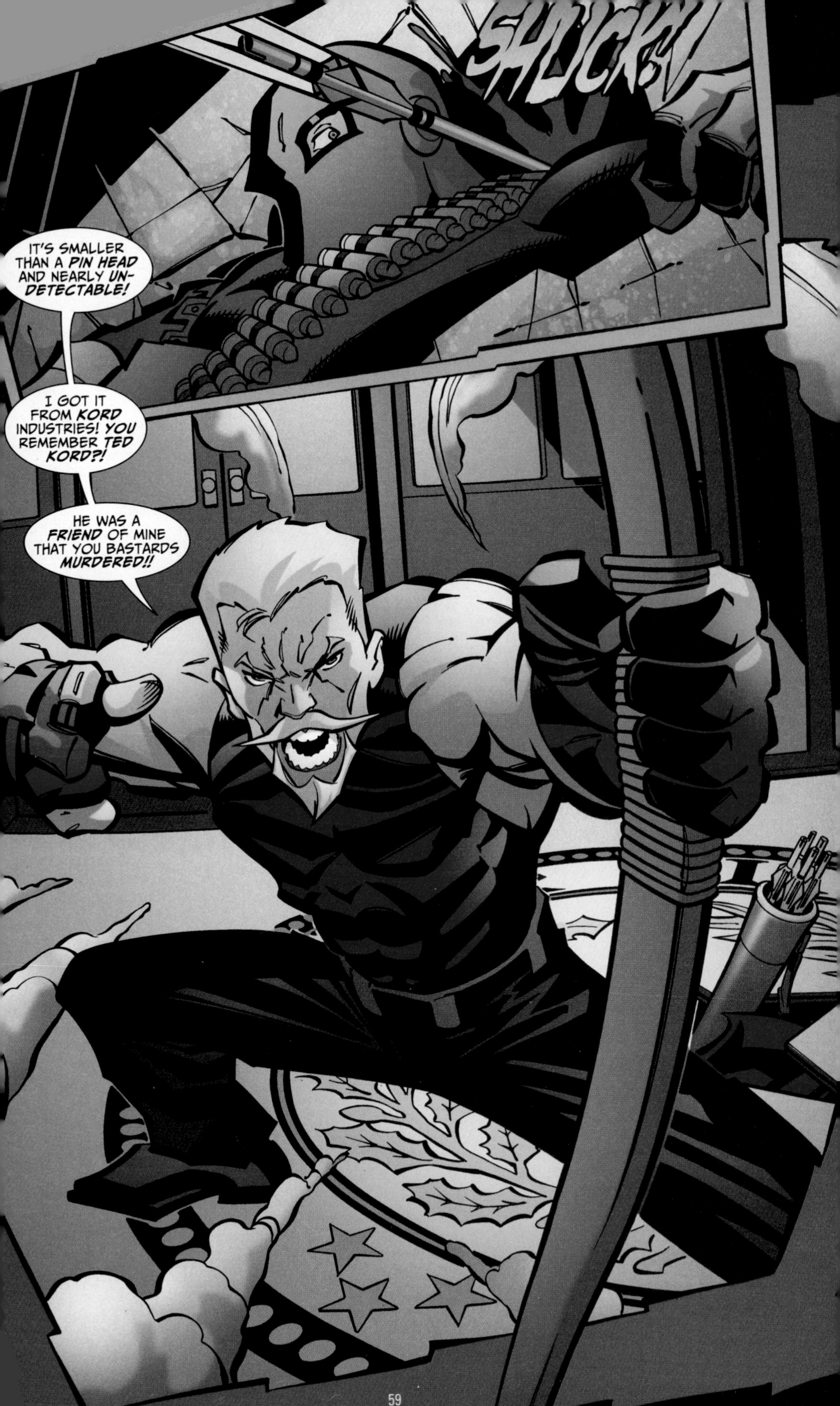
SHUCK!
IT'S SMALLER THAN A PIN HEAD AND NEARLY UN-DETECTABLE!
I GOT IT FROM KORD INDUSTRIES! YOU REMEMBER TED KORD?!
HE WAS A FRIEND OF MINE THAT YOU BASTARDS MURDERED!!

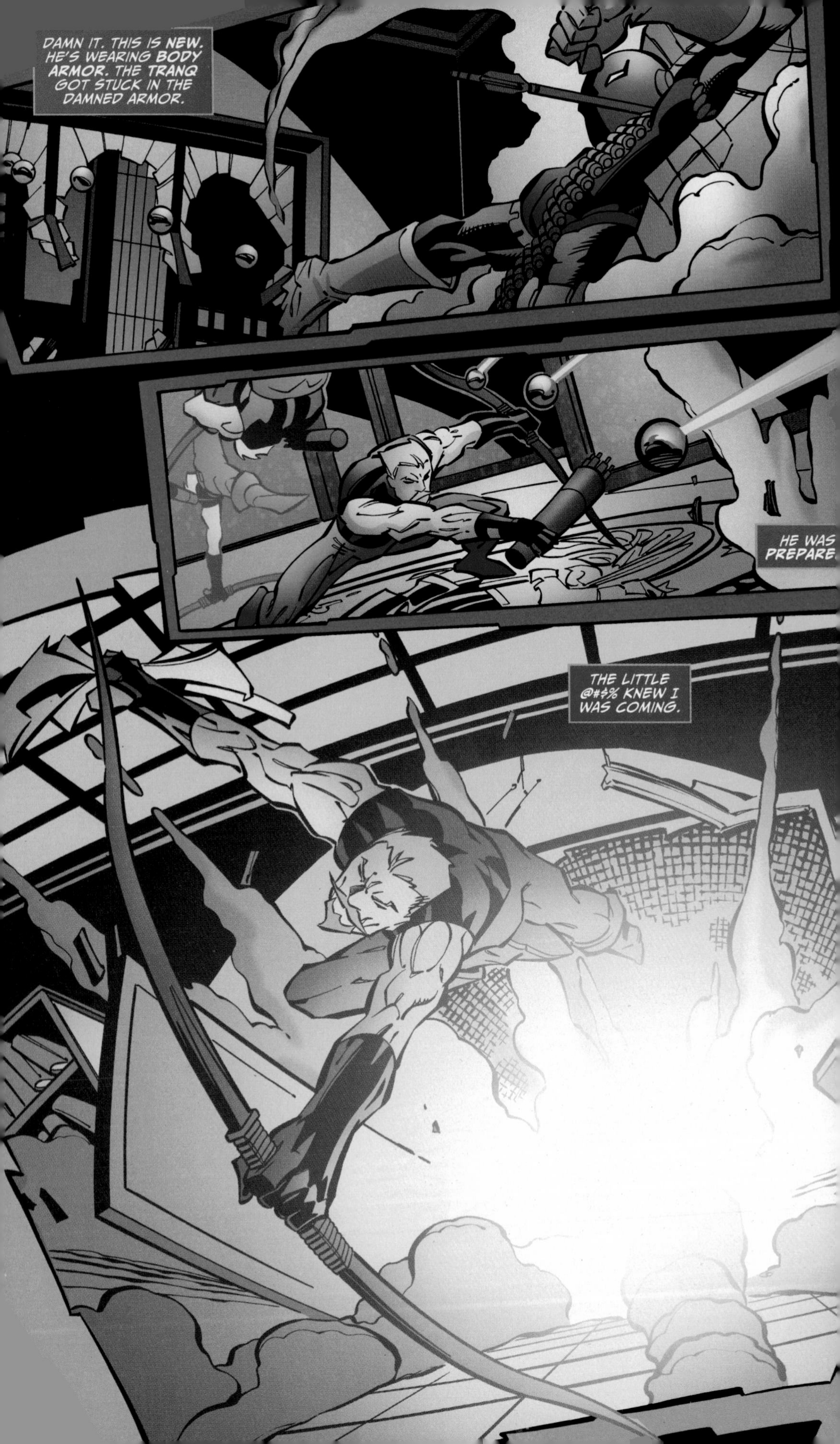
DAMN IT. THIS IS NEW. HE'S WEARING BODY ARMOR. THE TRANQ GOT STUCK IN THE DAMNED ARMOR.
HE WAS PREPARE
THE LITTLE @#$% KNEW I WAS COMING.

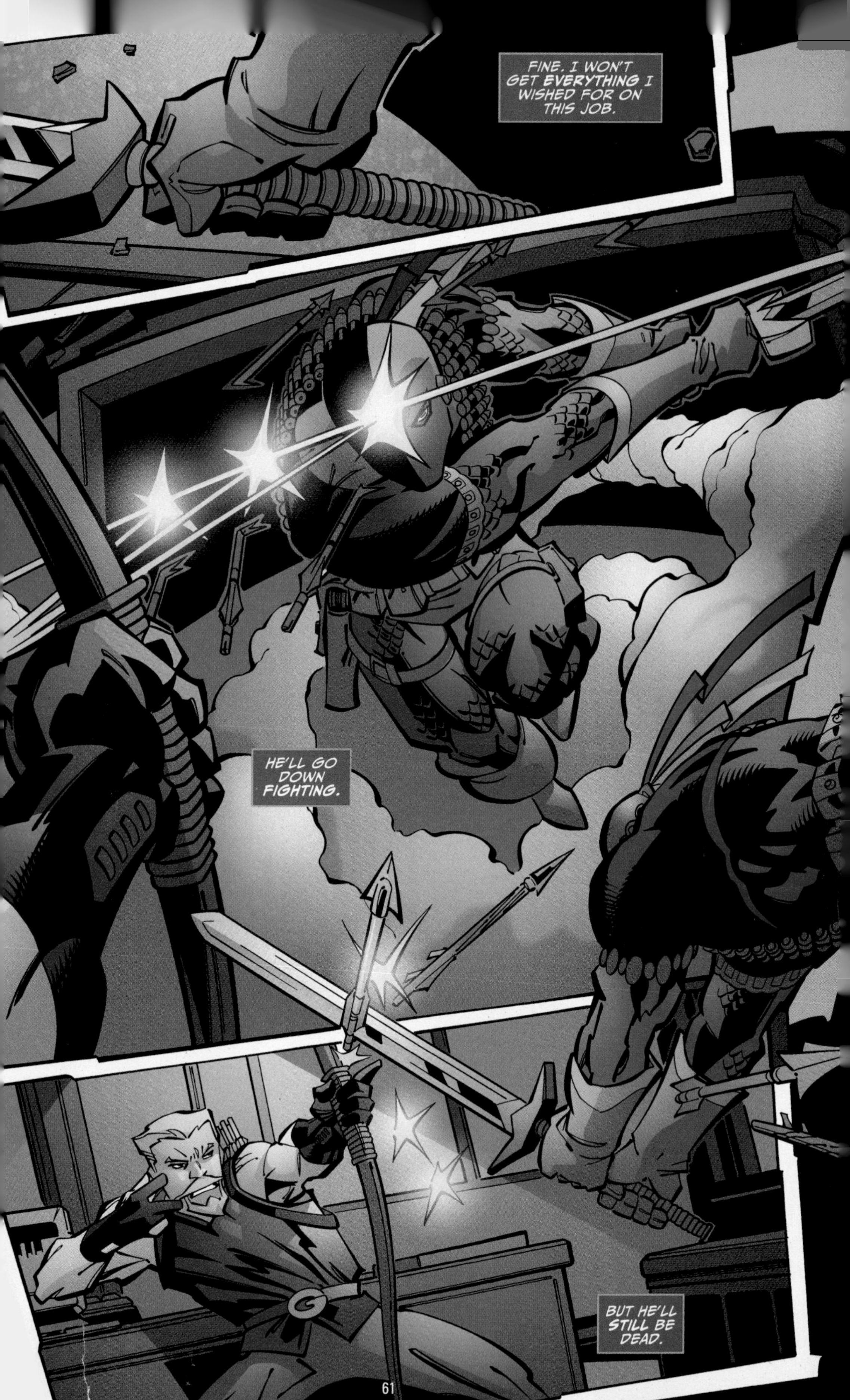
FINE. I WON'T GET EVERYTHING I WISHED FOR ON THIS JOB.
HE'LL GO DOWN FIGHTING.
BUT HE'LL STILL BE DEAD.

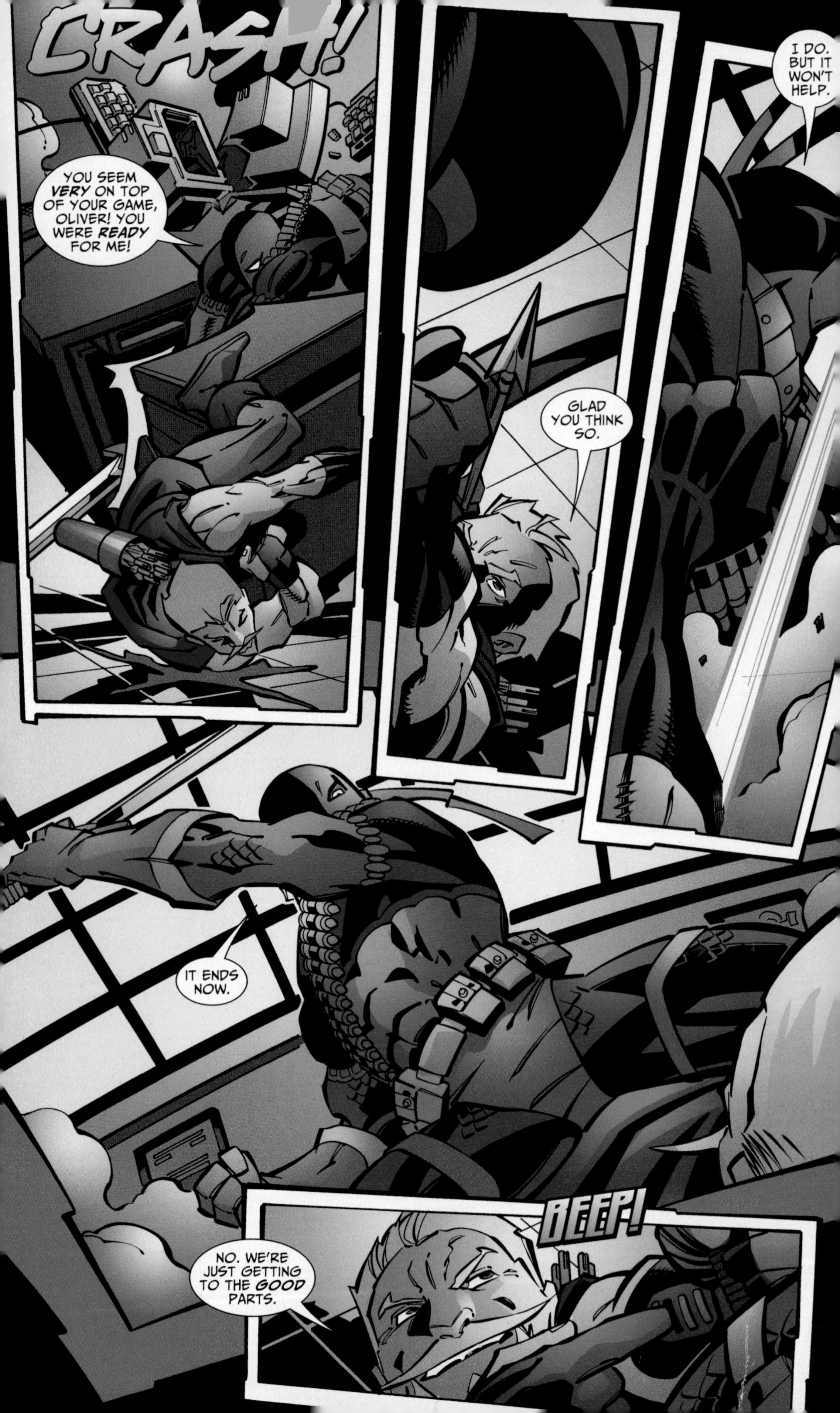
CRASH!
YOU SEEM VERY ON TOP OF YOUR GAME, OLIVER! YOU WERE READY FOR ME!
GLAD YOU THINK SO.
I DO. BUT IT WON'T HELP.
IT ENDS NOW.
BEEP!
NO. WE'RE JUST GETTING TO THE GOOD PARTS.

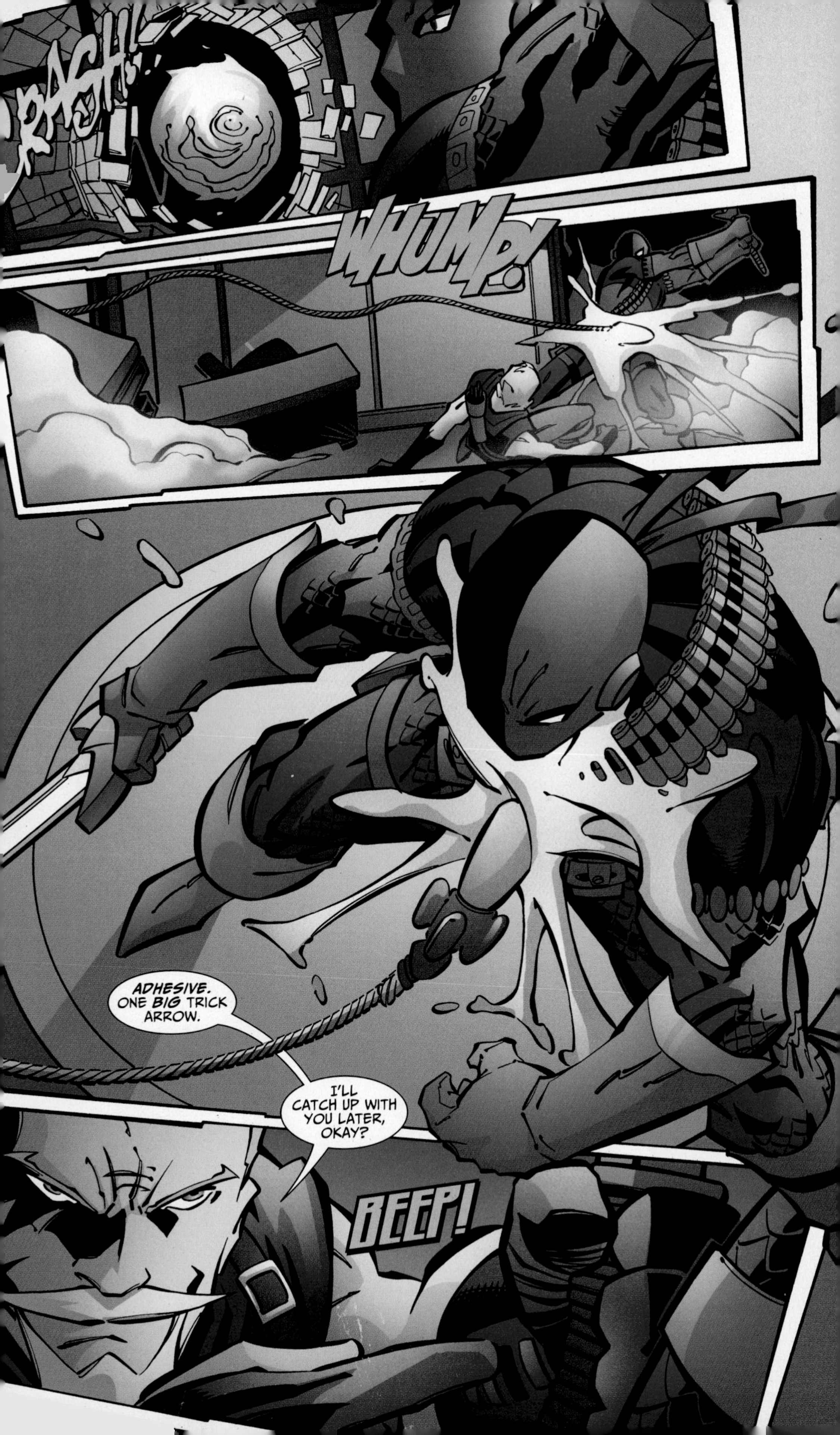

CRASH!!
WHUMP!
ADHESIVE. ONE BIG TRICK ARROW.
I'LL CATCH UP WITH YOU LATER, OKAY?
BEEP!

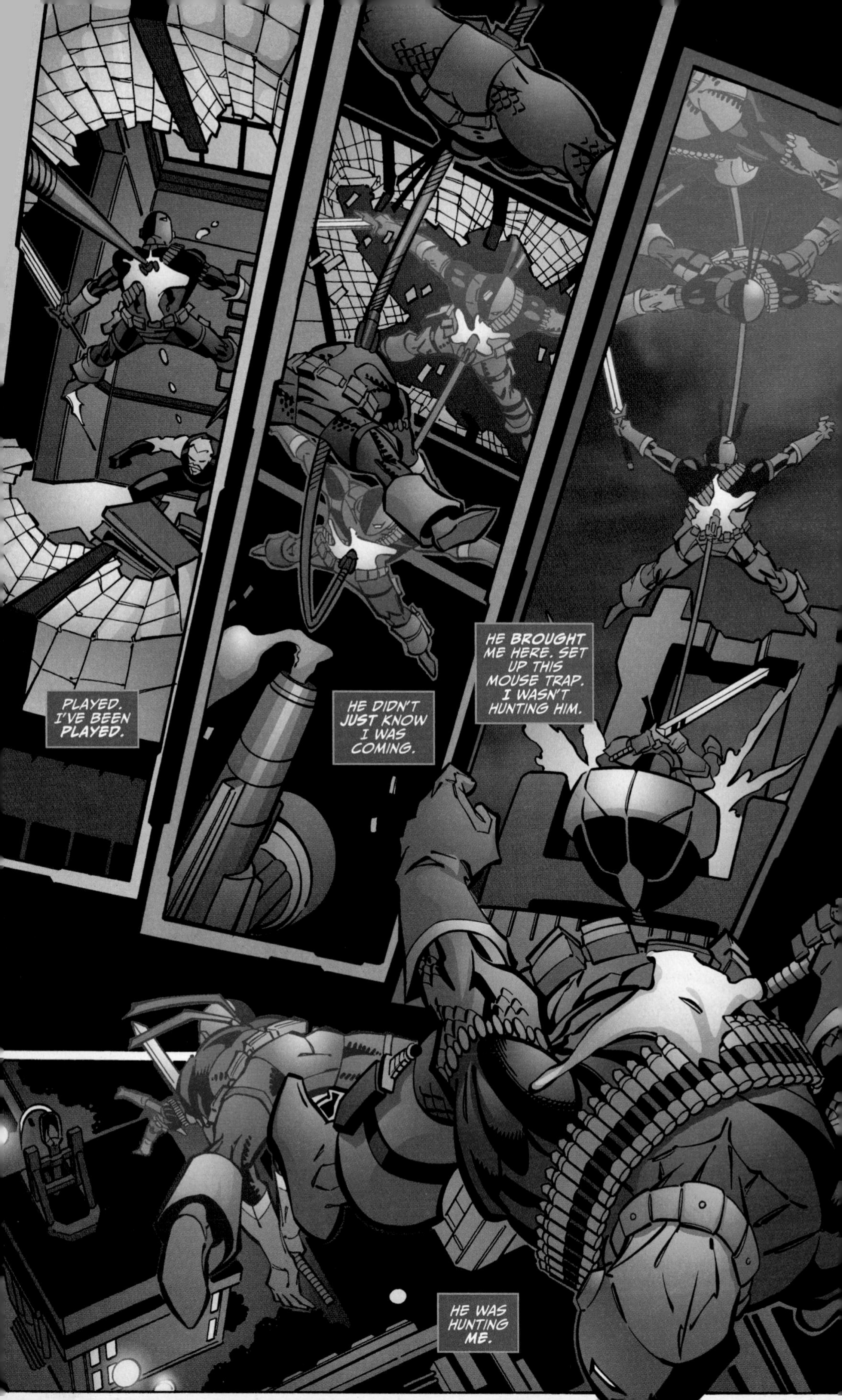
PLAYED. I'VE BEEN PLAYED.
HE DIDN'T JUST KNOW I WAS COMING.
HE BROUGHT ME HERE. SET UP THIS MOUSE TRAP. I WASN'T HUNTING HIM.
HE WAS HUNTING ME.

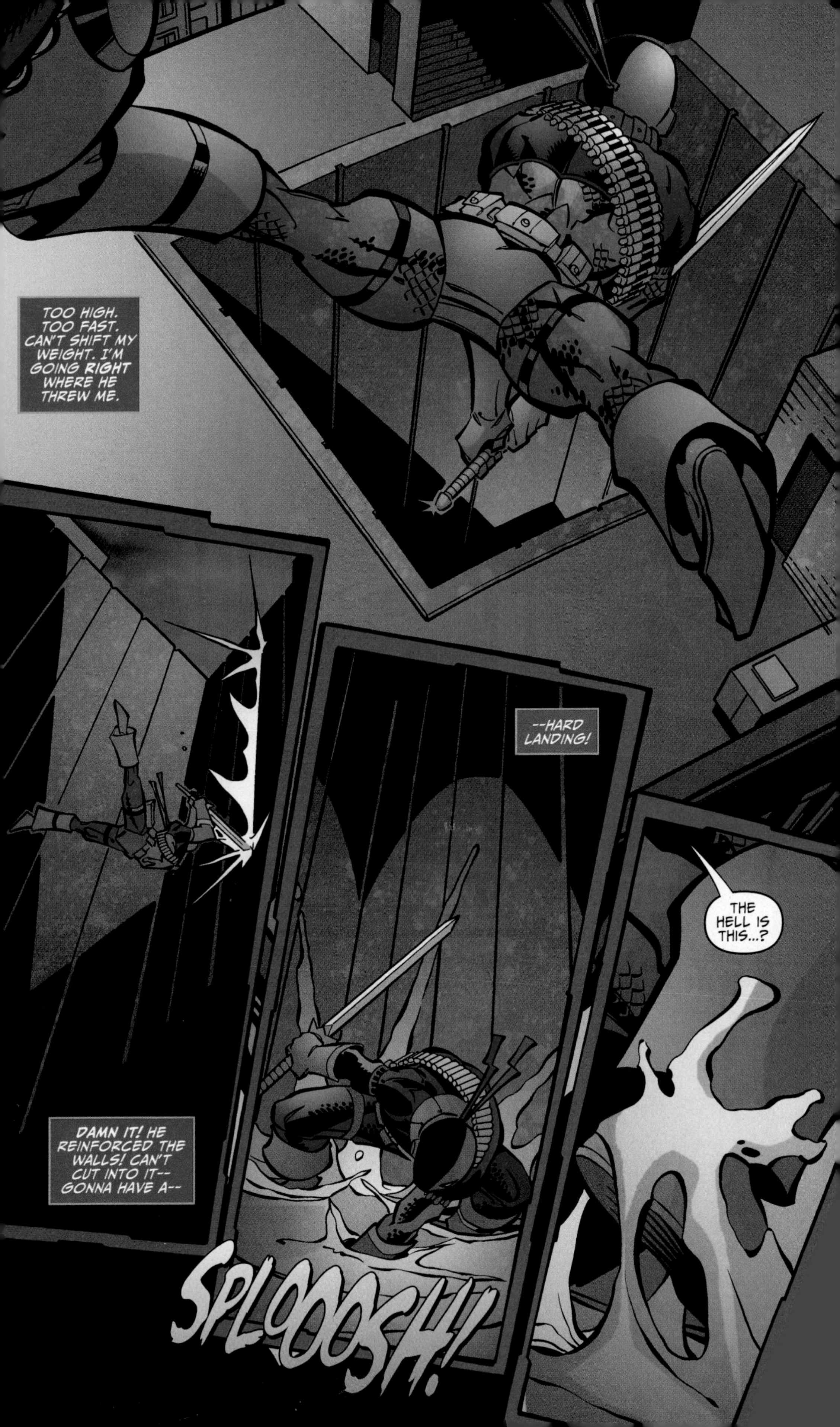
TOO HIGH. TOO FAST. CAN'T SHIFT MY WEIGHT. I'M GOING RIGHT WHERE HE THREW ME.
DAMN IT! HE REINFORCED THE WALLS! CAN'T CUT INTO IT-- GONNA HAVE A--
--HARD LANDING!
SPLOOOSH!
THE HELL IS THIS...?

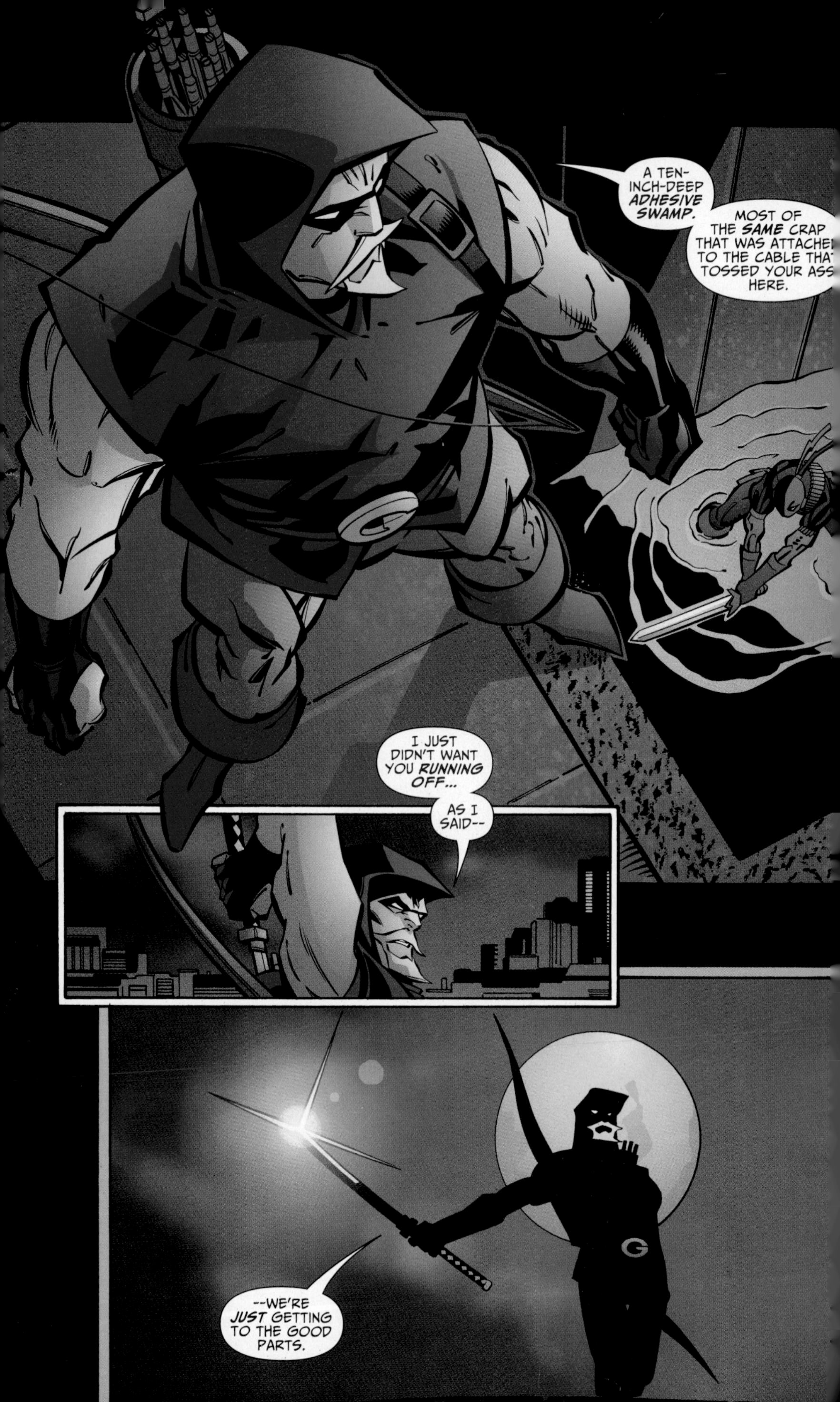
A TEN-INCH-DEEP *ADHESIVE SWAMP.*
MOST OF THE ***SAME*** CRAP THAT WAS ATTACHED TO THE CABLE THAT TOSSED YOUR ASS HERE.
I JUST DIDN'T WANT YOU *RUNNING OFF...*
AS I SAID--
--WE'RE *JUST* GETTING TO THE GOOD PARTS.

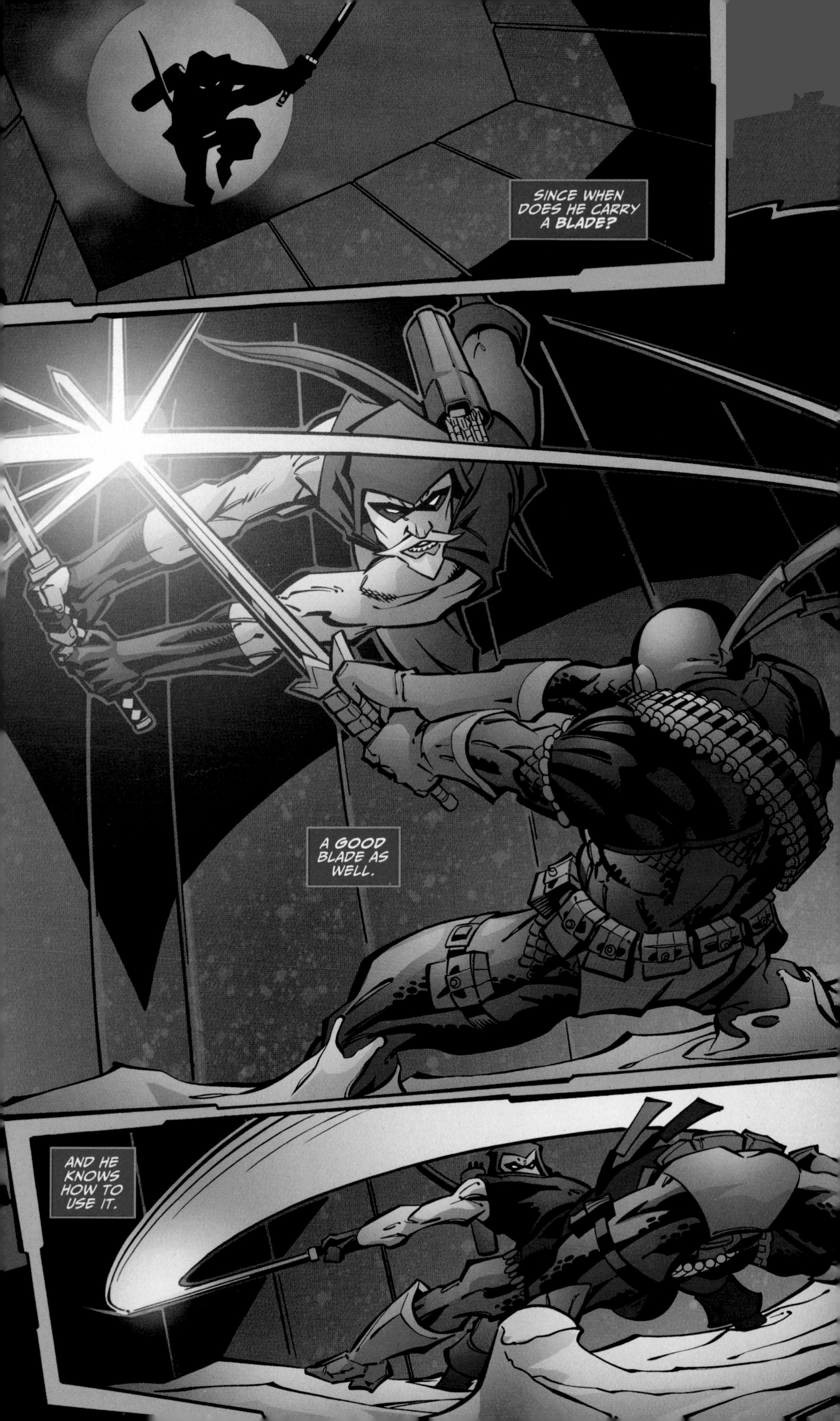
SINCE WHEN DOES HE CARRY A BLADE?
A GOOD BLADE AS WELL.
AND HE KNOWS HOW TO USE IT.

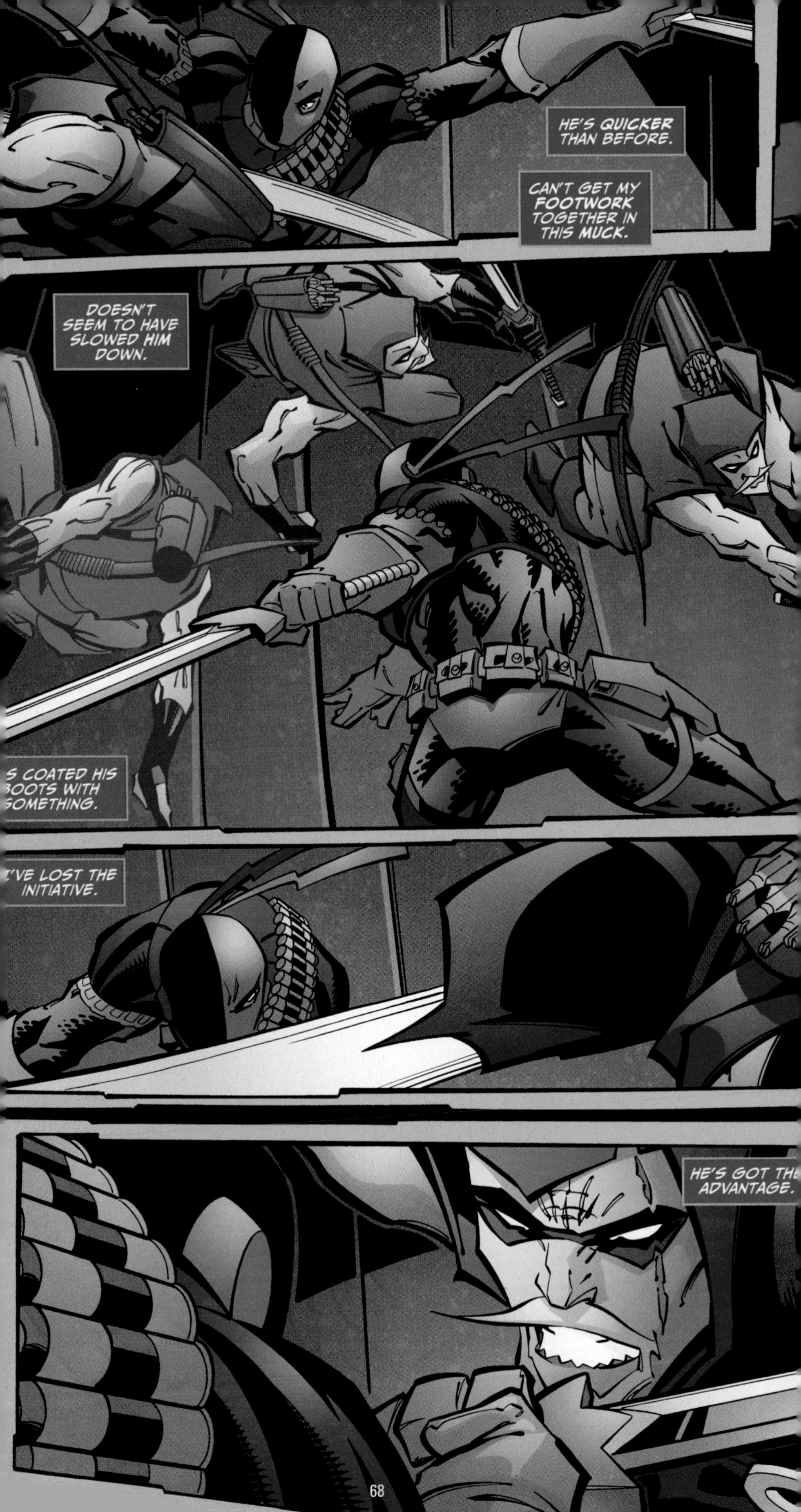
HE'S QUICKER THAN BEFORE.
CAN'T GET MY FOOTWORK TOGETHER IN THIS MUCK.
DOESN'T SEEM TO HAVE SLOWED HIM DOWN.
S COATED HIS BOOTS WITH SOMETHING.
I'VE LOST THE INITIATIVE.
HE'S GOT TH ADVANTAGE.

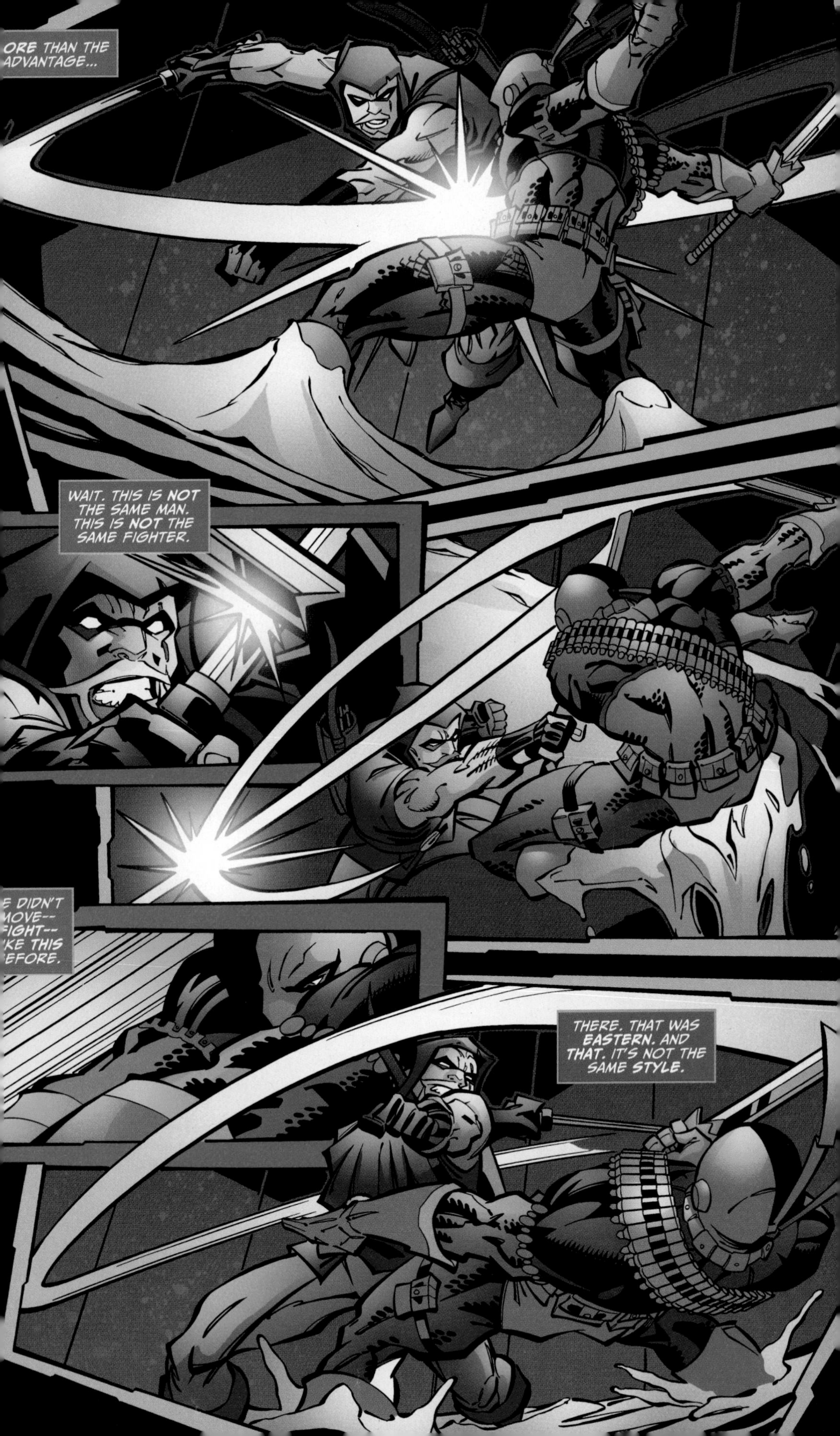
ORE THAN THE ADVANTAGE...
WAIT. THIS IS NOT THE SAME MAN. THIS IS NOT THE SAME FIGHTER.
E DIDN'T MOVE-- FIGHT-- KE THIS EFORE.
THERE. THAT WAS EASTERN. AND THAT. IT'S NOT THE SAME STYLE.

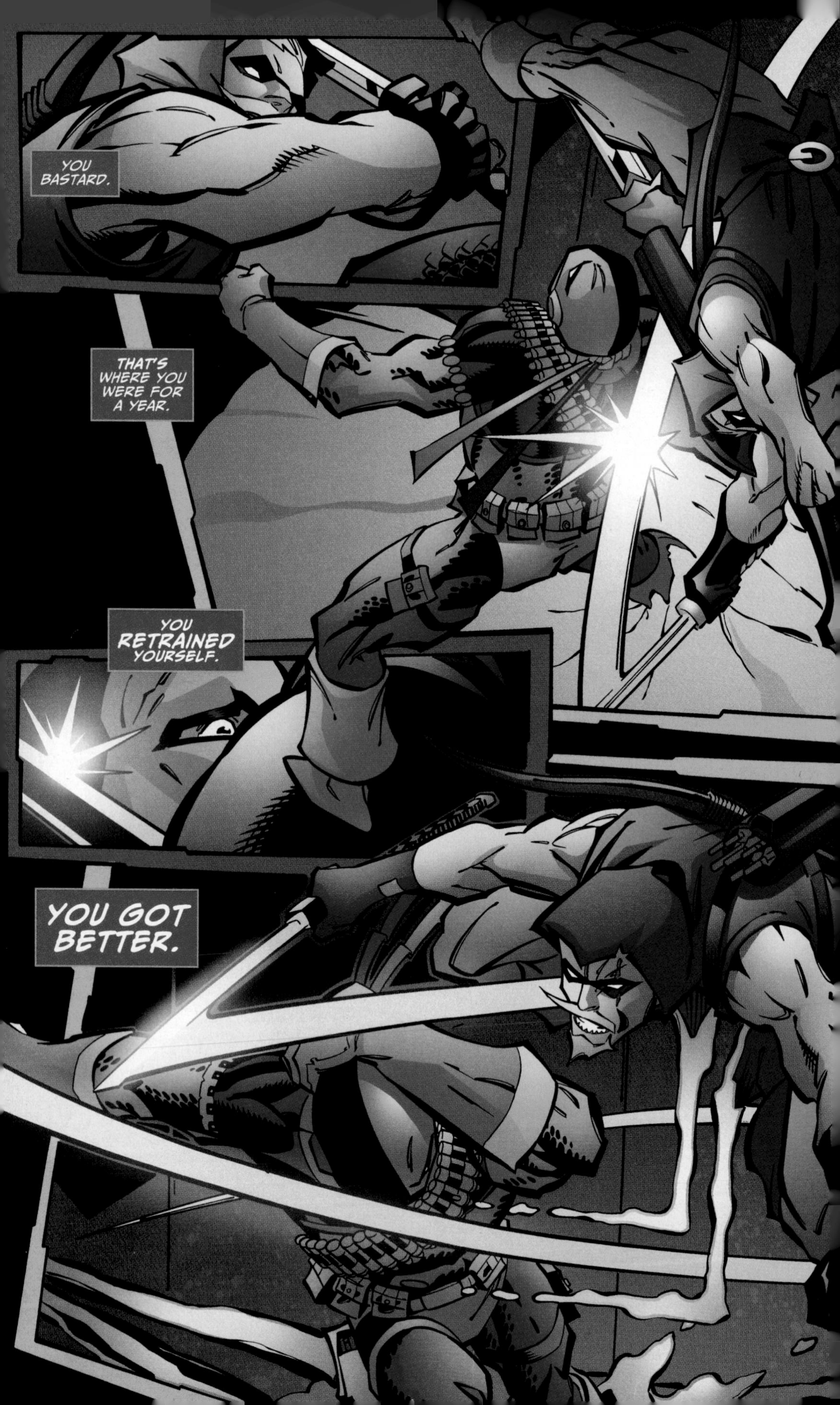
YOU BASTARD.
THAT'S WHERE YOU WERE FOR A YEAR.
YOU RETRAINED YOURSELF.
YOU GOT BETTER.

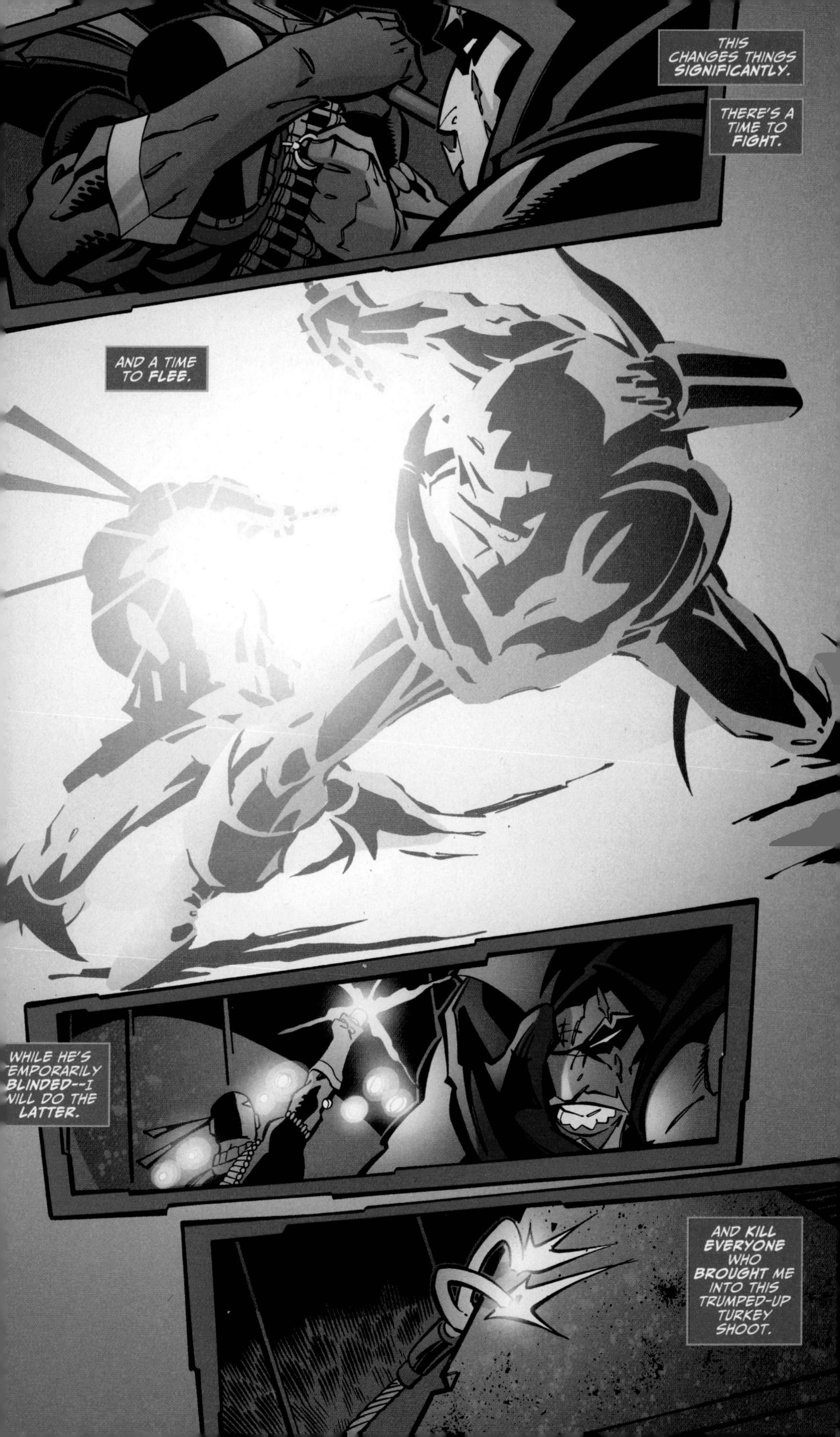
THIS CHANGES THINGS SIGNIFICANTLY.
THERE'S A TIME TO FIGHT.
AND A TIME TO FLEE.
WHILE HE'S EMPORARILY BLINDED--I VILL DO THE LATTER.
AND KILL EVERYONE WHO BROUGHT ME INTO THIS TRUMPED-UP TURKEY SHOOT.

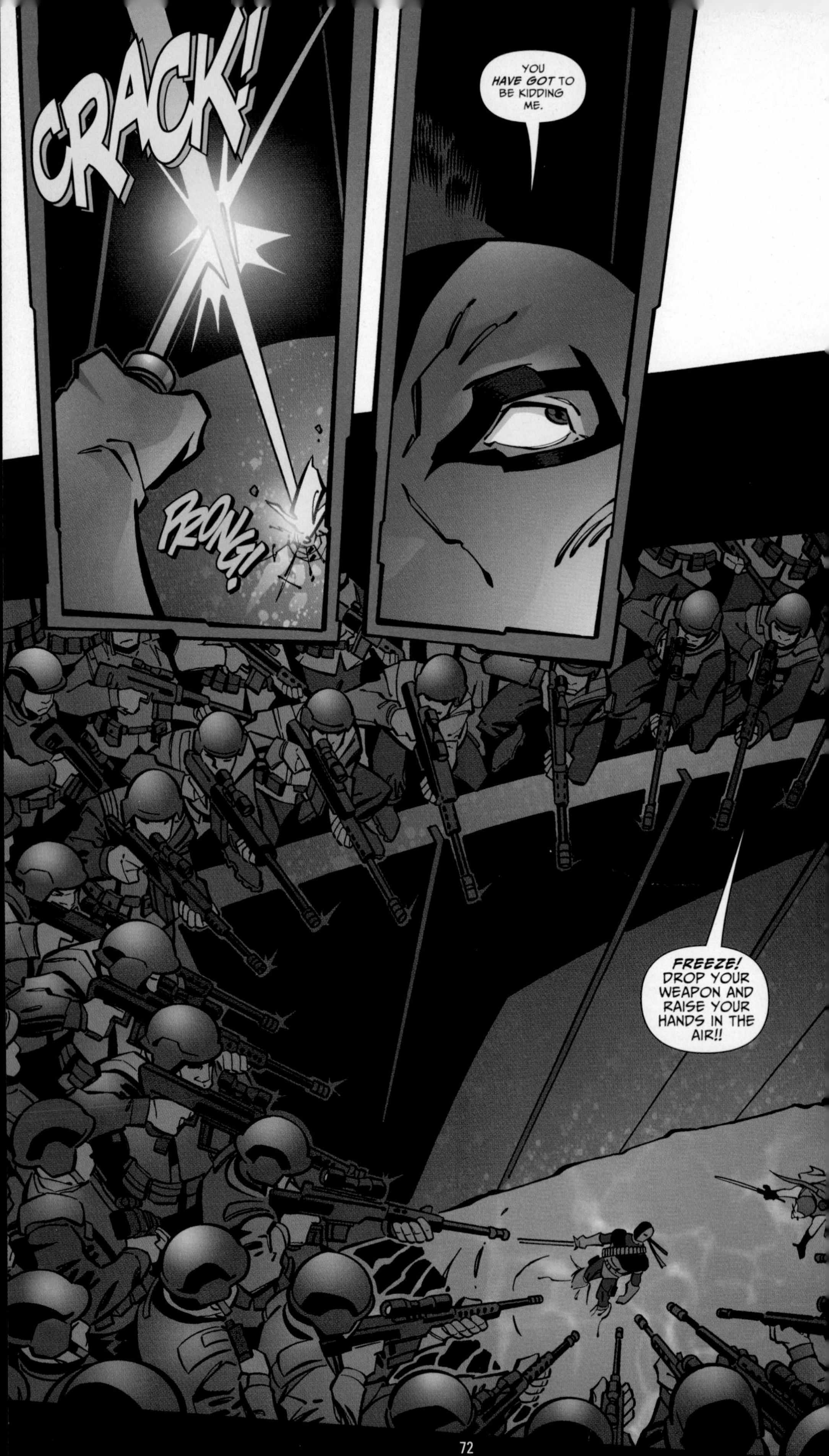
CRACK!
PRONG!!
YOU *HAVE GOT* TO BE KIDDING ME.
FREEZE! DROP YOUR WEAPON AND RAISE YOUR HANDS IN THE AIR!!

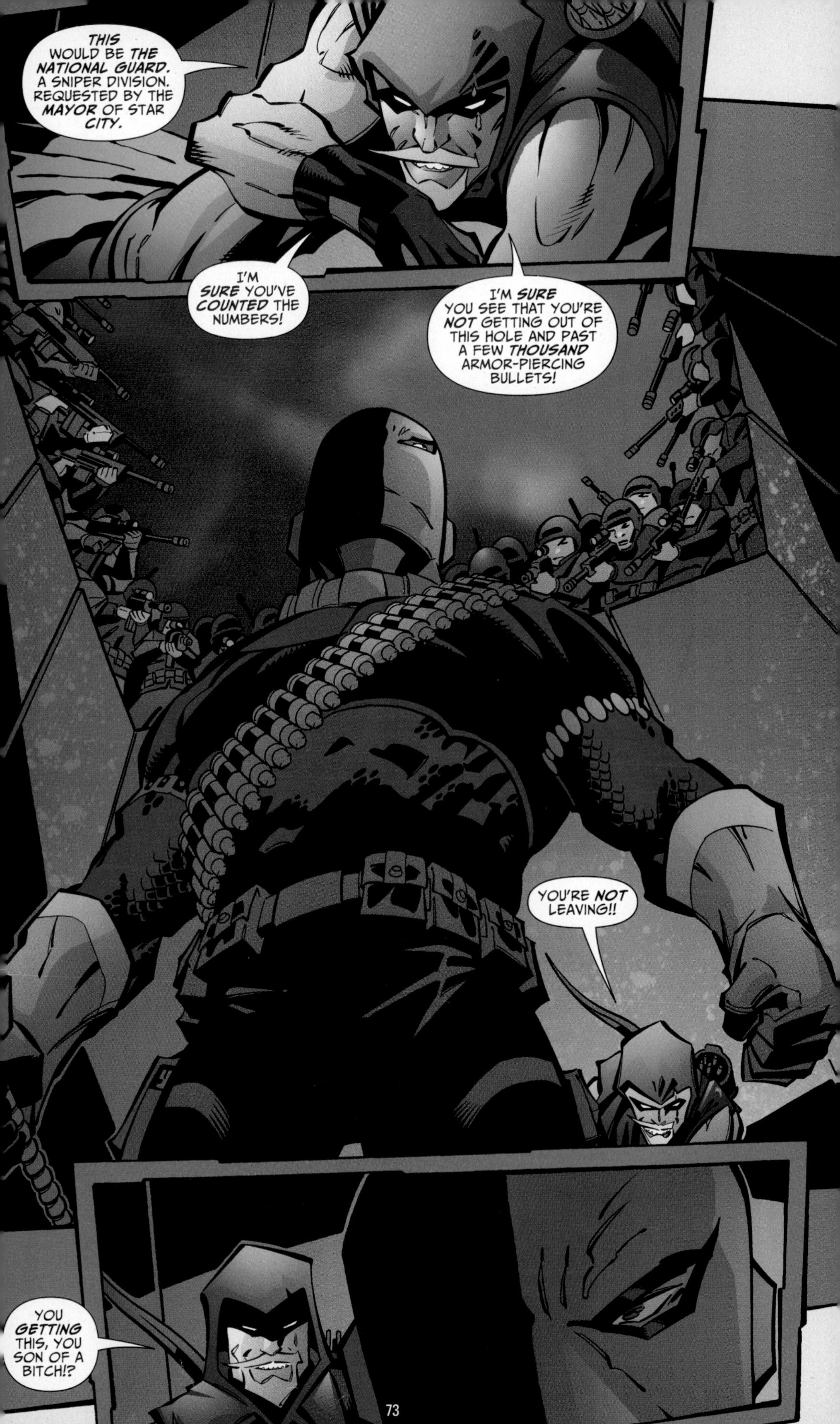
THIS WOULD BE THE NATIONAL GUARD. A SNIPER DIVISION. REQUESTED BY THE MAYOR OF STAR CITY.
I'M SURE YOU'VE COUNTED THE NUMBERS!
I'M SURE YOU SEE THAT YOU'RE NOT GETTING OUT OF THIS HOLE AND PAST A FEW THOUSAND ARMOR-PIERCING BULLETS!
YOU'RE NOT LEAVING!!
YOU GETTING THIS, YOU SON OF A BITCH!?

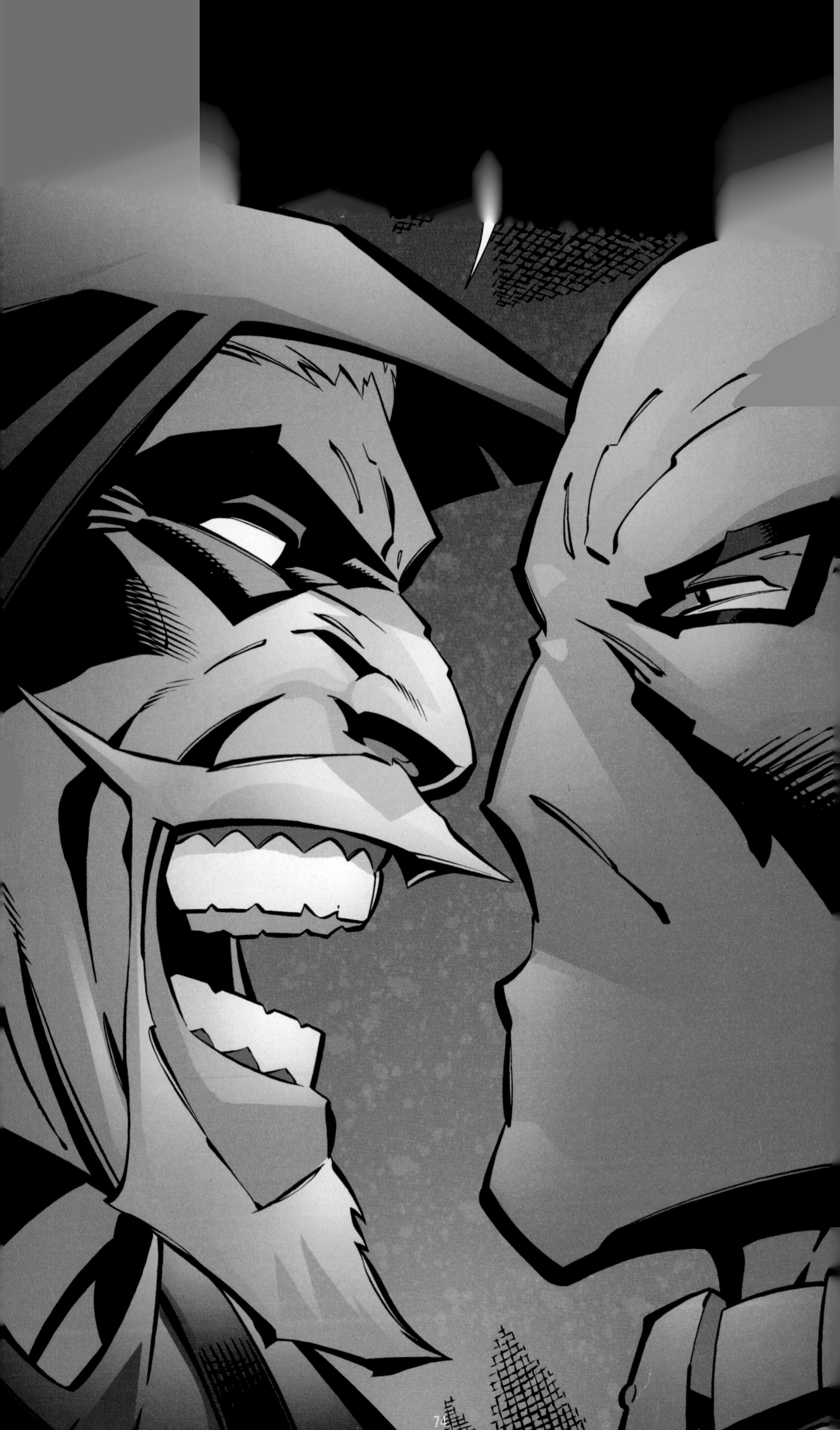

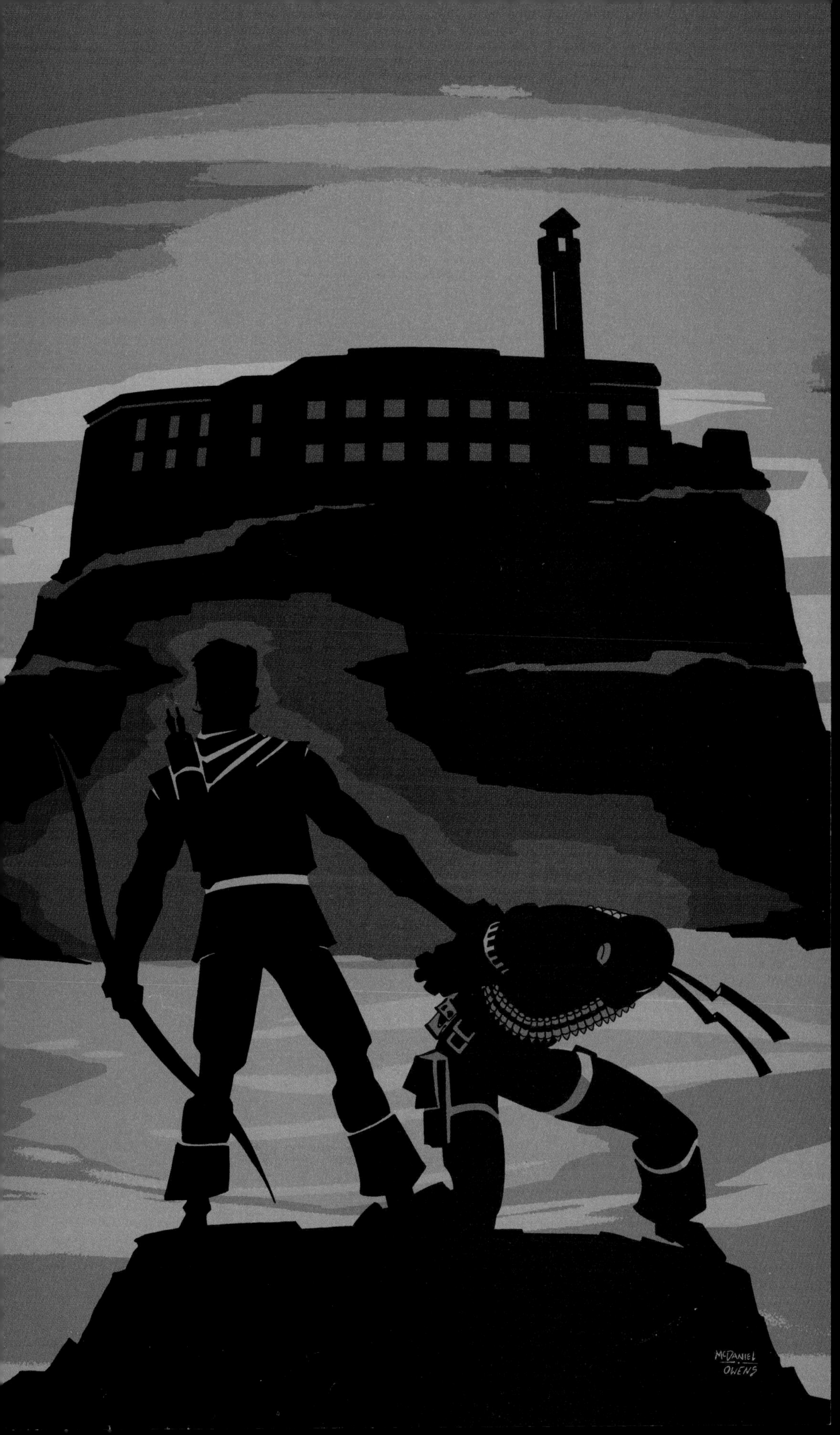
McDANIEL
OWENS

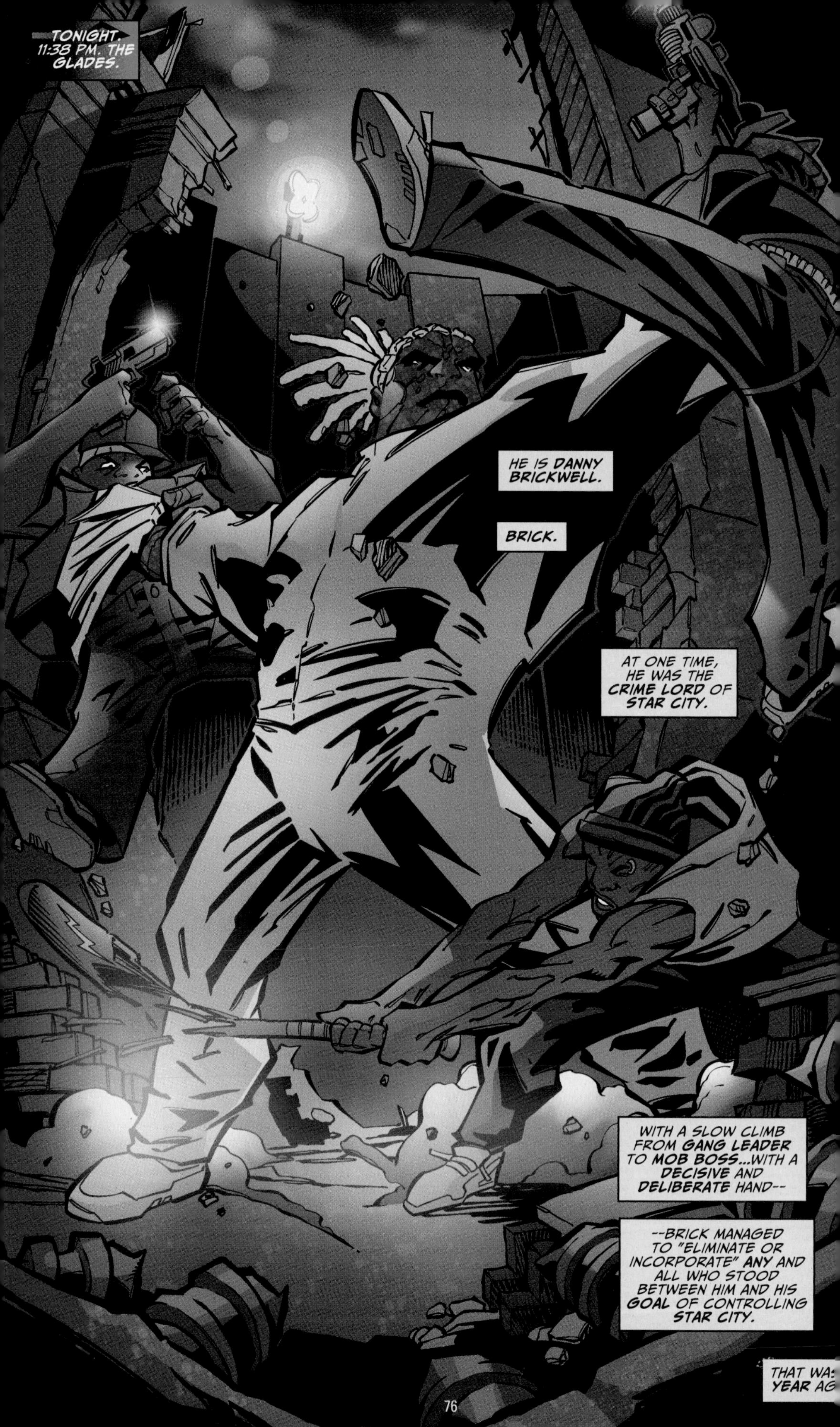
TONIGHT. 11:38 PM. THE GLADES.
HE IS DANNY BRICKWELL.
BRICK.
AT ONE TIME, HE WAS THE CRIME LORD OF STAR CITY.
WITH A SLOW CLIMB FROM GANG LEADER TO MOB BOSS...WITH A DECISIVE AND DELIBERATE HAND--
--BRICK MANAGED TO "ELIMINATE OR INCORPORATE" ANY AND ALL WHO STOOD BETWEEN HIM AND HIS GOAL OF CONTROLLING STAR CITY.
THAT WAS
YEAR AG

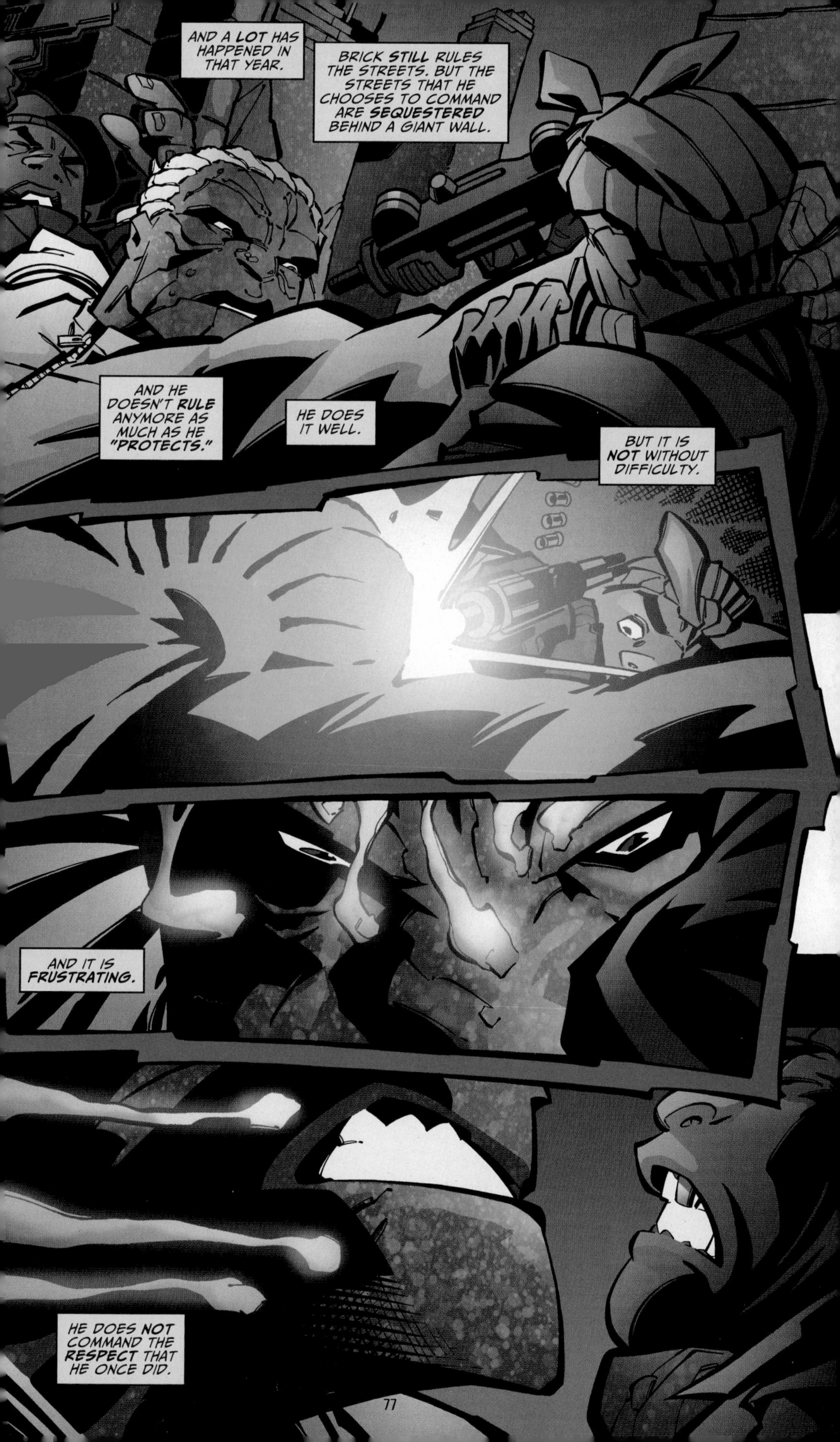
AND A LOT HAS HAPPENED IN THAT YEAR.
BRICK STILL RULES THE STREETS. BUT THE STREETS THAT HE CHOOSES TO COMMAND ARE SEQUESTERED BEHIND A GIANT WALL.
AND HE DOESN'T RULE ANYMORE AS MUCH AS HE "PROTECTS."
HE DOES IT WELL.
BUT IT IS NOT WITHOUT DIFFICULTY.
AND IT IS FRUSTRATING.
HE DOES NOT COMMAND THE RESPECT THAT HE ONCE DID.

THEY ALL SEEM TO FEAR HIM A LITTLE *LESS*.

HE THINKS *SOMETIMES* IT WAS JUST EASIER WHEN HE TOOK *MONEY* AND *KILLED* PEOPLE.

IT WAS A *LESS* CONFUSING TIME.

THE *HELL*-- WHAT TH HELL IS T MATTE WITH YO MAN?!

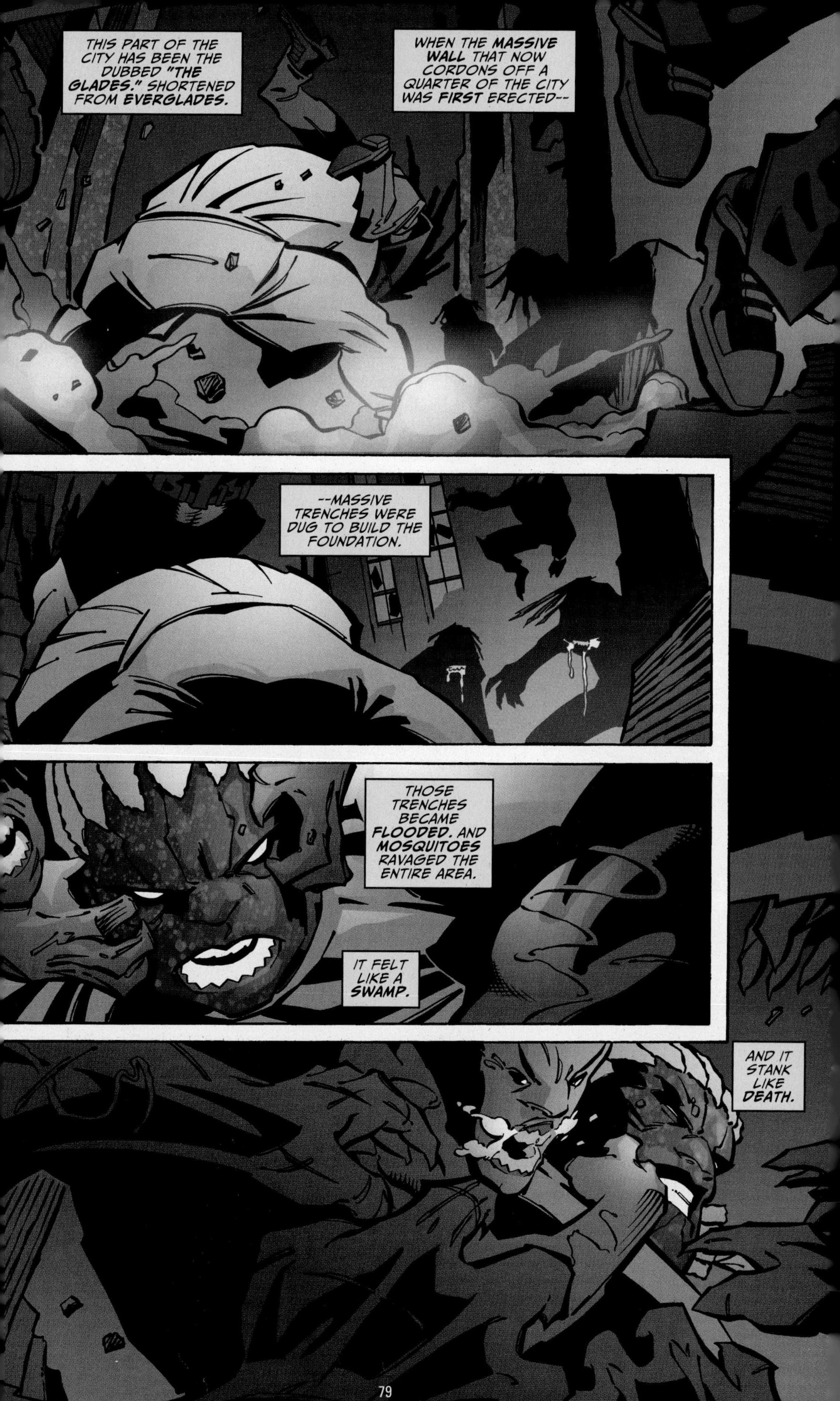
THIS PART OF THE CITY HAS BEEN THE DUBBED "THE GLADES." SHORTENED FROM EVERGLADES.
WHEN THE MASSIVE WALL THAT NOW CORDONS OFF A QUARTER OF THE CITY WAS FIRST ERECTED--
--MASSIVE TRENCHES WERE DUG TO BUILD THE FOUNDATION.
THOSE TRENCHES BECAME FLOODED. AND MOSQUITOES RAVAGED THE ENTIRE AREA.
IT FELT LIKE A SWAMP.
AND IT STANK LIKE DEATH.

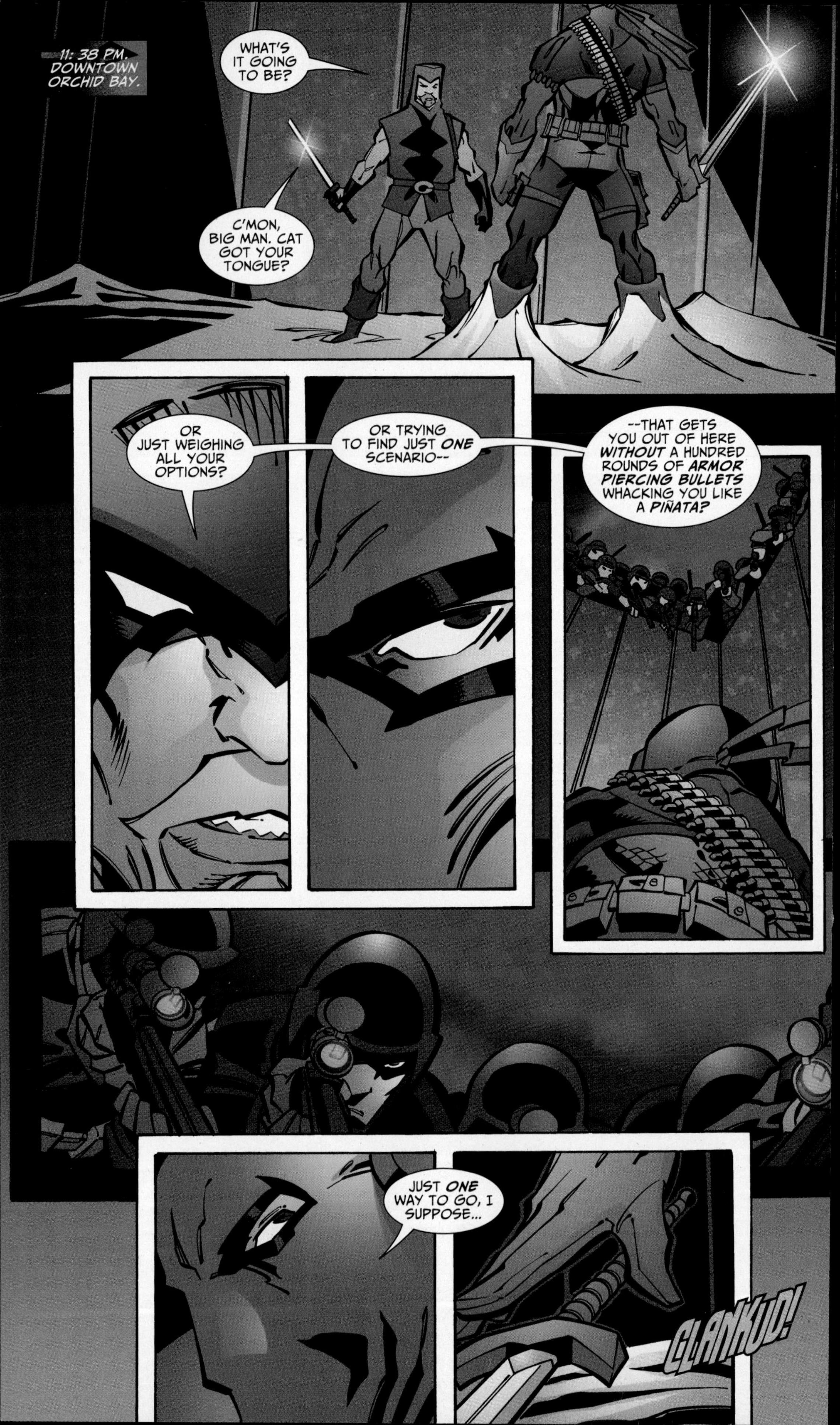
11:38 PM. DOWNTOWN ORCHID BAY.
WHAT'S IT GOING TO BE?
C'MON, BIG MAN. CAT GOT YOUR TONGUE?
OR JUST WEIGHING ALL YOUR OPTIONS?
OR TRYING TO FIND JUST ONE SCENARIO--
--THAT GETS YOU OUT OF HERE WITHOUT A HUNDRED ROUNDS OF ARMOR PIERCING BULLETS WHACKING YOU LIKE A PIÑATA?
JUST ONE WAY TO GO, I SUPPOSE...
CLANKUD!

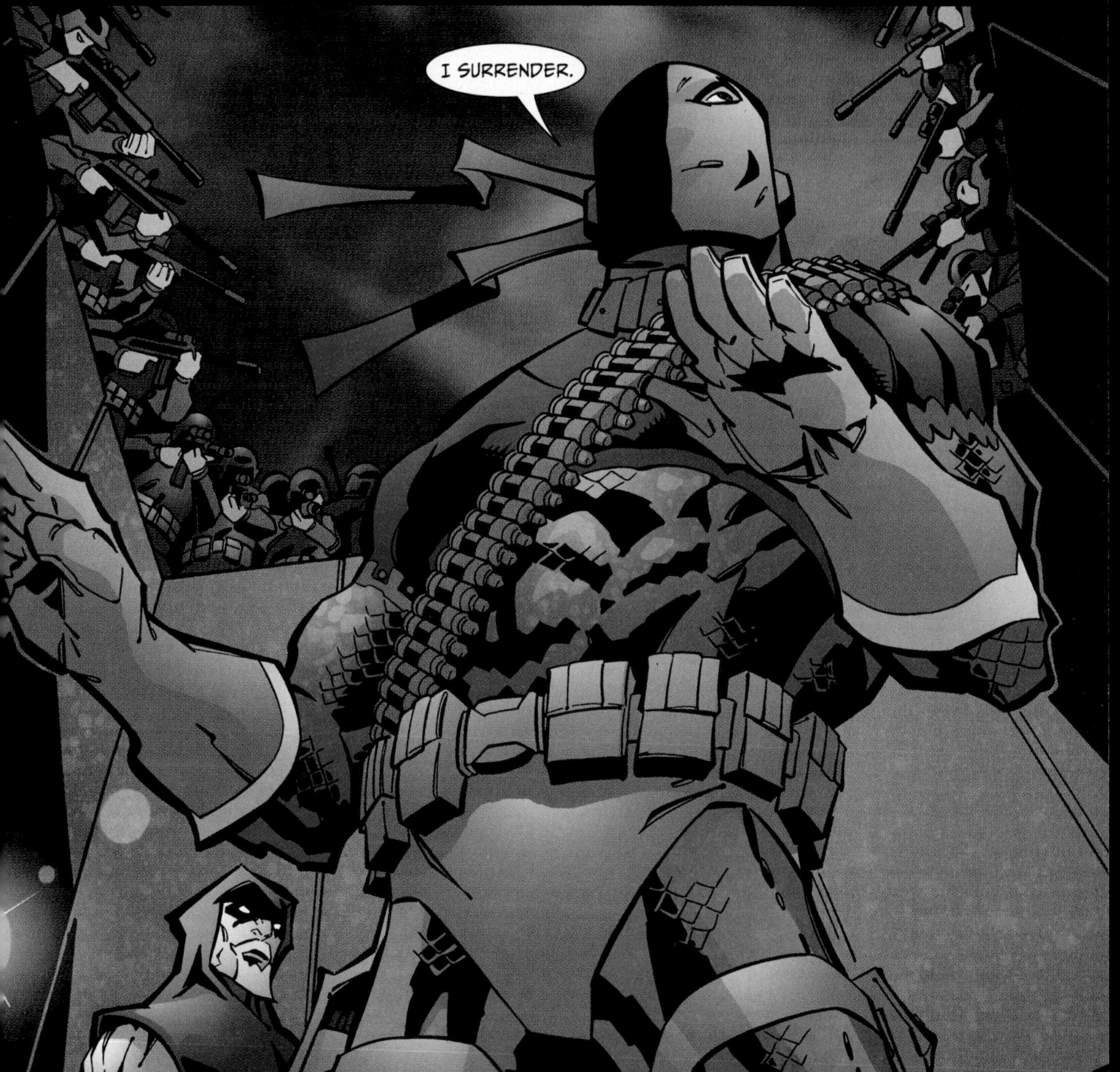
I SURRENDER.

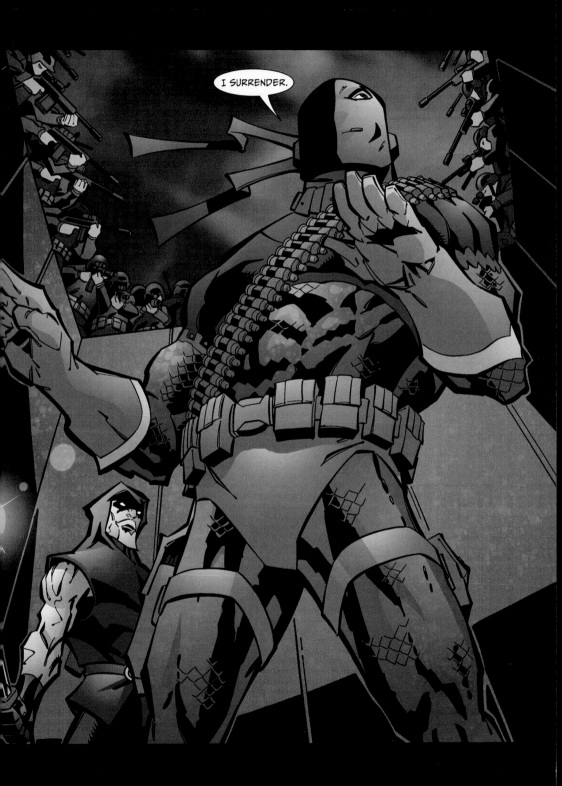

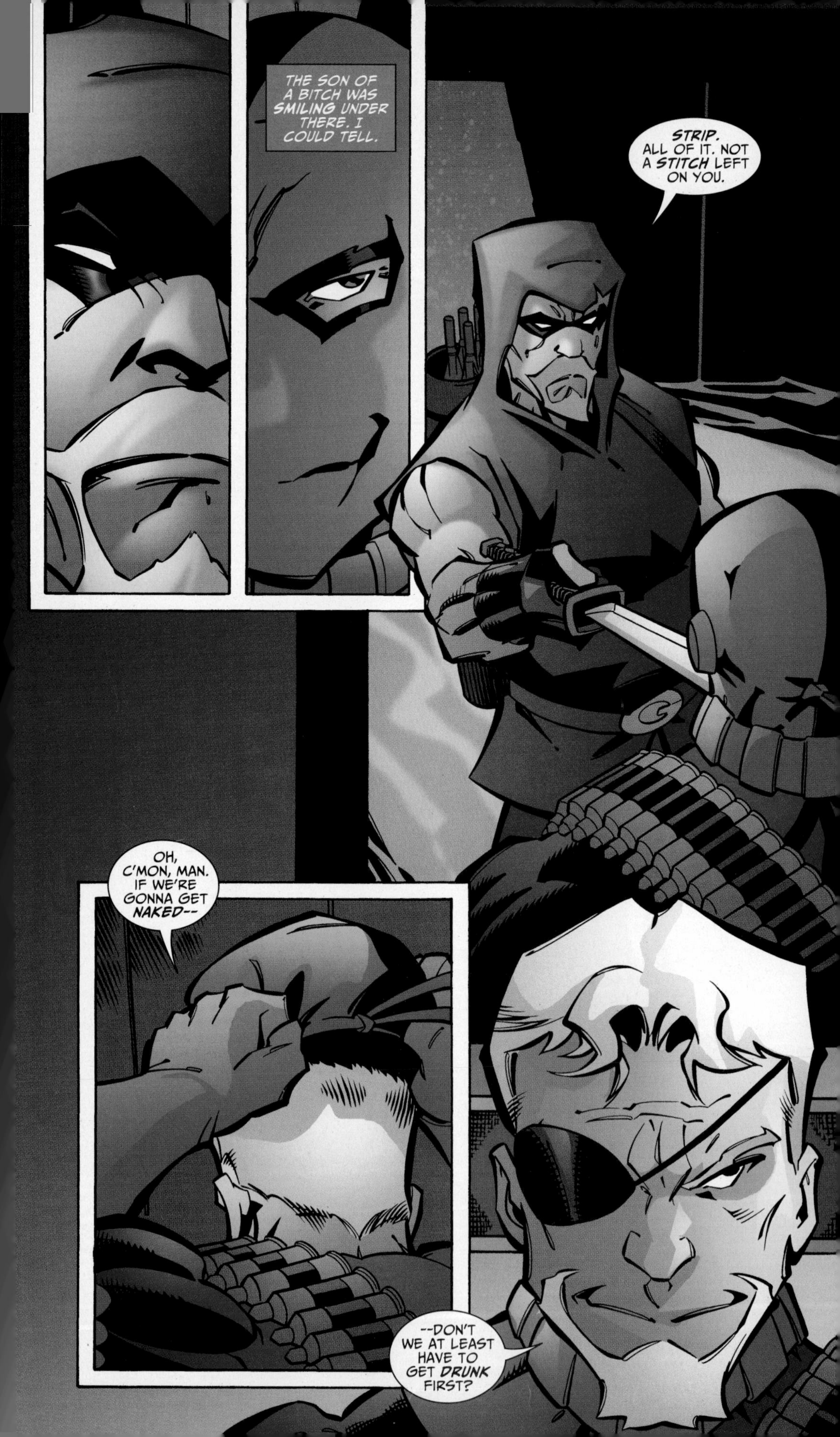
THE SON OF A BITCH WAS SMILING UNDER THERE. I COULD TELL.
STRIP. ALL OF IT. NOT A STITCH LEFT ON YOU.
OH, C'MON, MAN. IF WE'RE GONNA GET NAKED--
--DON'T WE AT LEAST HAVE TO GET DRUNK FIRST?

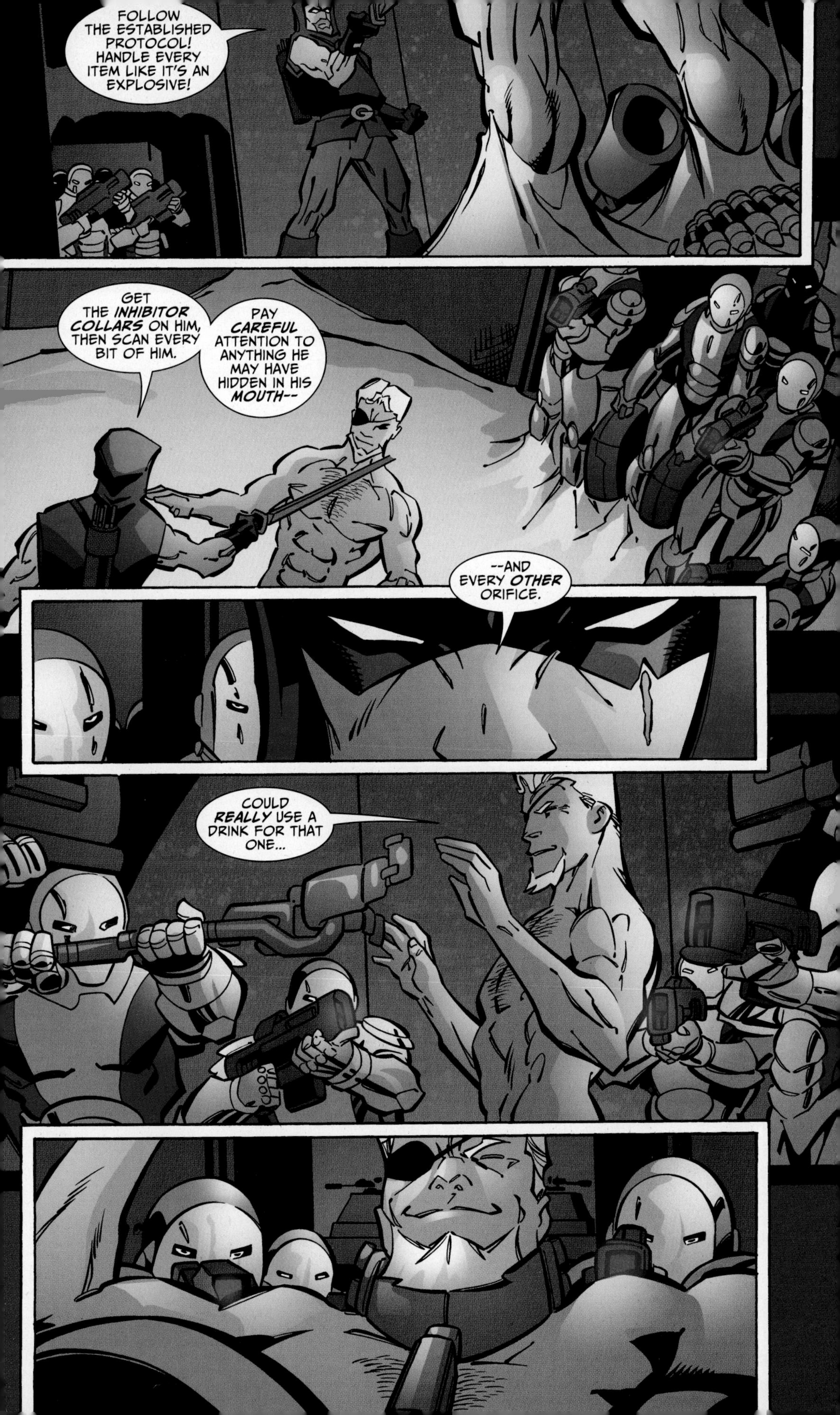
FOLLOW THE ESTABLISHED PROTOCOL! HANDLE EVERY ITEM LIKE IT'S AN EXPLOSIVE!
GET THE INHIBITOR COLLARS ON HIM, THEN SCAN EVERY BIT OF HIM.
PAY CAREFUL ATTENTION TO ANYTHING HE MAY HAVE HIDDEN IN HIS MOUTH--
--AND EVERY OTHER ORIFICE.
COULD REALLY USE A DRINK FOR THAT ONE...

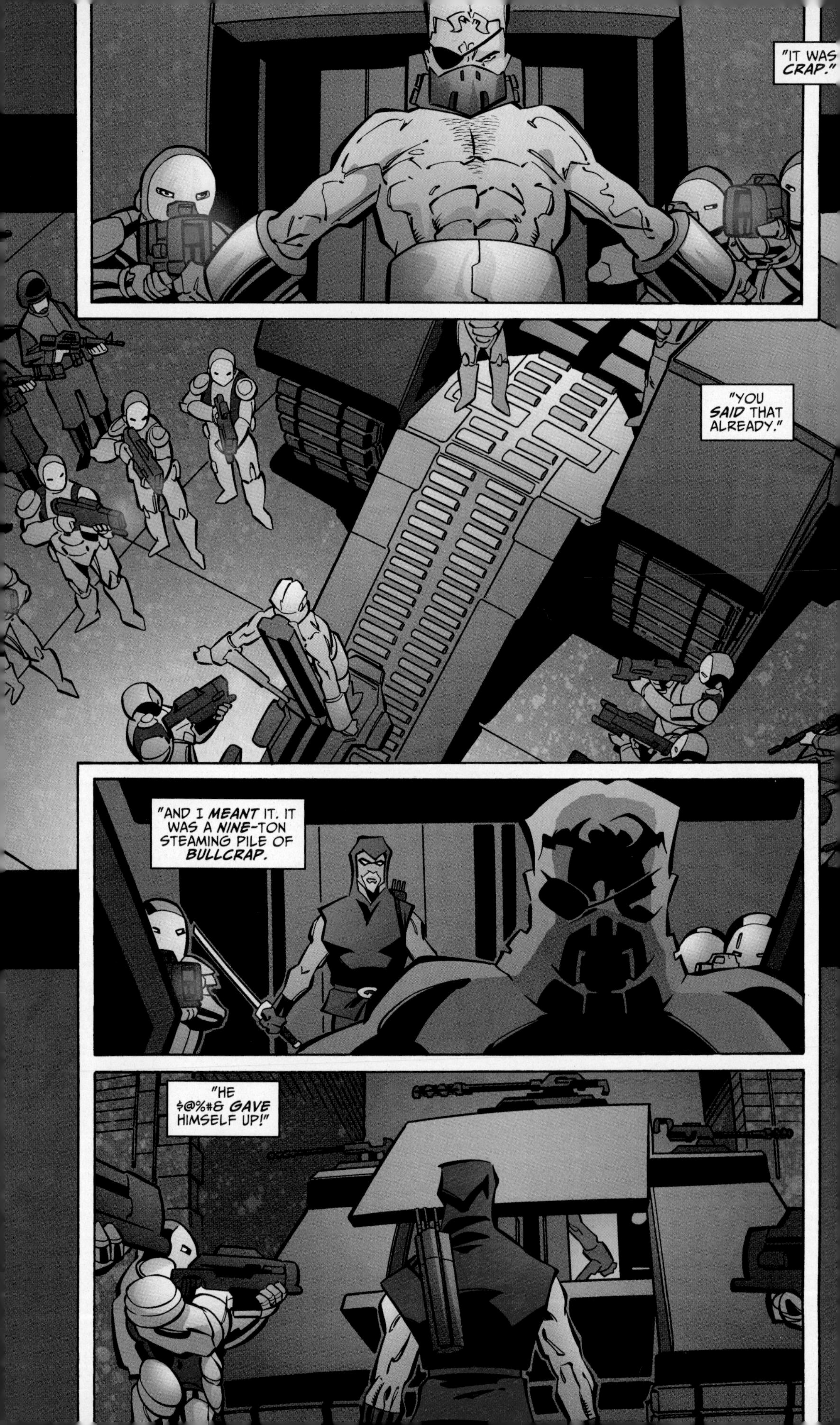
"IT WAS *CRAP.*"
"YOU *SAID* THAT ALREADY."
"AND I *MEANT* IT. IT WAS A *NINE*-TON STEAMING PILE OF *BULLCRAP.*
"HE $@%#& *GAVE* HIMSELF UP!"

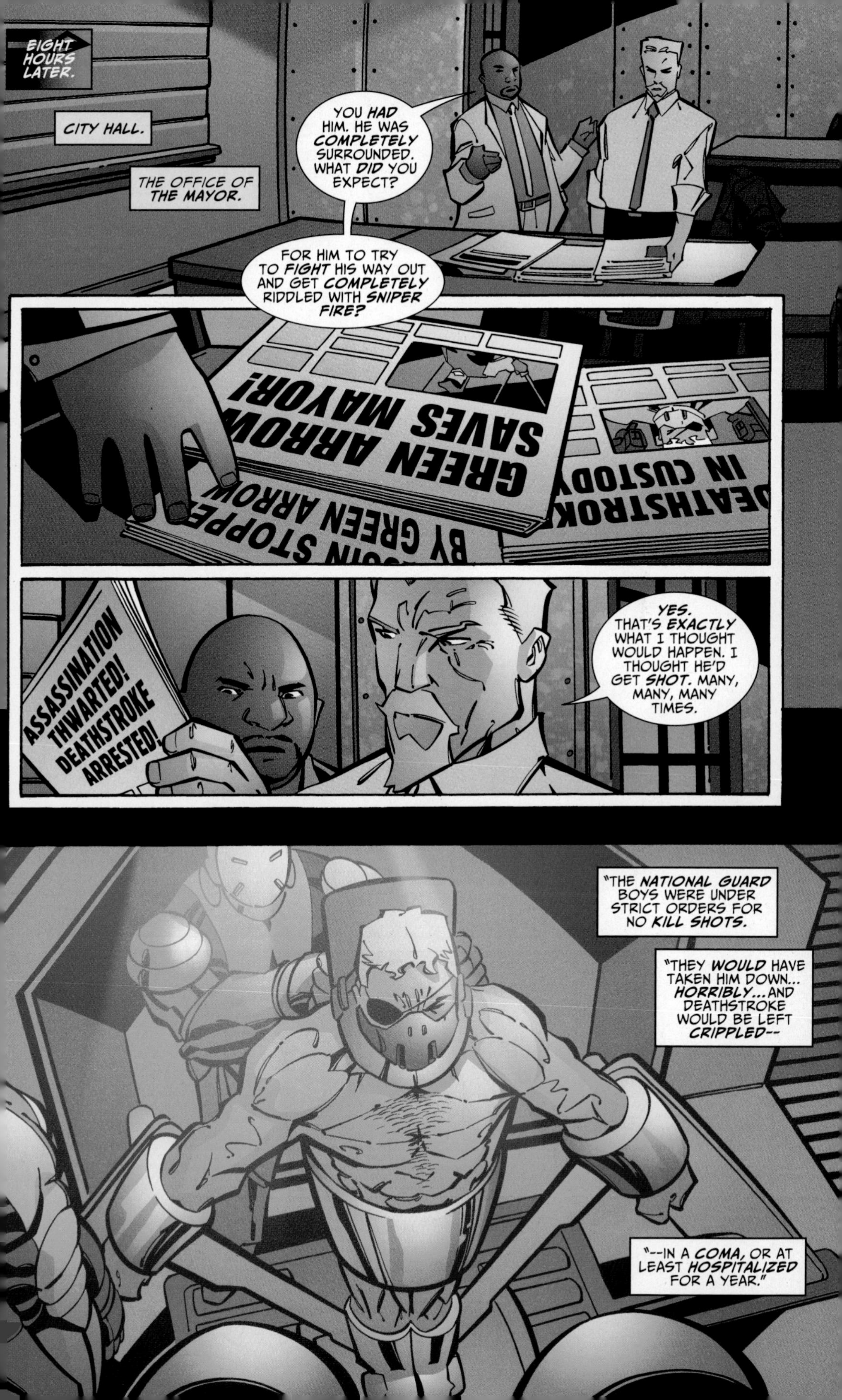
EIGHT HOURS LATER.
CITY HALL.
THE OFFICE OF THE MAYOR.
YOU HAD HIM. HE WAS COMPLETELY SURROUNDED. WHAT DID YOU EXPECT?
FOR HIM TO TRY TO FIGHT HIS WAY OUT AND GET COMPLETELY RIDDLED WITH SNIPER FIRE?
GREEN ARROW SAVES MAYOR!
BY GREEN ARROW
DEATHSTROKE IN CUSTODY
ASSASSINATION THWARTED! DEATHSTROKE ARRESTED!
YES. THAT'S EXACTLY WHAT I THOUGHT WOULD HAPPEN. I THOUGHT HE'D GET SHOT. MANY, MANY, MANY TIMES.
"THE NATIONAL GUARD BOYS WERE UNDER STRICT ORDERS FOR NO KILL SHOTS.
"THEY WOULD HAVE TAKEN HIM DOWN... HORRIBLY... AND DEATHSTROKE WOULD BE LEFT CRIPPLED--
"--IN A COMA, OR AT LEAST HOSPITALIZED FOR A YEAR."

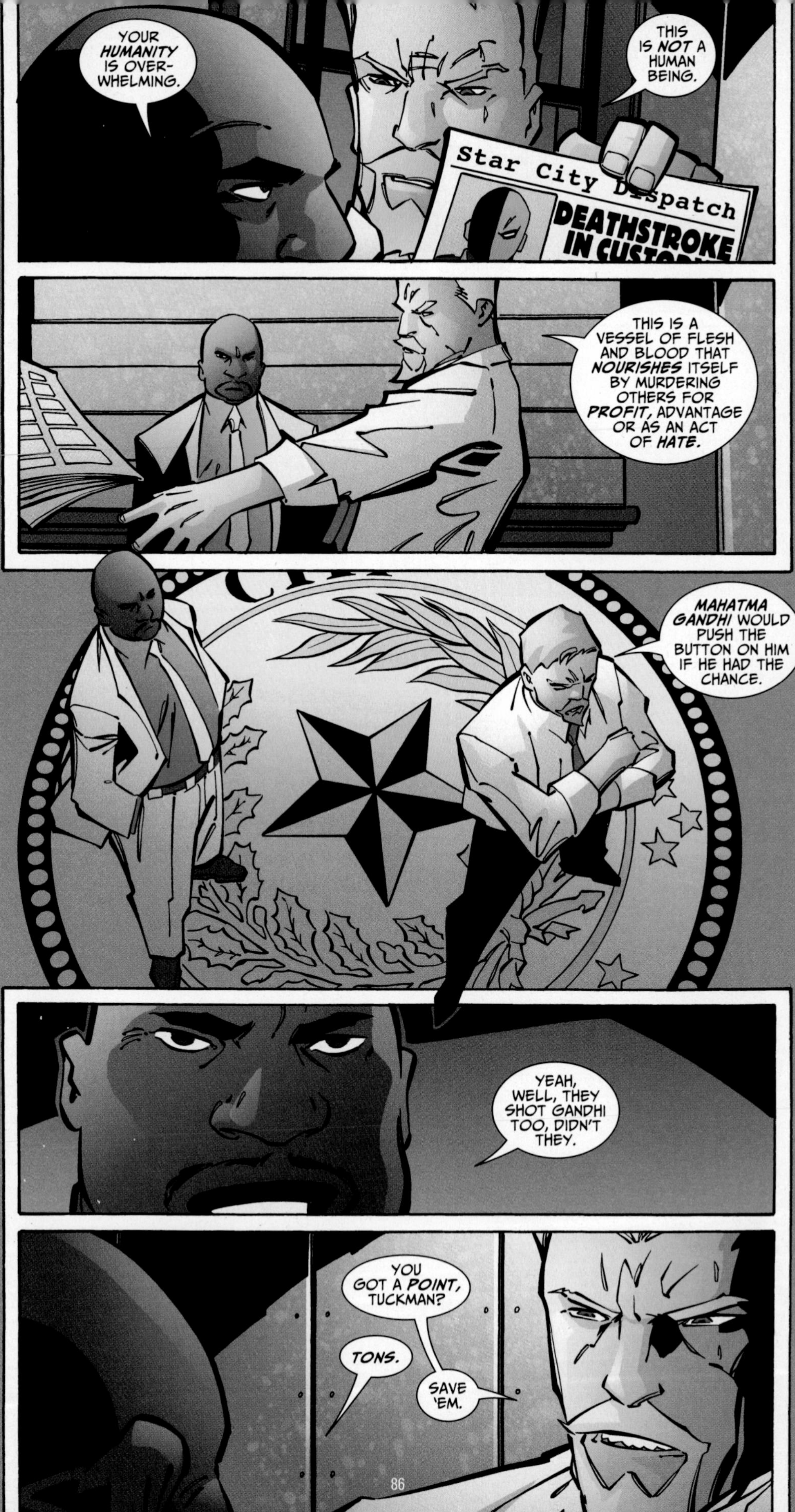
YOUR HUMANITY IS OVER-WHELMING.
THIS IS NOT A HUMAN BEING.
Star City Dispatch
DEATHSTROKE IN CUSTO
THIS IS A VESSEL OF FLESH AND BLOOD THAT NOURISHES ITSELF BY MURDERING OTHERS FOR PROFIT, ADVANTAGE OR AS AN ACT OF HATE.
MAHATMA GANDHI WOULD PUSH THE BUTTON ON HIM IF HE HAD THE CHANCE.
YEAH, WELL, THEY SHOT GANDHI TOO, DIDN'T THEY.
YOU GOT A POINT, TUCKMAN?
TONS.
SAVE 'EM.

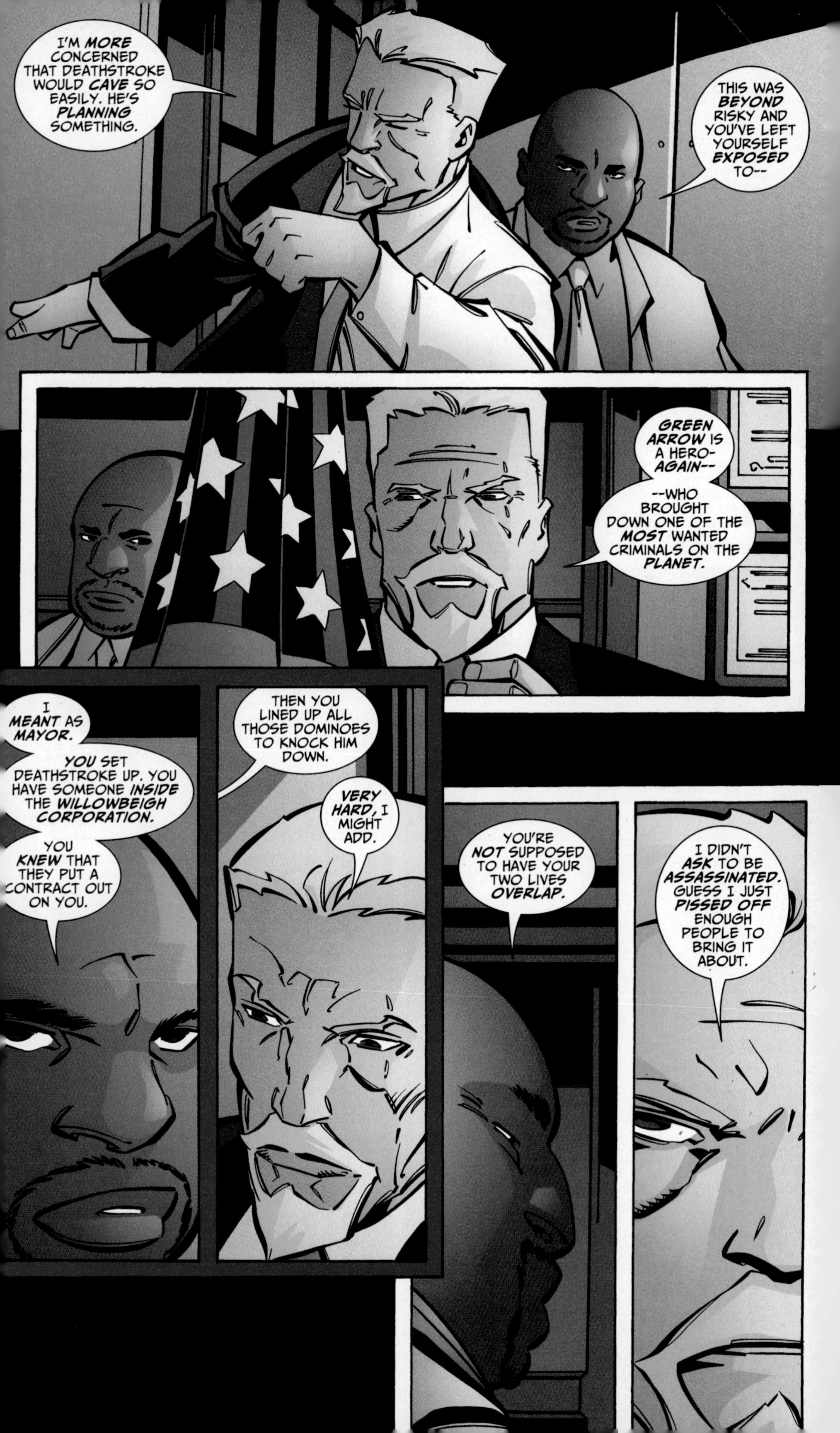
I'M MORE CONCERNED THAT DEATHSTROKE WOULD CAVE SO EASILY. HE'S PLANNING SOMETHING.
THIS WAS BEYOND RISKY AND YOU'VE LEFT YOURSELF EXPOSED TO--
GREEN ARROW IS A HERO-AGAIN--
--WHO BROUGHT DOWN ONE OF THE MOST WANTED CRIMINALS ON THE PLANET.
I MEANT AS MAYOR.
YOU SET DEATHSTROKE UP. YOU HAVE SOMEONE INSIDE THE WILLOWBEIGH CORPORATION.
YOU KNEW THAT THEY PUT A CONTRACT OUT ON YOU.
THEN YOU LINED UP ALL THOSE DOMINOES TO KNOCK HIM DOWN.
VERY HARD, I MIGHT ADD.
YOU'RE NOT SUPPOSED TO HAVE YOUR TWO LIVES OVERLAP.
I DIDN'T ASK TO BE ASSASSINATED. GUESS I JUST PISSED OFF ENOUGH PEOPLE TO BRING IT ABOUT.

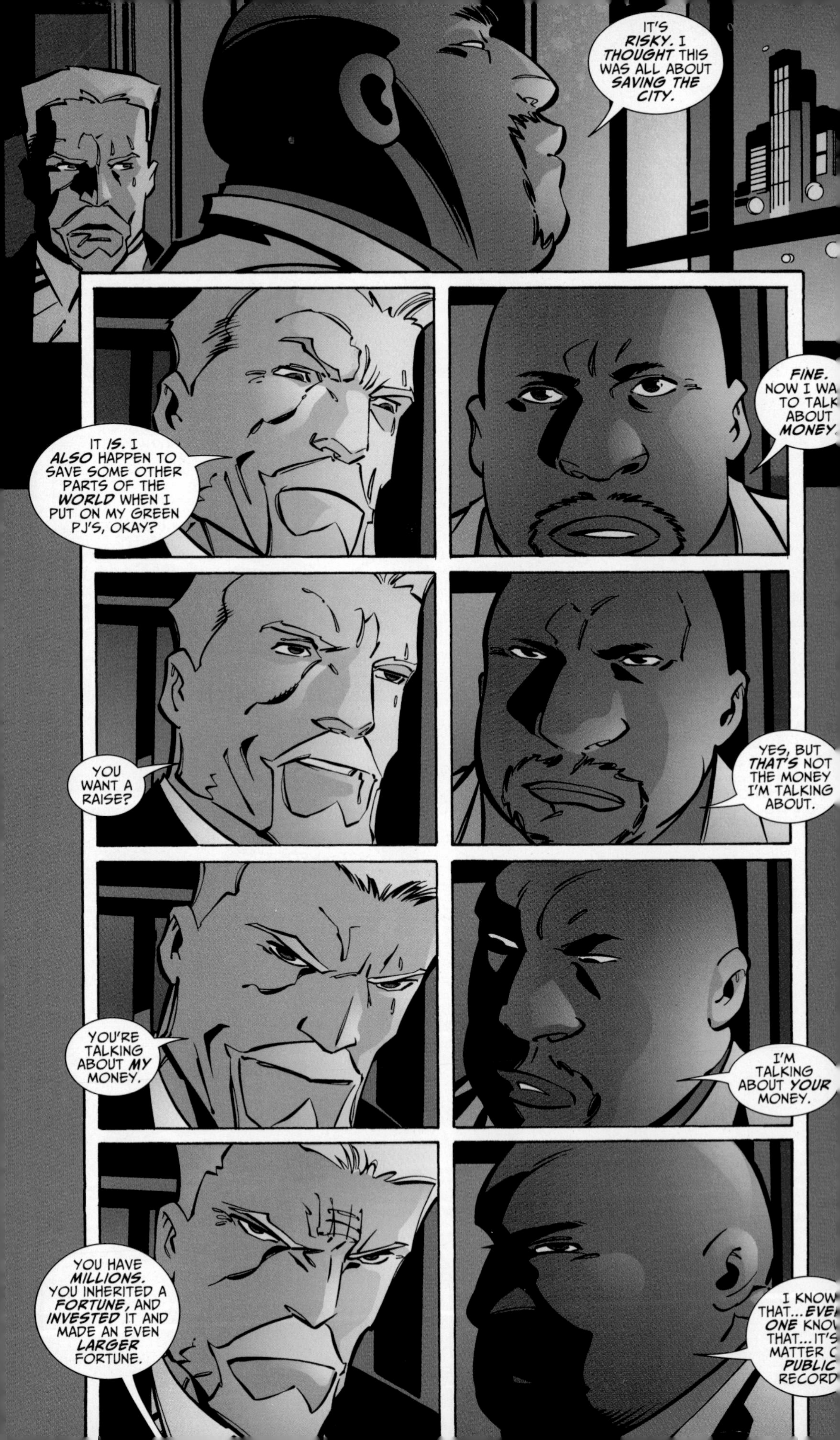
IT'S RISKY. I THOUGHT THIS WAS ALL ABOUT SAVING THE CITY.
IT IS. I ALSO HAPPEN TO SAVE SOME OTHER PARTS OF THE WORLD WHEN I PUT ON MY GREEN PJ'S, OKAY?
FINE. NOW I WA TO TALK ABOUT MONEY.
YOU WANT A RAISE?
YES, BUT THAT'S NOT THE MONEY I'M TALKING ABOUT.
YOU'RE TALKING ABOUT MY MONEY.
I'M TALKING ABOUT YOUR MONEY.
YOU HAVE MILLIONS. YOU INHERITED A FORTUNE, AND INVESTED IT AND MADE AN EVEN LARGER FORTUNE.
I KNOW THAT... EVE ONE KNOW THAT... IT'S MATTER PUBLIC RECORD

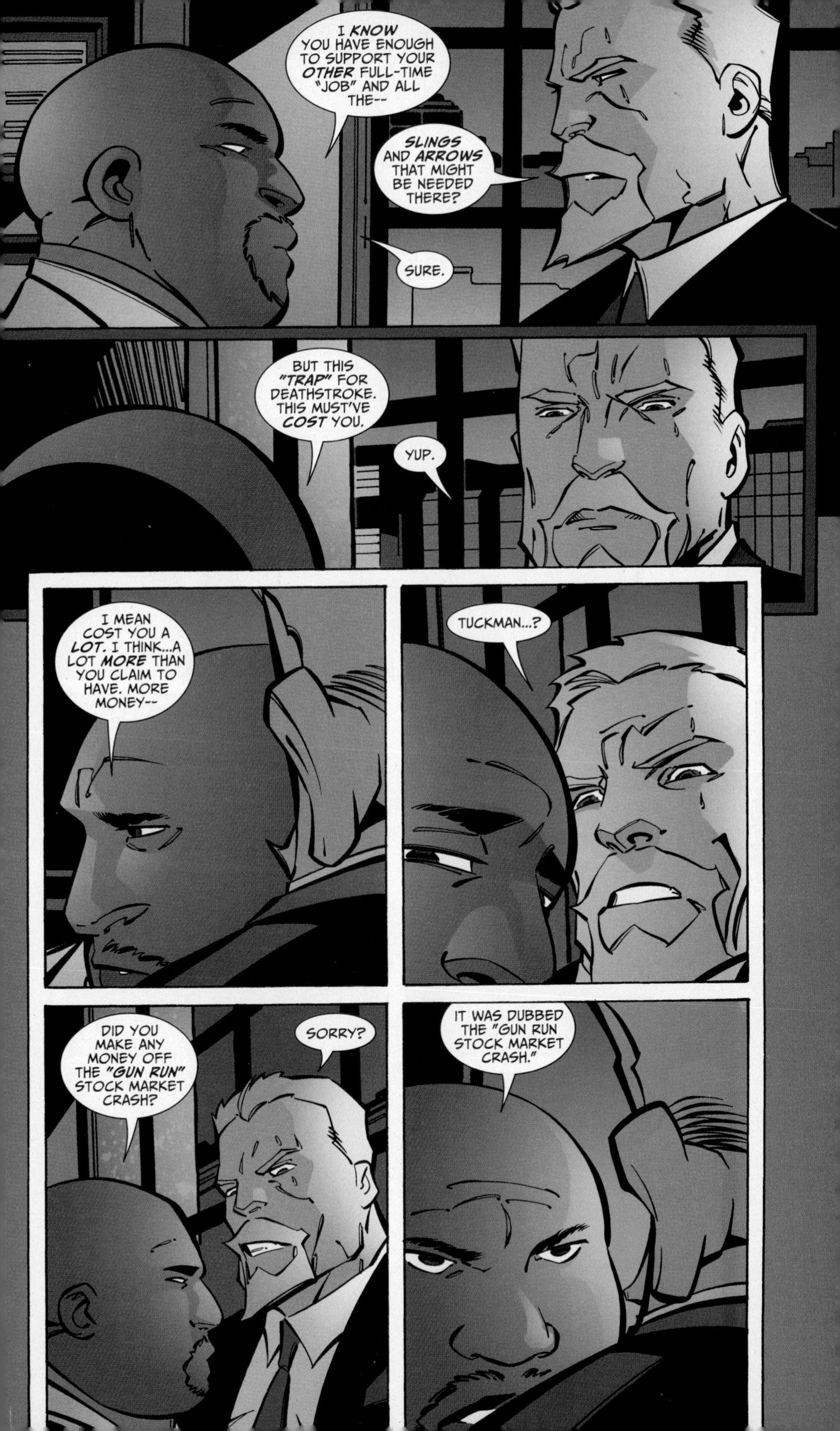
I KNOW YOU HAVE ENOUGH TO SUPPORT YOUR OTHER FULL-TIME "JOB" AND ALL THE--
SLINGS AND ARROWS THAT MIGHT BE NEEDED THERE?
SURE.
BUT THIS "TRAP" FOR DEATHSTROKE. THIS MUST'VE COST YOU.
YUP.
I MEAN COST YOU A LOT. I THINK...A LOT MORE THAN YOU CLAIM TO HAVE. MORE MONEY--
TUCKMAN...?
DID YOU MAKE ANY MONEY OFF THE "GUN RUN" STOCK MARKET CRASH?
SORRY?
IT WAS DUBBED THE "GUN RUN STOCK MARKET CRASH."

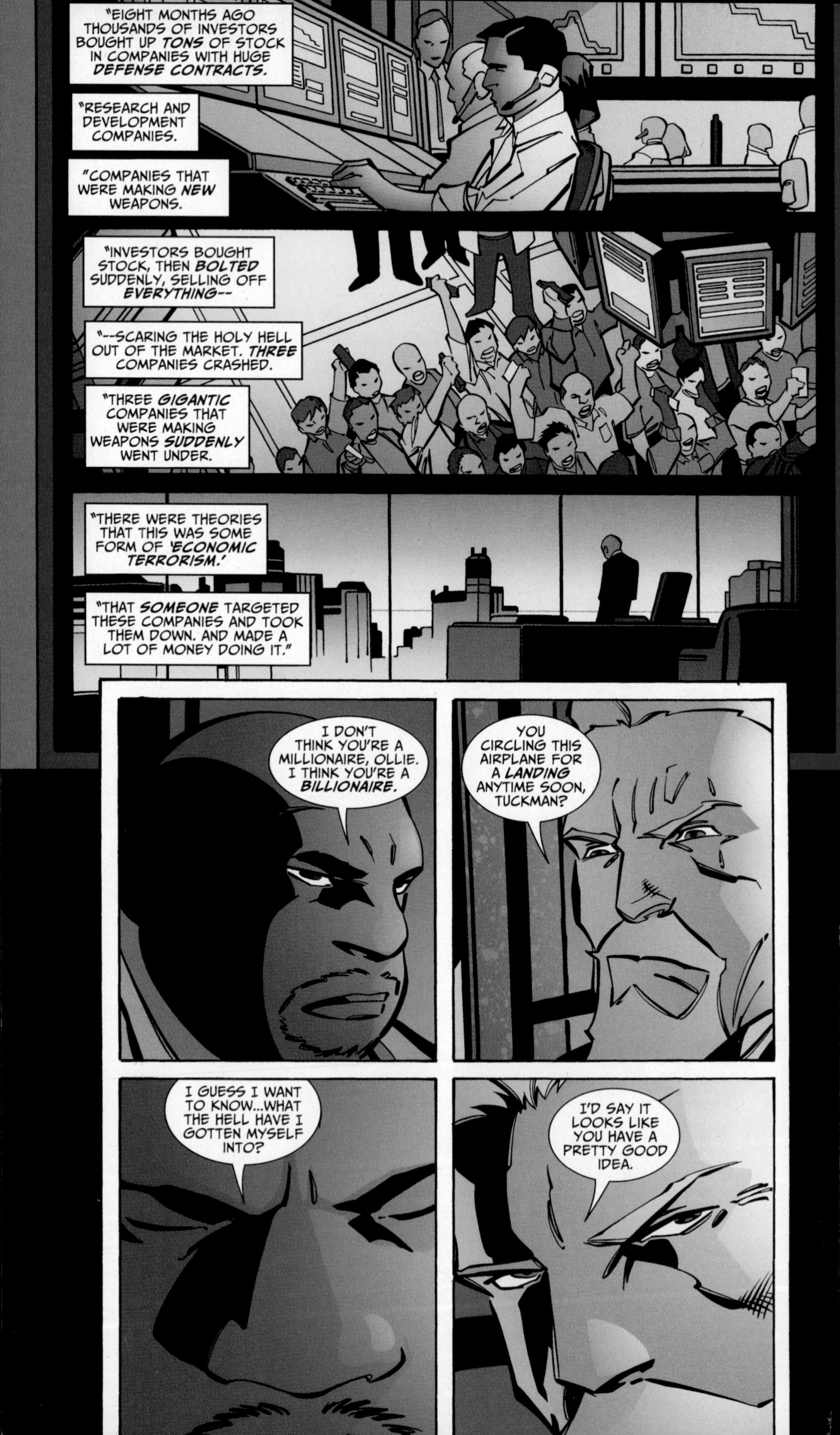
"EIGHT MONTHS AGO THOUSANDS OF INVESTORS BOUGHT UP TONS OF STOCK IN COMPANIES WITH HUGE DEFENSE CONTRACTS.
"RESEARCH AND DEVELOPMENT COMPANIES.
"COMPANIES THAT WERE MAKING NEW WEAPONS.
"INVESTORS BOUGHT STOCK, THEN BOLTED SUDDENLY, SELLING OFF EVERYTHING--
"--SCARING THE HOLY HELL OUT OF THE MARKET. THREE COMPANIES CRASHED.
"THREE GIGANTIC COMPANIES THAT WERE MAKING WEAPONS SUDDENLY WENT UNDER.
"THERE WERE THEORIES THAT THIS WAS SOME FORM OF 'ECONOMIC TERRORISM.'
"THAT SOMEONE TARGETED THESE COMPANIES AND TOOK THEM DOWN. AND MADE A LOT OF MONEY DOING IT."
I DON'T THINK YOU'RE A MILLIONAIRE, OLLIE. I THINK YOU'RE A BILLIONAIRE.
YOU CIRCLING THIS AIRPLANE FOR A LANDING ANYTIME SOON, TUCKMAN?
I GUESS I WANT TO KNOW...WHAT THE HELL HAVE I GOTTEN MYSELF INTO?
I'D SAY IT LOOKS LIKE YOU HAVE A PRETTY GOOD IDEA.

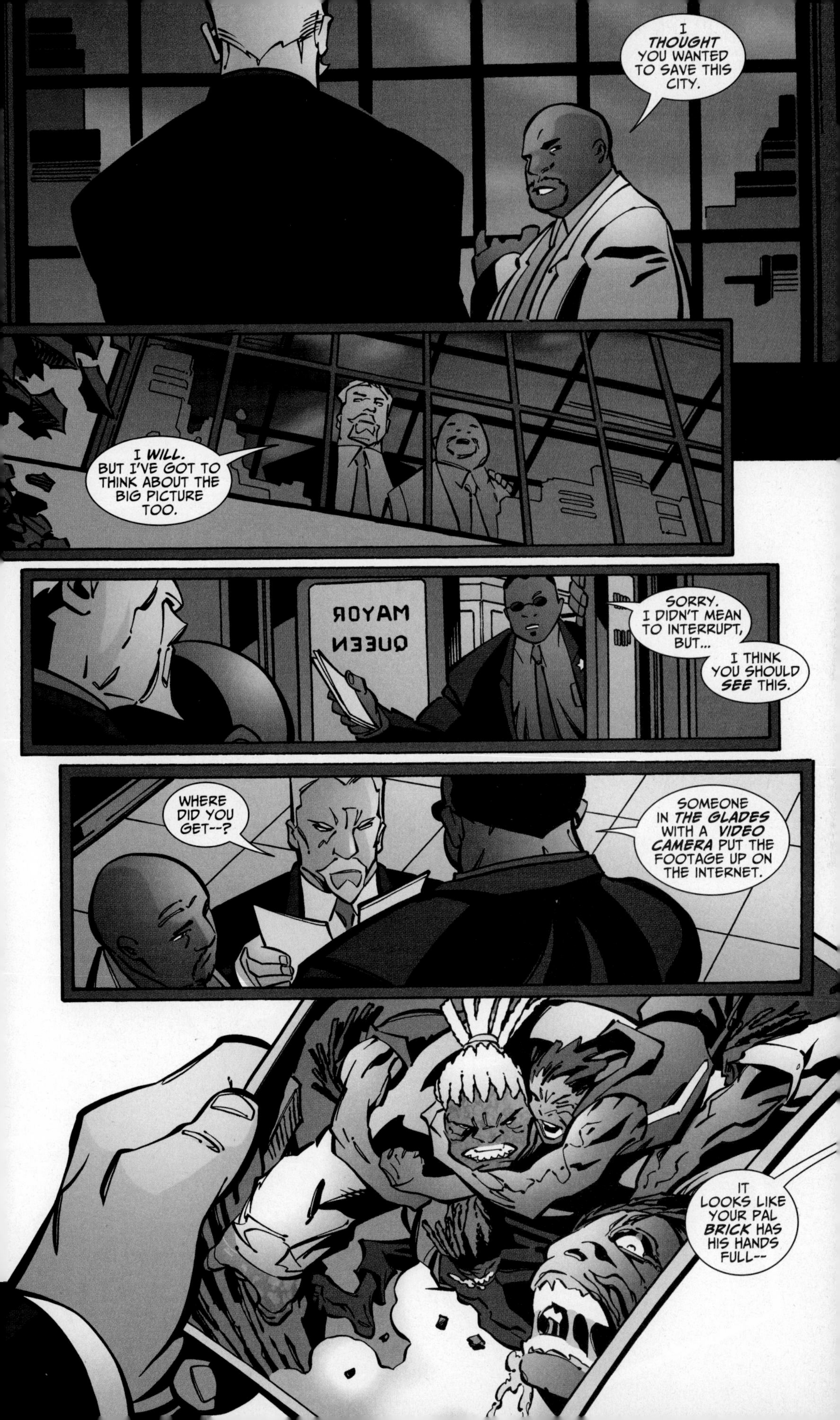
I THOUGHT YOU WANTED TO SAVE THIS CITY.
I WILL. BUT I'VE GOT TO THINK ABOUT THE BIG PICTURE TOO.
MAYOR QUEEN
SORRY. I DIDN'T MEAN TO INTERRUPT, BUT...
I THINK YOU SHOULD SEE THIS.
WHERE DID YOU GET--?
SOMEONE IN THE GLADES WITH A VIDEO CAMERA PUT THE FOOTAGE UP ON THE INTERNET.
IT LOOKS LIKE YOUR PAL BRICK HAS HIS HANDS FULL--

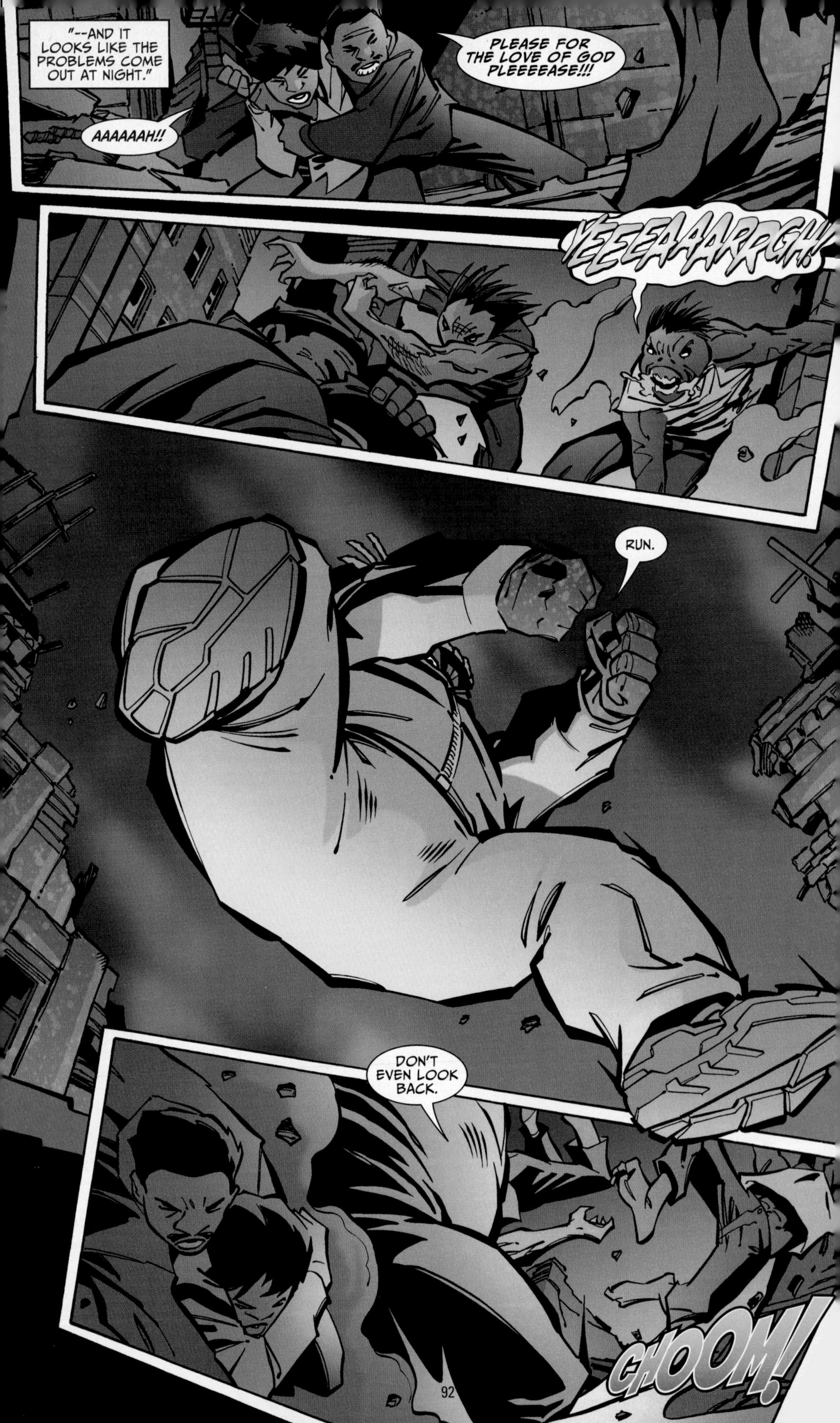
"--AND IT LOOKS LIKE THE PROBLEMS COME OUT AT NIGHT."
PLEASE FOR THE LOVE OF GOD PLEEEEASE!!!
AAAAAAH!!
YEEEAAARRGH!
RUN.
DON'T EVEN LOOK BACK.
CHOOM!

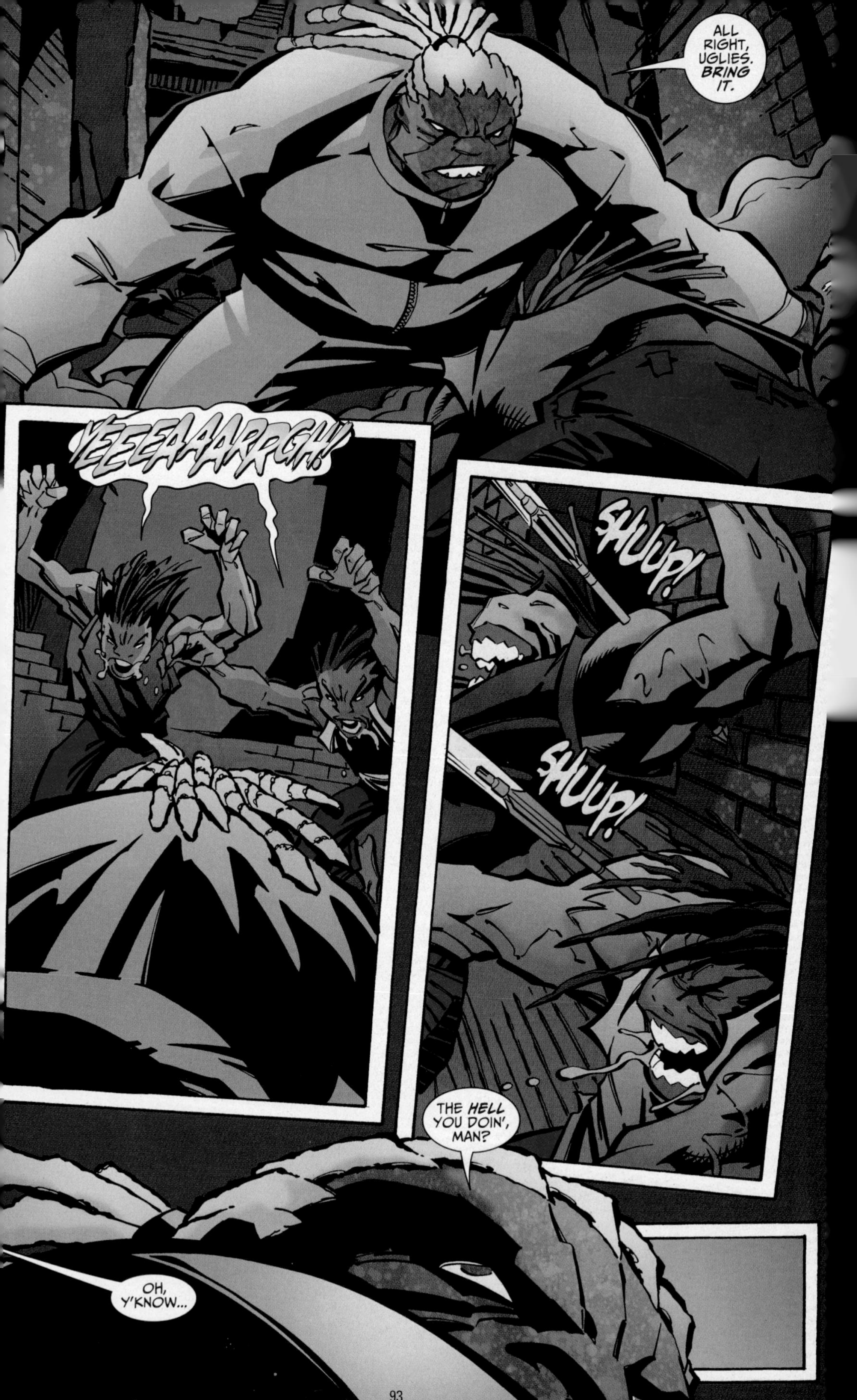
ALL RIGHT, UGLIES. BRING IT.
YEEEAAARRGH!
SHUUP!
SHUUP!
THE HELL YOU DOIN', MAN?
OH, Y'KNOW...

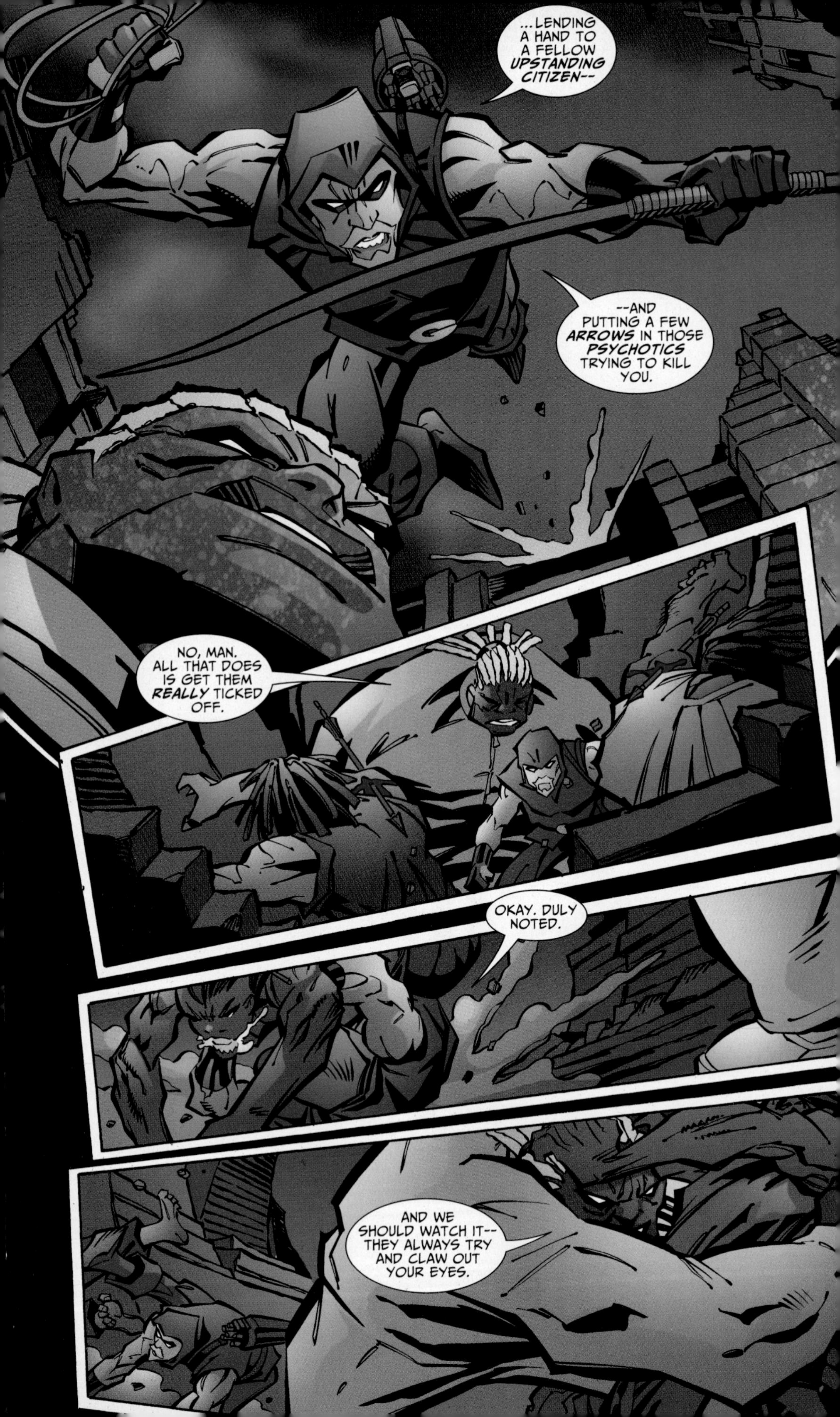
...LENDING A HAND TO A FELLOW *UPSTANDING CITIZEN*--
--AND PUTTING A FEW *ARROWS* IN THOSE *PSYCHOTICS* TRYING TO KILL YOU.
NO, MAN. ALL THAT DOES IS GET THEM *REALLY* TICKED OFF.
OKAY. DULY NOTED.
AND WE SHOULD WATCH IT-- THEY ALWAYS TRY AND CLAW OUT YOUR EYES.

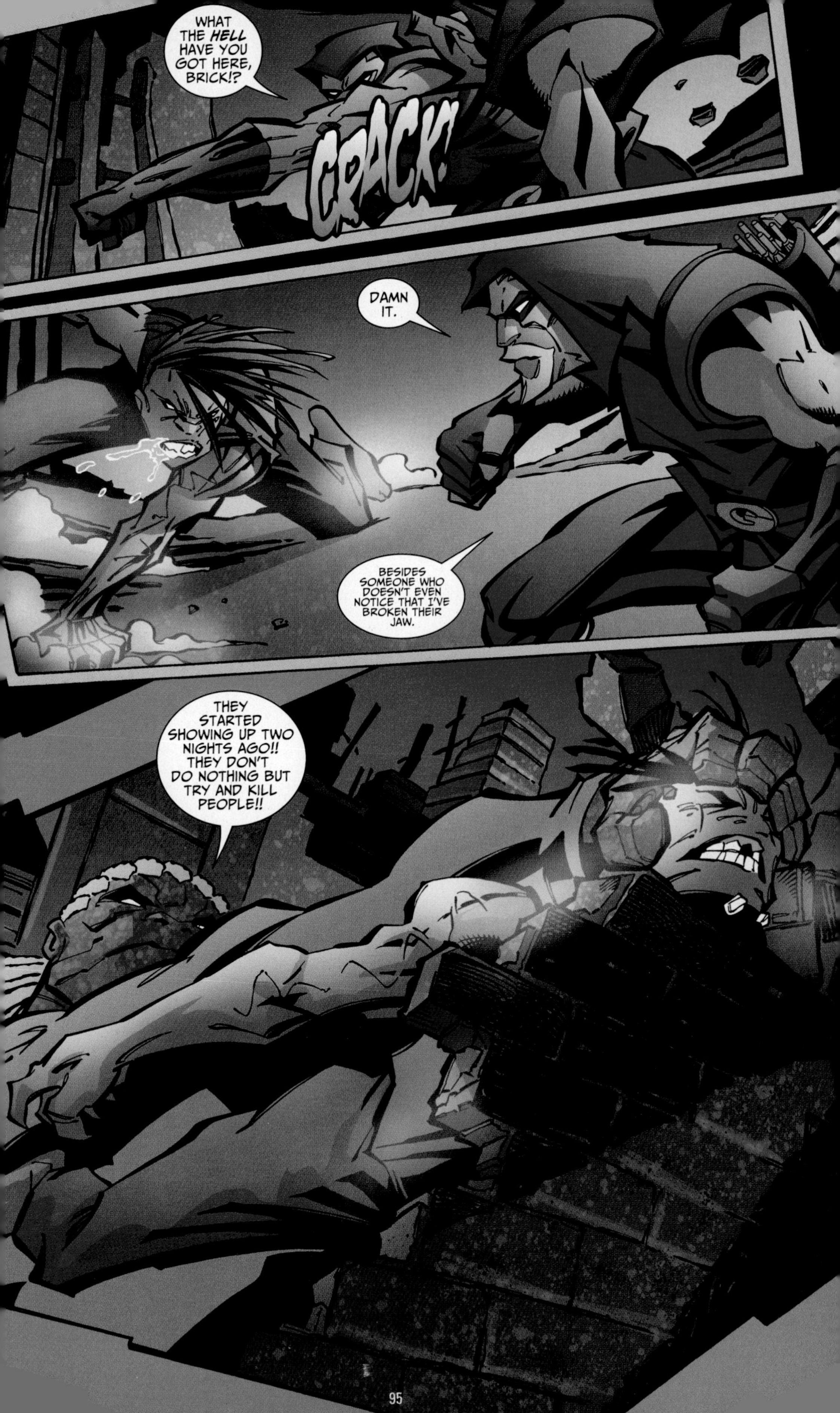
WHAT THE HELL HAVE YOU GOT HERE, BRICK!?
CRACK!
DAMN IT.
BESIDES SOMEONE WHO DOESN'T EVEN NOTICE THAT I'VE BROKEN THEIR JAW.
THEY STARTED SHOWING UP TWO NIGHTS AGO!! THEY DON'T DO NOTHING BUT TRY AND KILL PEOPLE!!

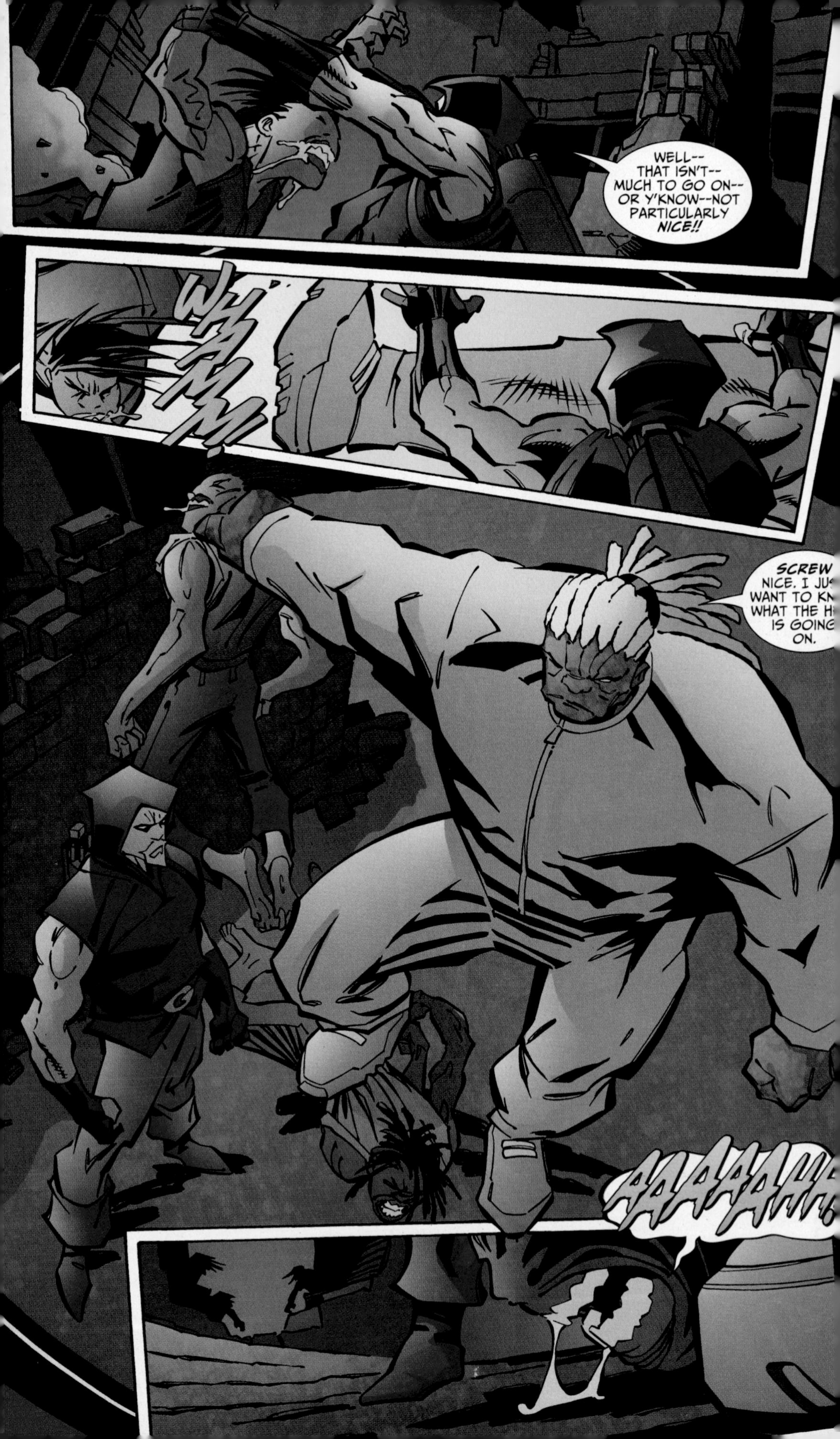

WELL-- THAT ISN'T-- MUCH TO GO ON-- OR Y'KNOW--NOT PARTICULARLY NICE!!
WHAMM!
SCREW NICE. I JUS WANT TO KN WHAT THE H IS GOING ON.
AAAAAHH

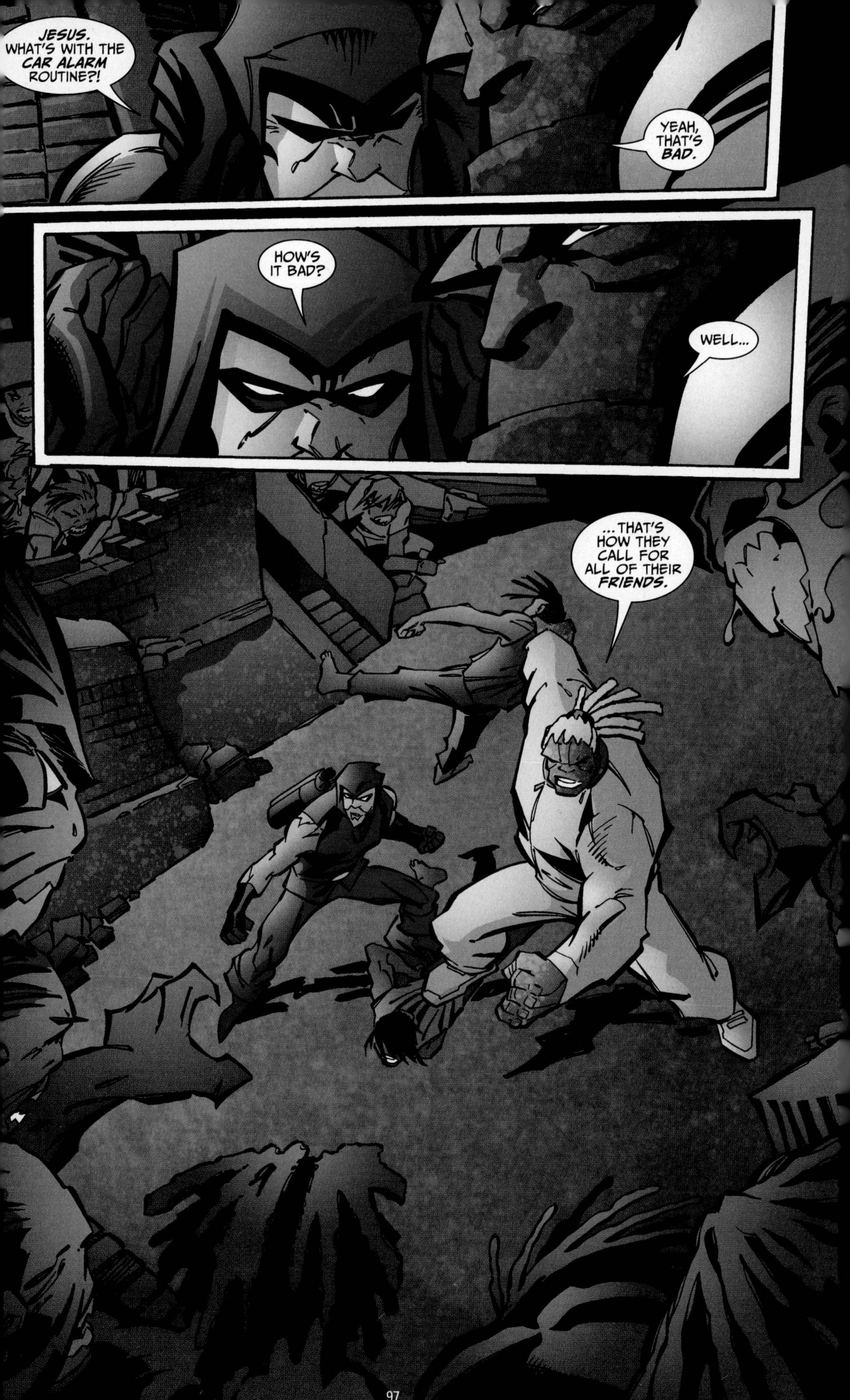
JESUS. WHAT'S WITH THE CAR ALARM ROUTINE?!
YEAH, THAT'S BAD.
HOW'S IT BAD?
WELL...
...THAT'S HOW THEY CALL FOR ALL OF THEIR FRIENDS.

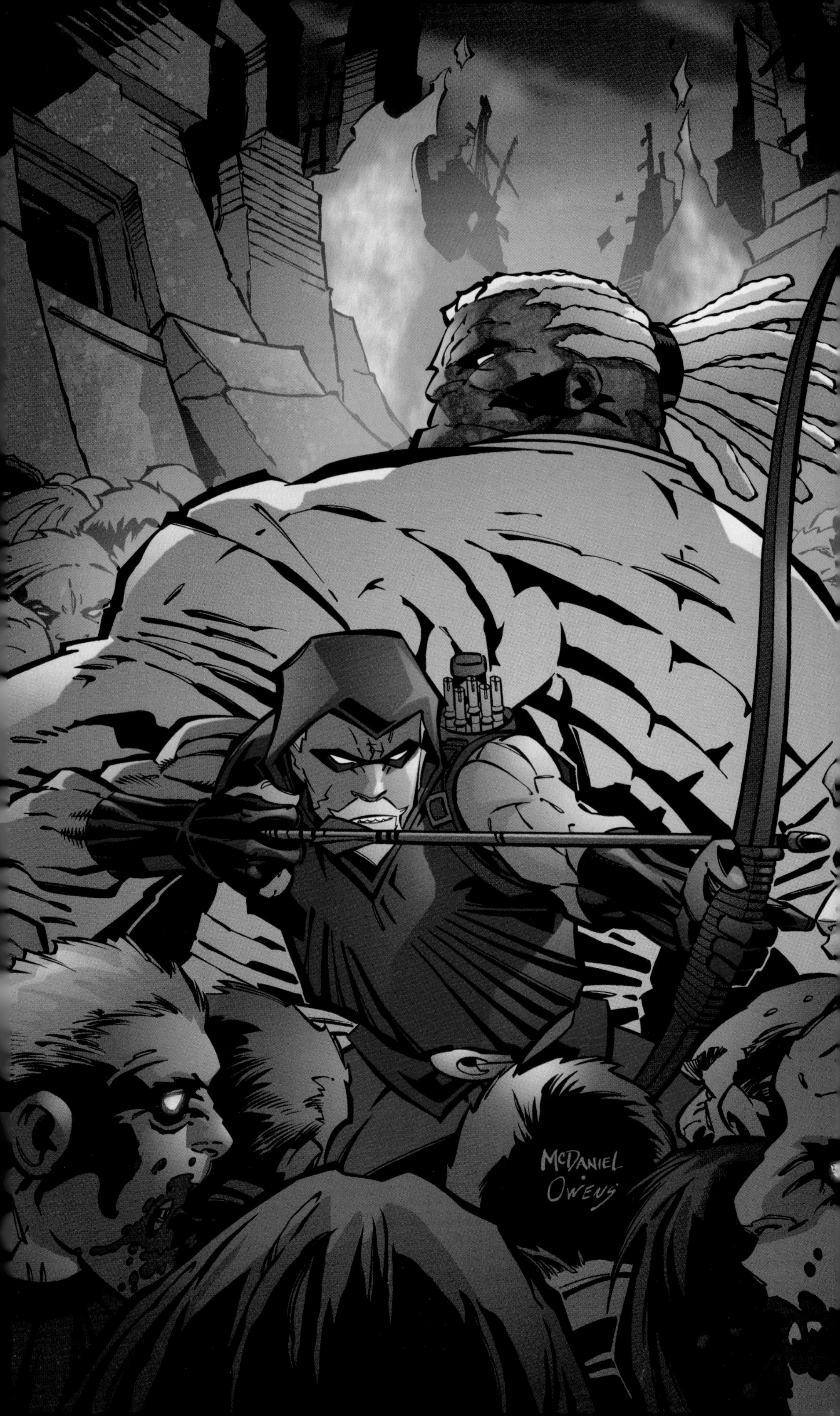
McDANIEL
OWENS

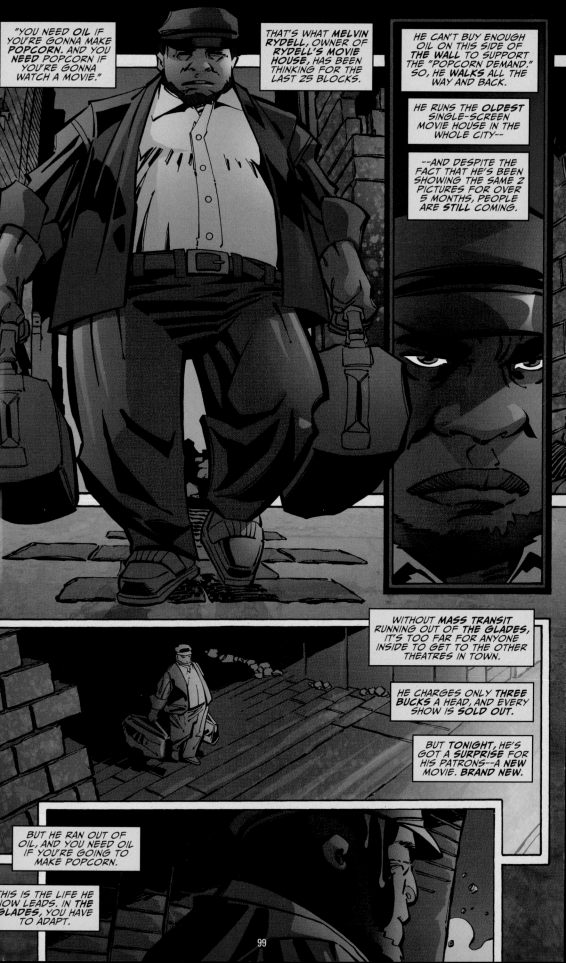

"YOU NEED OIL IF YOU'RE GONNA MAKE POPCORN. AND YOU NEED POPCORN IF YOU'RE GONNA WATCH A MOVIE."

THAT'S WHAT MELVIN RYDELL, OWNER OF RYDELL'S MOVIE HOUSE, HAS BEEN THINKING FOR THE LAST 25 BLOCKS.

HE CAN'T BUY ENOUGH OIL ON THIS SIDE OF THE WALL TO SUPPORT THE "POPCORN DEMAND." SO, HE WALKS ALL THE WAY AND BACK.

HE RUNS THE OLDEST SINGLE-SCREEN MOVIE HOUSE IN THE WHOLE CITY--

--AND DESPITE THE FACT THAT HE'S BEEN SHOWING THE SAME 2 PICTURES FOR OVER 5 MONTHS, PEOPLE ARE STILL COMING.

WITHOUT MASS TRANSIT RUNNING OUT OF THE GLADES, IT'S TOO FAR FOR ANYONE INSIDE TO GET TO THE OTHER THEATRES IN TOWN.

HE CHARGES ONLY THREE BUCKS A HEAD, AND EVERY SHOW IS SOLD OUT.

BUT TONIGHT, HE'S GOT A SURPRISE FOR HIS PATRONS--A NEW MOVIE. BRAND NEW.

BUT HE RAN OUT OF OIL, AND YOU NEED OIL IF YOU'RE GOING TO MAKE POPCORN.

THIS IS THE LIFE HE NOW LEADS. IN THE GLADES, YOU HAVE TO ADAPT.

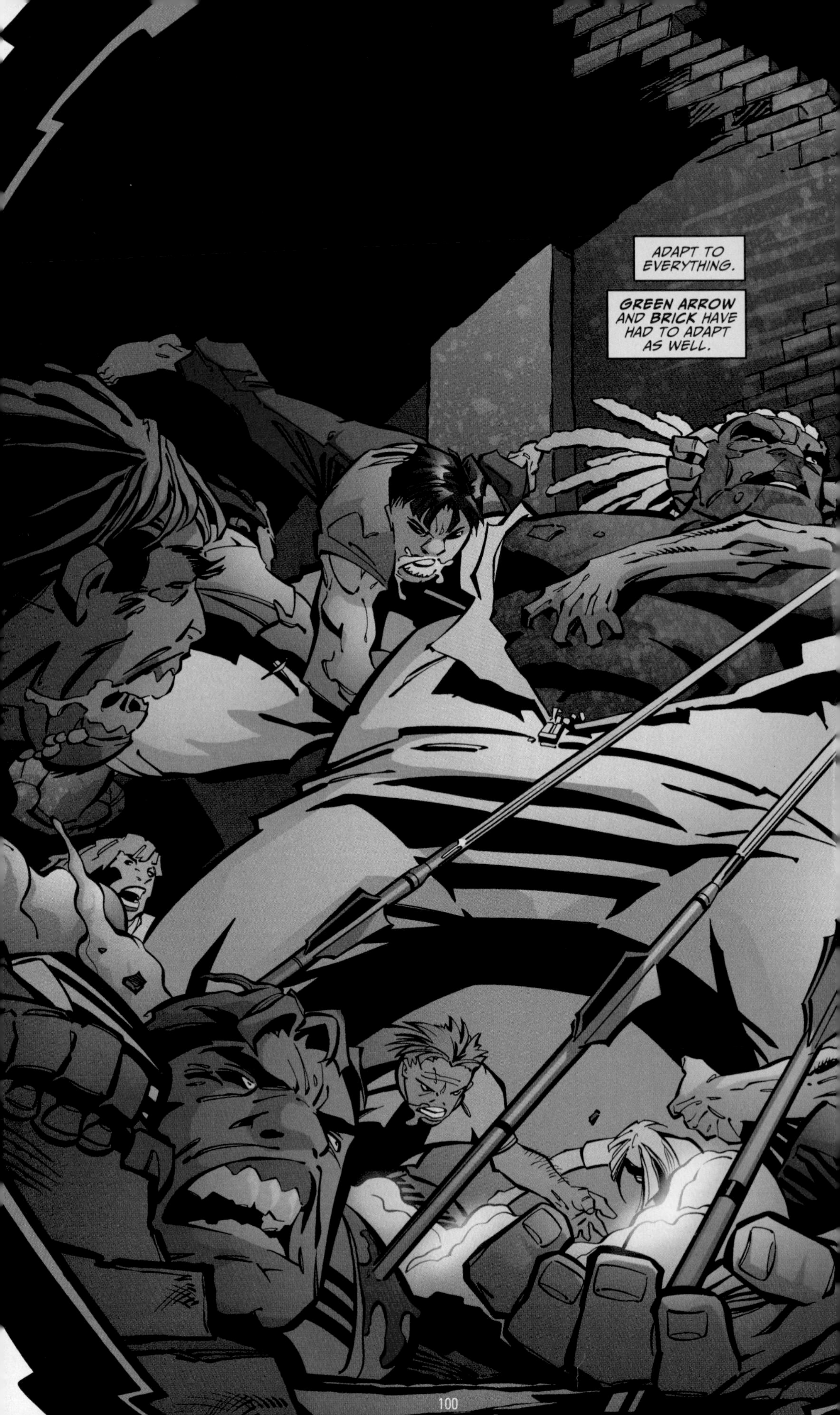
ADAPT TO EVERYTHING.
GREEN ARROW AND BRICK HAVE HAD TO ADAPT AS WELL.

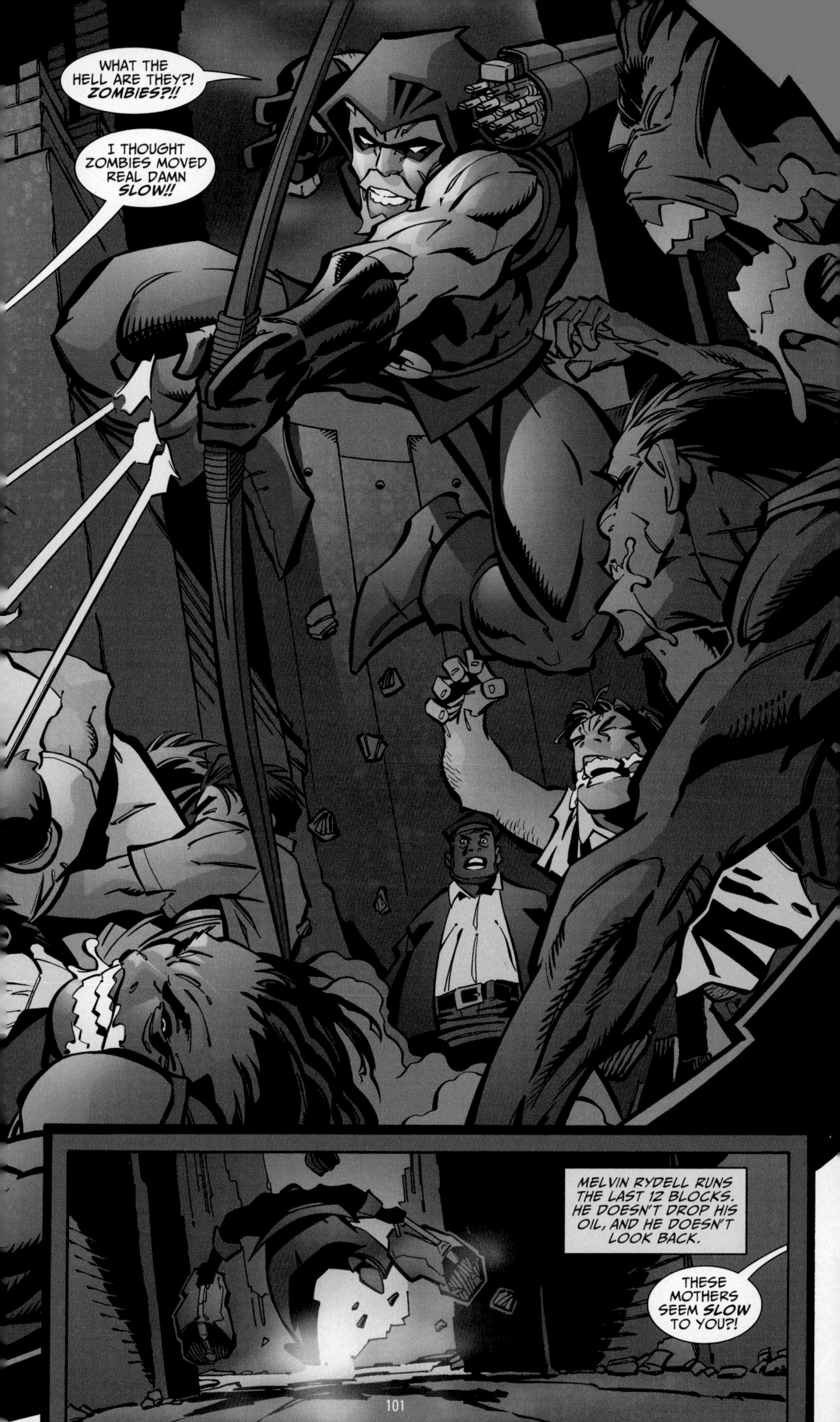
WHAT THE HELL ARE THEY?! ZOMBIES?!!
I THOUGHT ZOMBIES MOVED REAL DAMN SLOW!!
MELVIN RYDELL RUNS THE LAST 12 BLOCKS. HE DOESN'T DROP HIS OIL, AND HE DOESN'T LOOK BACK.
THESE MOTHERS SEEM SLOW TO YOU?!

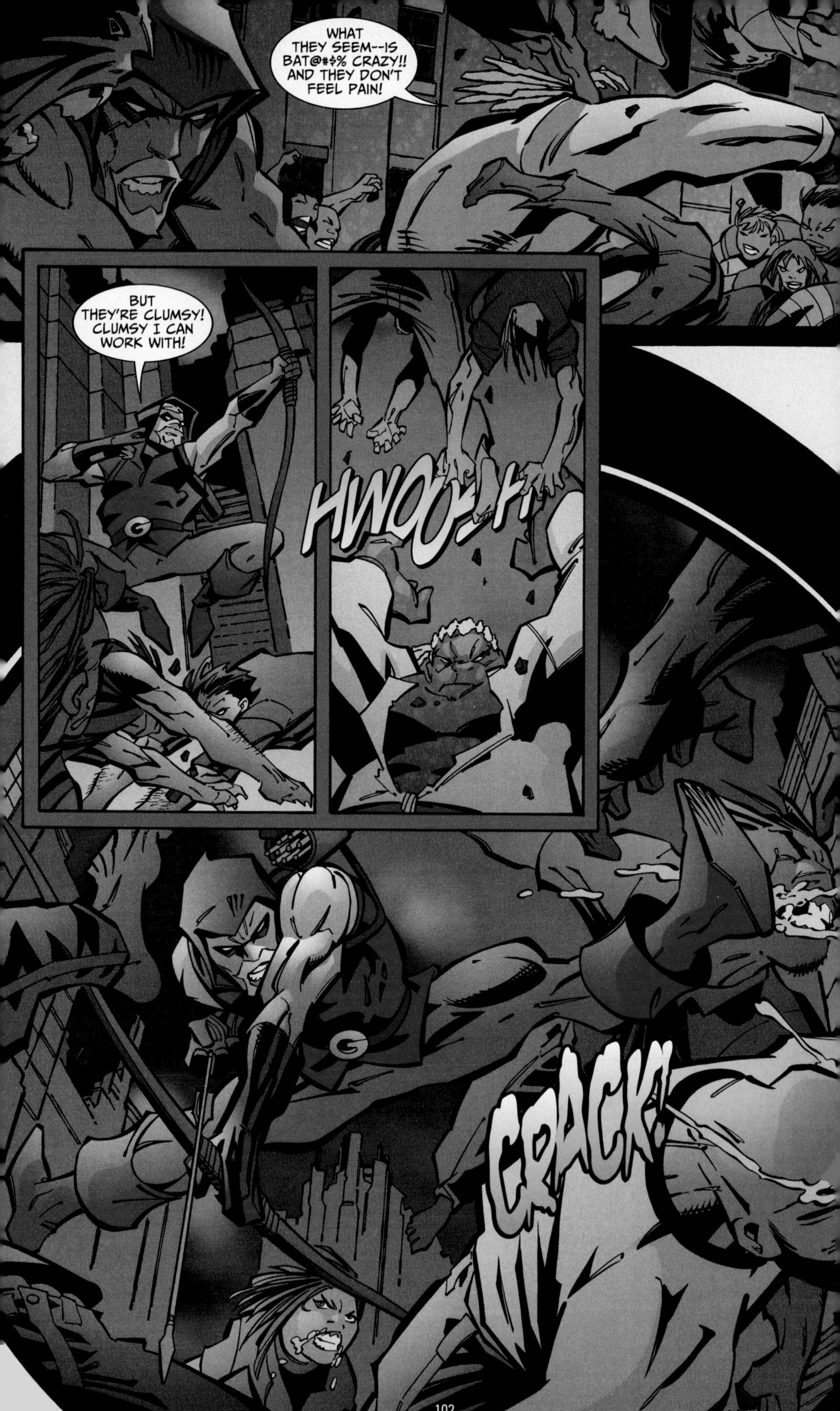

WHAT THEY SEEM--IS BAT@#$% CRAZY!! AND THEY DON'T FEEL PAIN!
BUT THEY'RE CLUMSY! CLUMSY I CAN WORK WITH!
HWOOSH
CRACK!

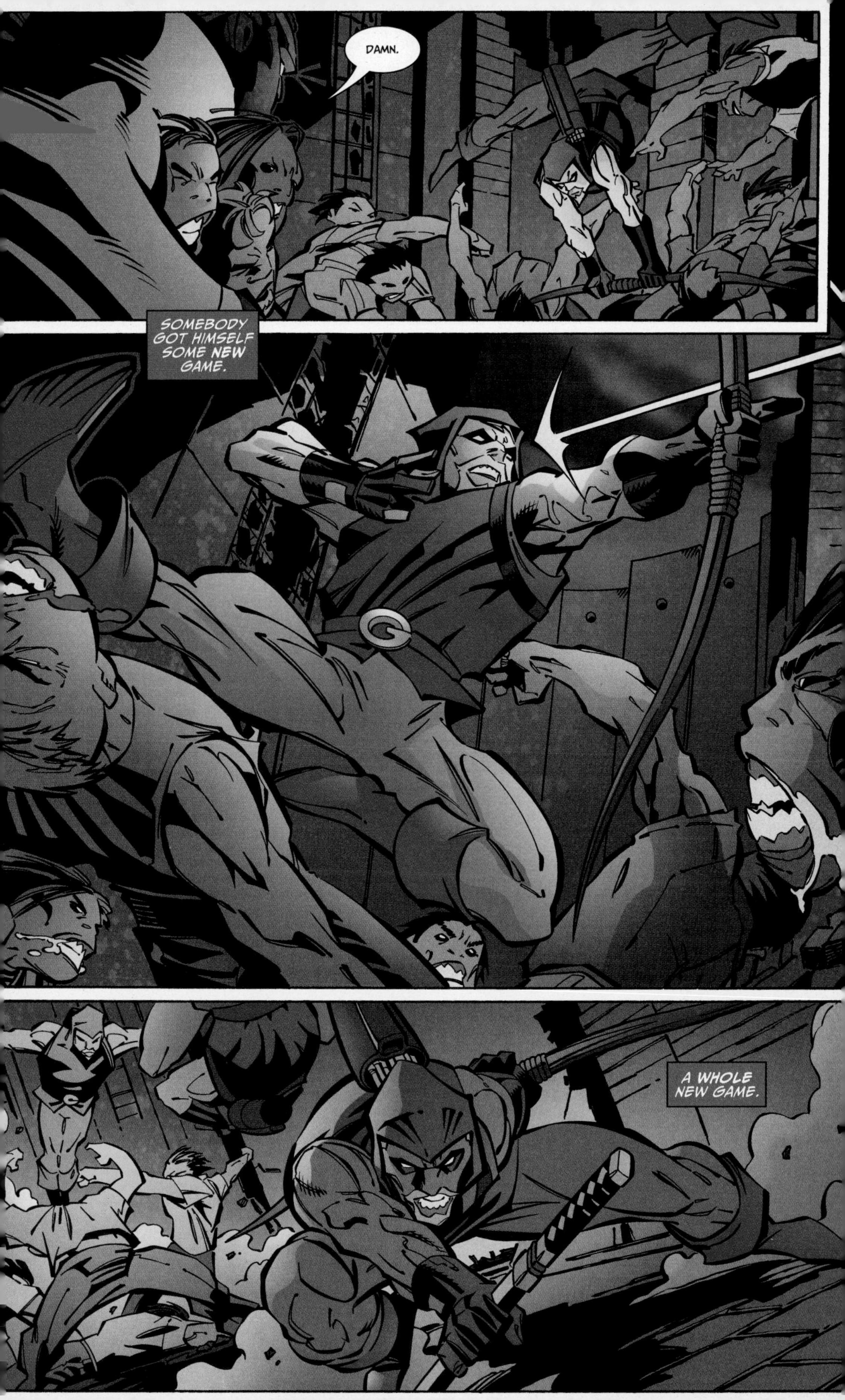

DAMN.
SOMEBODY GOT HIMSELF SOME NEW GAME.
A WHOLE NEW GAME.

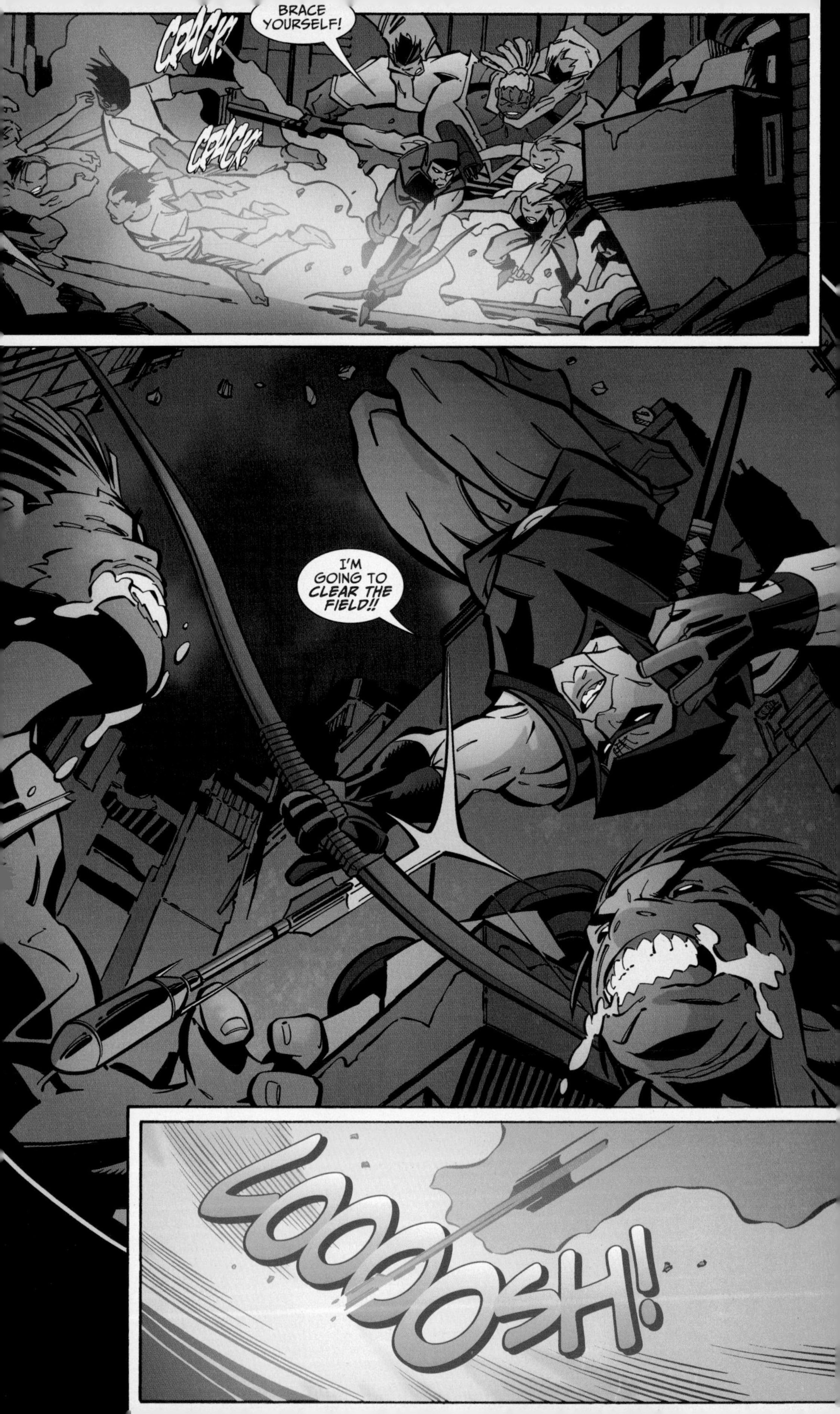
CRACK!
BRACE YOURSELF!
CRACK!
I'M GOING TO CLEAR THE FIELD!!
WOOOOSH!

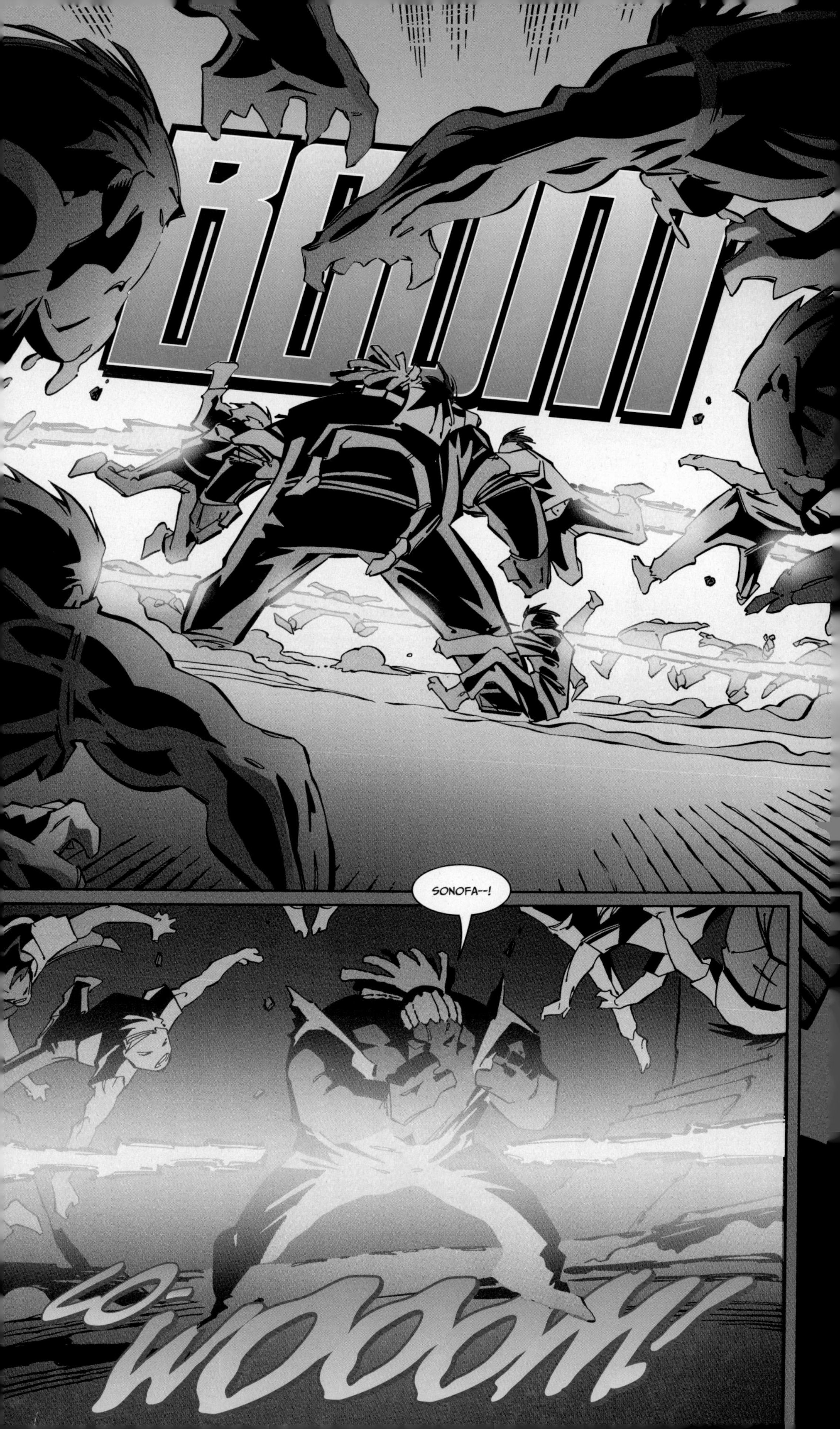
SONOFA--!

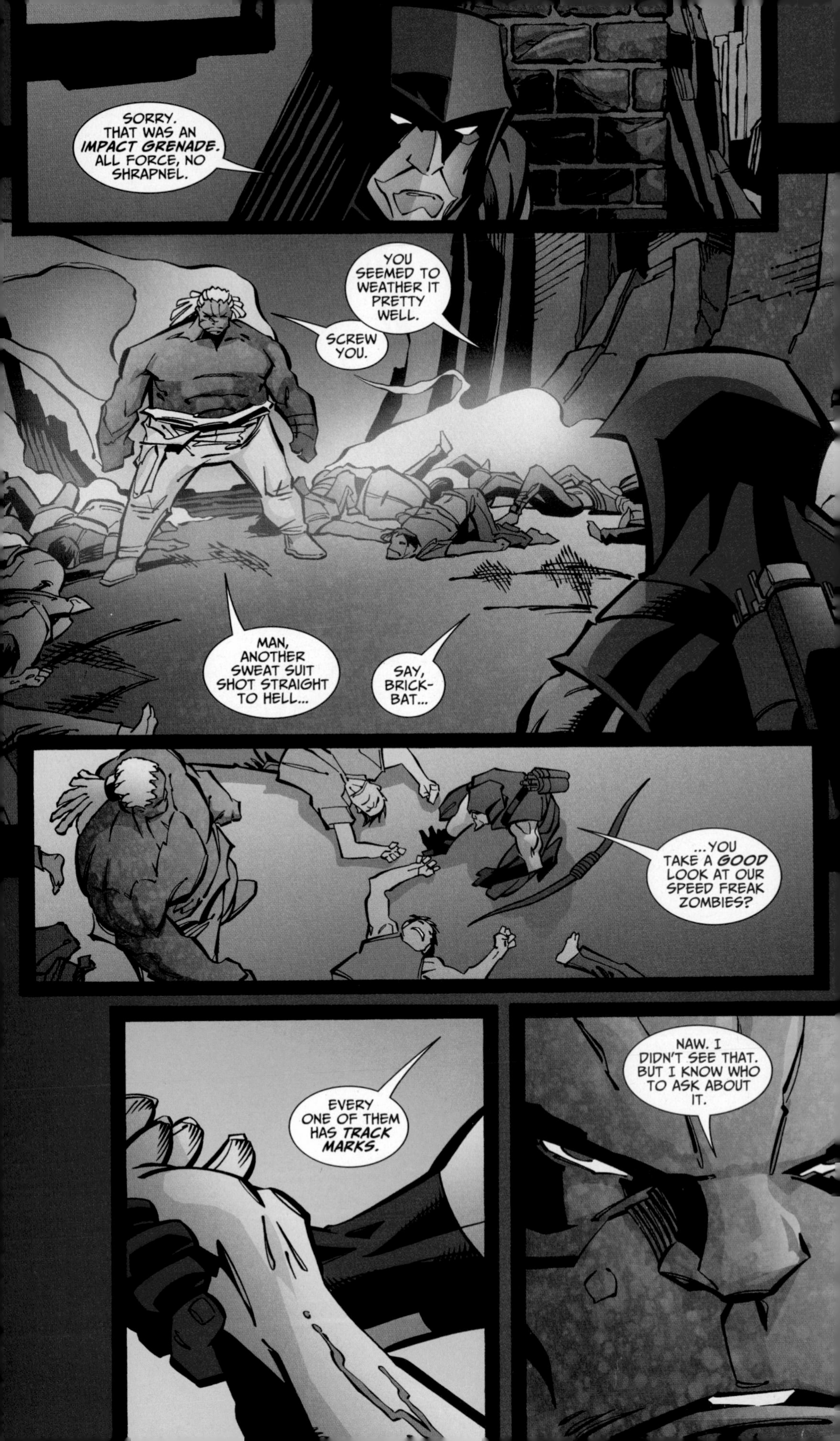
SORRY. THAT WAS AN IMPACT GRENADE. ALL FORCE, NO SHRAPNEL.
YOU SEEMED TO WEATHER IT PRETTY WELL.
SCREW YOU.
MAN, ANOTHER SWEAT SUIT SHOT STRAIGHT TO HELL...
SAY, BRICK-BAT...
...YOU TAKE A GOOD LOOK AT OUR SPEED FREAK ZOMBIES?
EVERY ONE OF THEM HAS TRACK MARKS.
NAW. I DIDN'T SEE THAT. BUT I KNOW WHO TO ASK ABOUT IT.

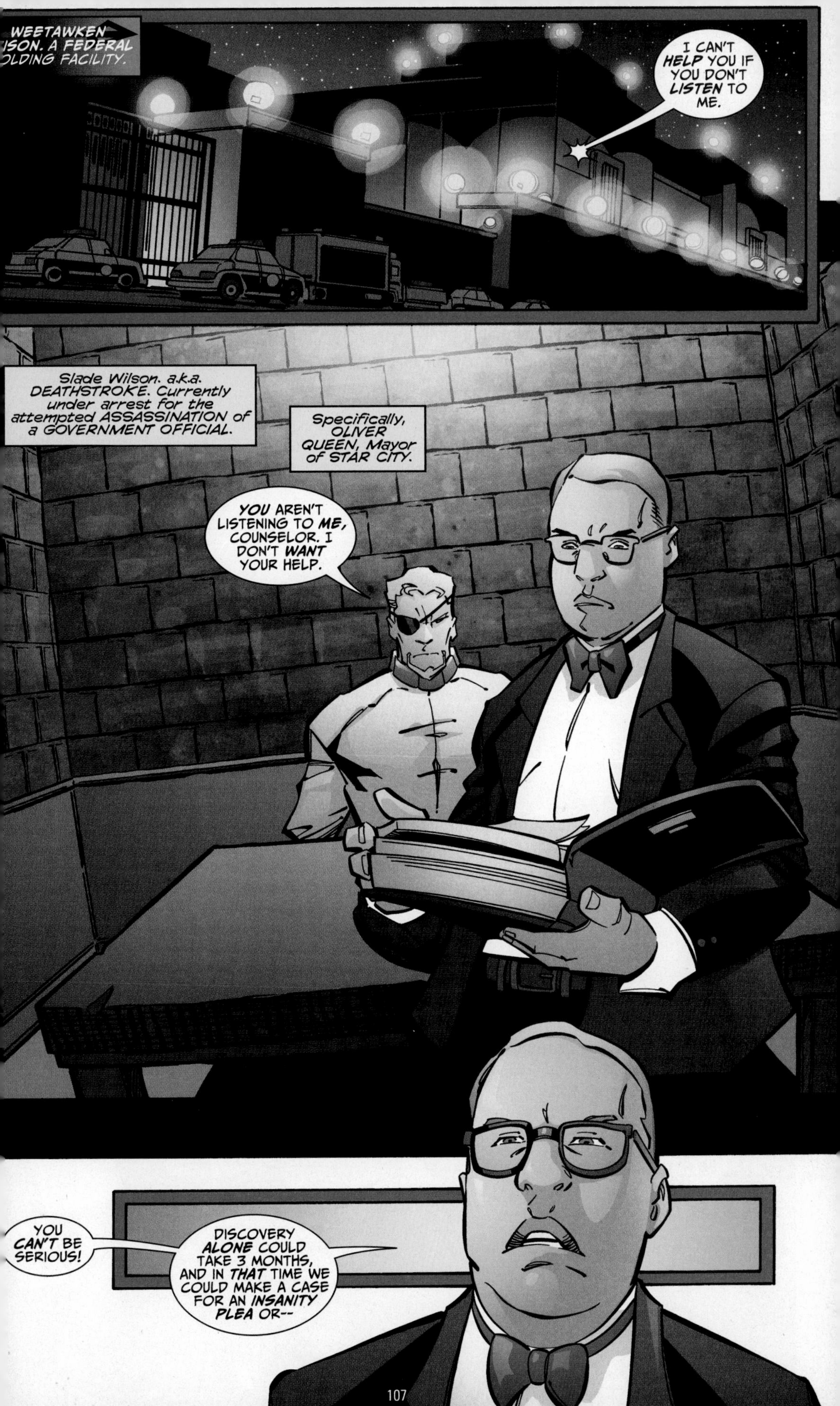
WEETAWKEN
ISON. A FEDERAL
OLDING FACILITY.
I CAN'T HELP YOU IF YOU DON'T LISTEN TO ME.
Slade Wilson. a.k.a. DEATHSTROKE. Currently under arrest for the attempted ASSASSINATION of a GOVERNMENT OFFICIAL.
Specifically, OLIVER QUEEN, Mayor of STAR CITY.
YOU AREN'T LISTENING TO ME, COUNSELOR. I DON'T WANT YOUR HELP.
YOU CAN'T BE SERIOUS!
DISCOVERY ALONE COULD TAKE 3 MONTHS, AND IN THAT TIME WE COULD MAKE A CASE FOR AN INSANITY PLEA OR--

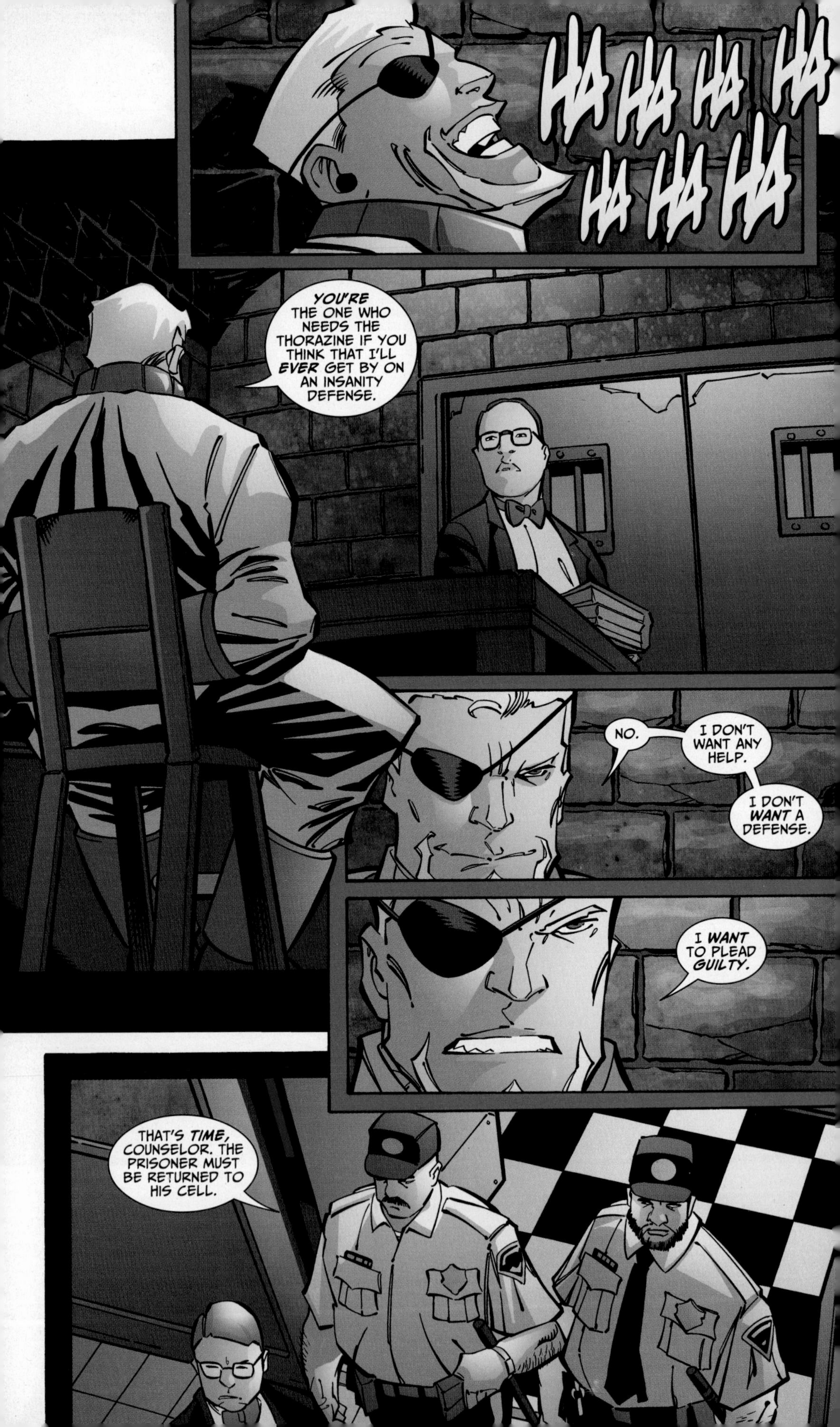
HA HA HA HA
HA HA HA
YOU'RE THE ONE WHO NEEDS THE THORAZINE IF YOU THINK THAT I'LL EVER GET BY ON AN INSANITY DEFENSE.
NO.
I DON'T WANT ANY HELP.
I DON'T WANT A DEFENSE.
I WANT TO PLEAD GUILTY.
THAT'S TIME, COUNSELOR. THE PRISONER MUST BE RETURNED TO HIS CELL.

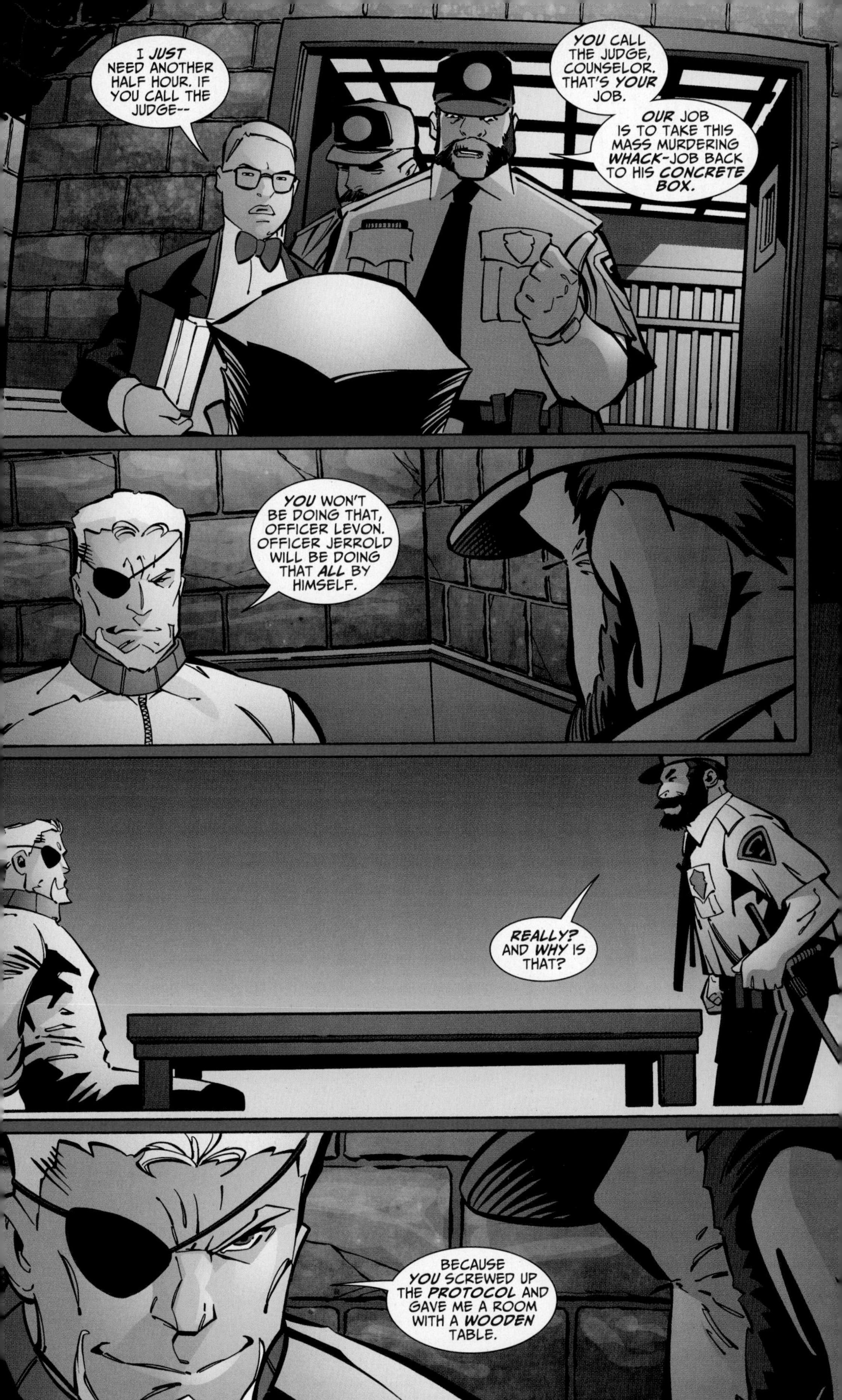
I JUST NEED ANOTHER HALF HOUR. IF YOU CALL THE JUDGE--
YOU CALL THE JUDGE, COUNSELOR. THAT'S YOUR JOB.
OUR JOB IS TO TAKE THIS MASS MURDERING WHACK-JOB BACK TO HIS CONCRETE BOX.
YOU WON'T BE DOING THAT, OFFICER LEVON. OFFICER JERROLD WILL BE DOING THAT ALL BY HIMSELF.
REALLY? AND WHY IS THAT?
BECAUSE YOU SCREWED UP THE PROTOCOL AND GAVE ME A ROOM WITH A WOODEN TABLE.

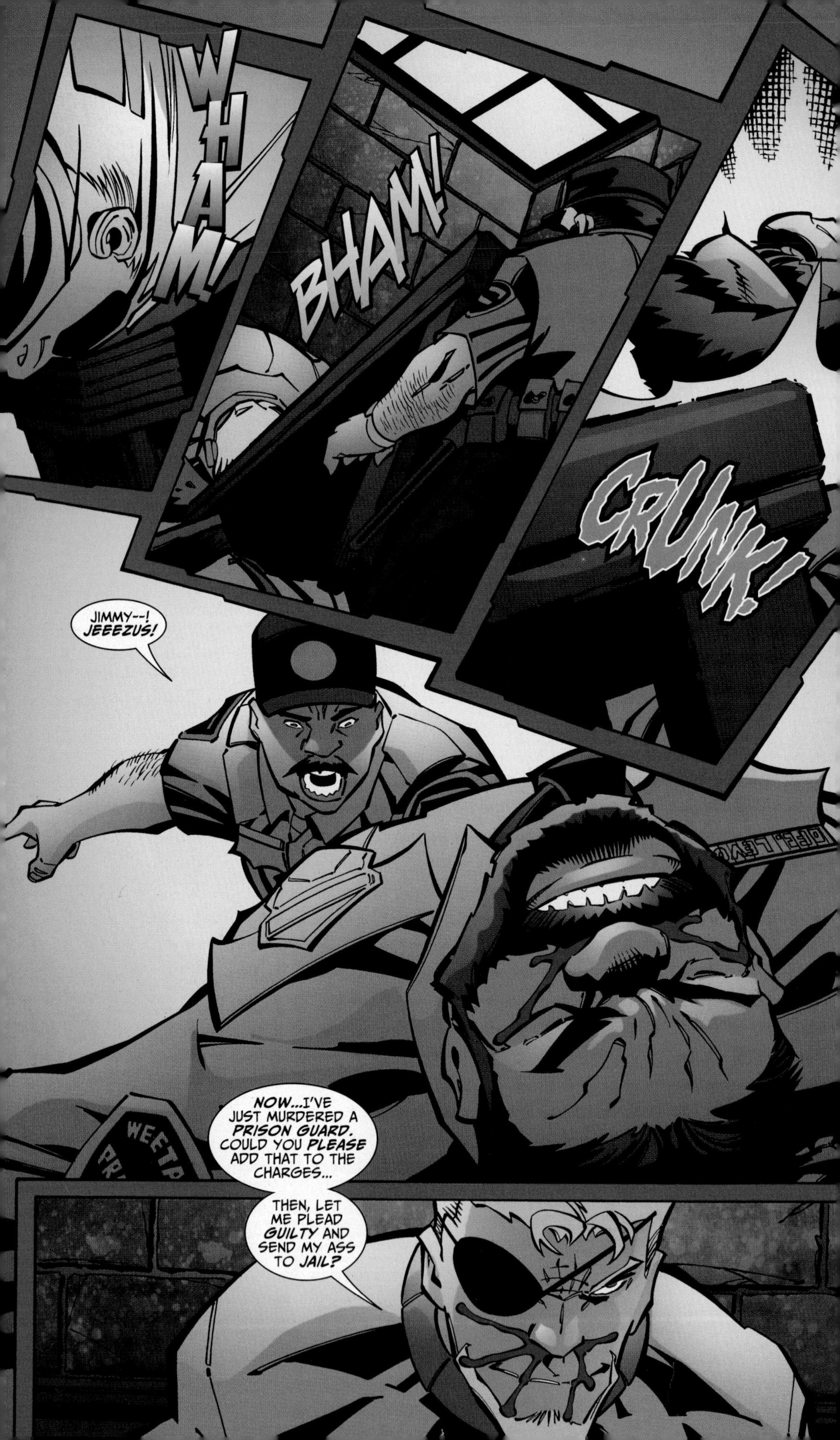
WHAM!
BHAM!
CRUNK!
JIMMY--! *JEEEZUS!*
NOW...I'VE JUST MURDERED A *PRISON GUARD*. COULD YOU *PLEASE* ADD THAT TO THE CHARGES...
THEN, LET ME PLEAD *GUILTY* AND SEND MY ASS TO *JAIL?*

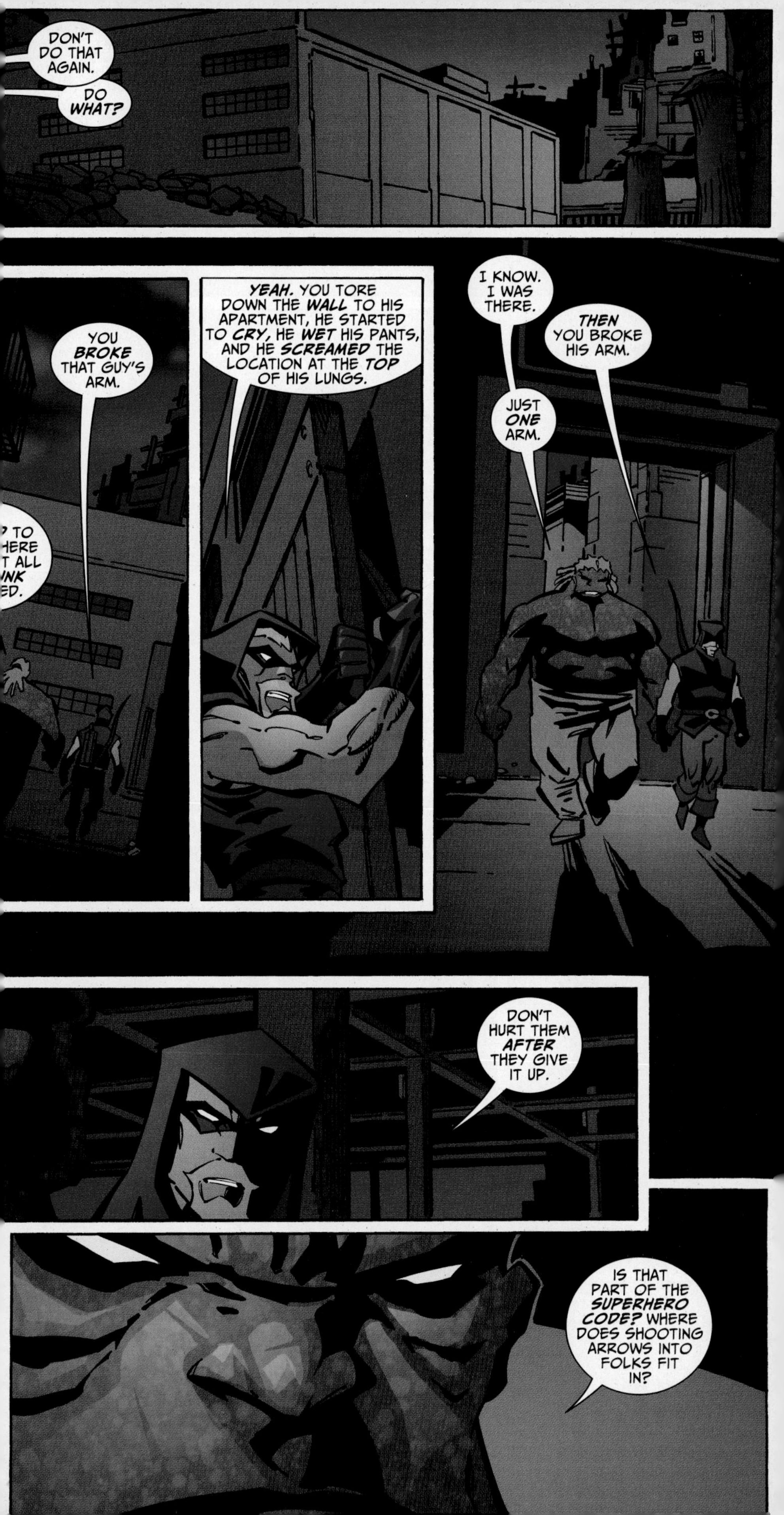
DON'T DO THAT AGAIN.
DO WHAT?
YOU BROKE THAT GUY'S ARM.
YEAH. YOU TORE DOWN THE WALL TO HIS APARTMENT, HE STARTED TO CRY, HE WET HIS PANTS, AND HE SCREAMED THE LOCATION AT THE TOP OF HIS LUNGS.
I KNOW. I WAS THERE.
JUST ONE ARM.
THEN YOU BROKE HIS ARM.
DON'T HURT THEM AFTER THEY GIVE IT UP.
IS THAT PART OF THE SUPERHERO CODE? WHERE DOES SHOOTING ARROWS INTO FOLKS FIT IN?

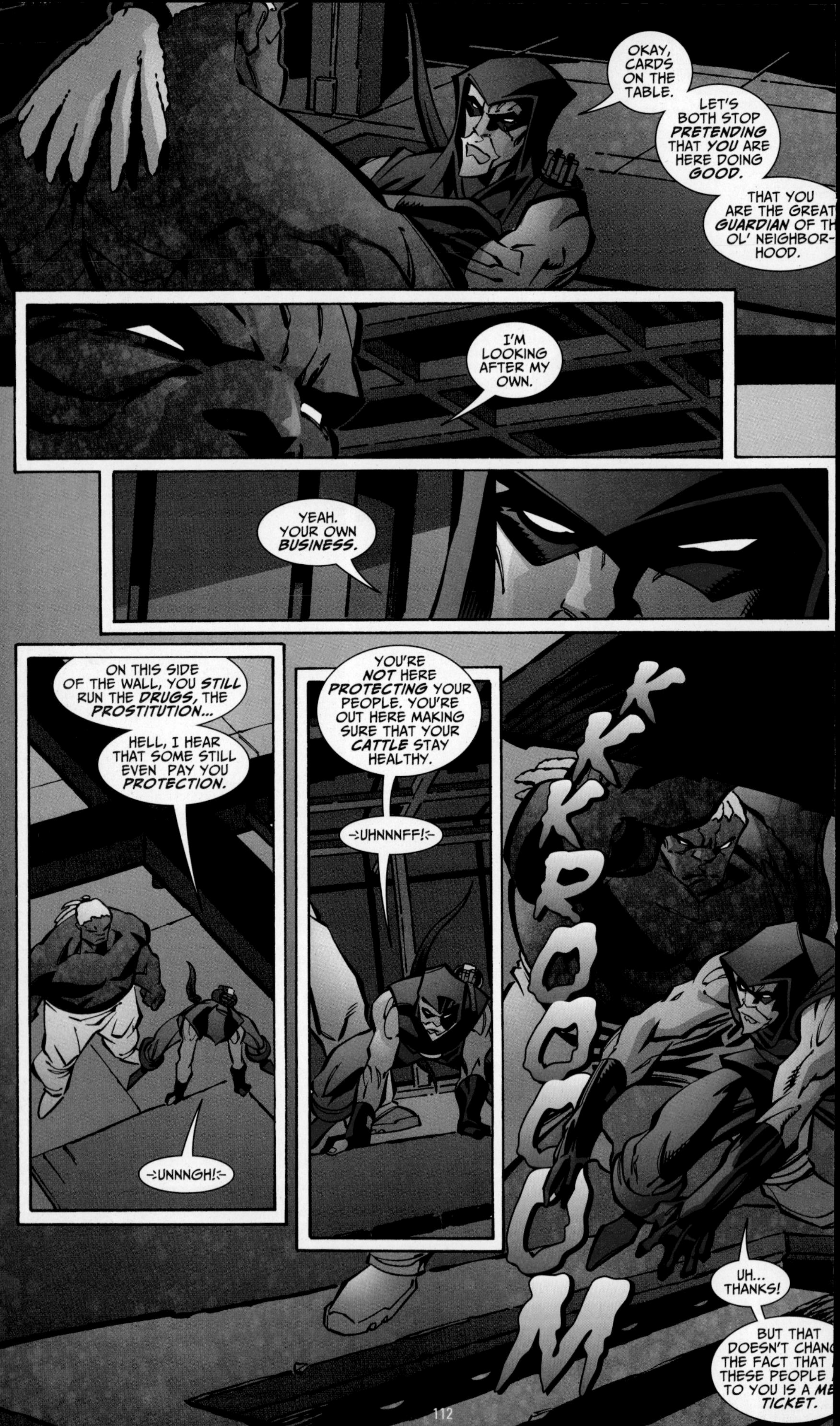
OKAY, CARDS ON THE TABLE.
LET'S BOTH STOP PRETENDING THAT YOU ARE HERE DOING GOOD.
THAT YOU ARE THE GREAT GUARDIAN OF TH OL' NEIGHBOR-HOOD.
I'M LOOKING AFTER MY OWN.
YEAH. YOUR OWN BUSINESS.
ON THIS SIDE OF THE WALL, YOU STILL RUN THE DRUGS, THE PROSTITUTION...
HELL, I HEAR THAT SOME STILL EVEN PAY YOU PROTECTION.
-UNNNGH!-
YOU'RE NOT HERE PROTECTING YOUR PEOPLE. YOU'RE OUT HERE MAKING SURE THAT YOUR CATTLE STAY HEALTHY.
-UHNNNFF!-
KKKKROOOOOOM
UH... THANKS!
BUT THAT DOESN'T CHANG THE FACT THAT THESE PEOPLE TO YOU IS A ME TICKET.

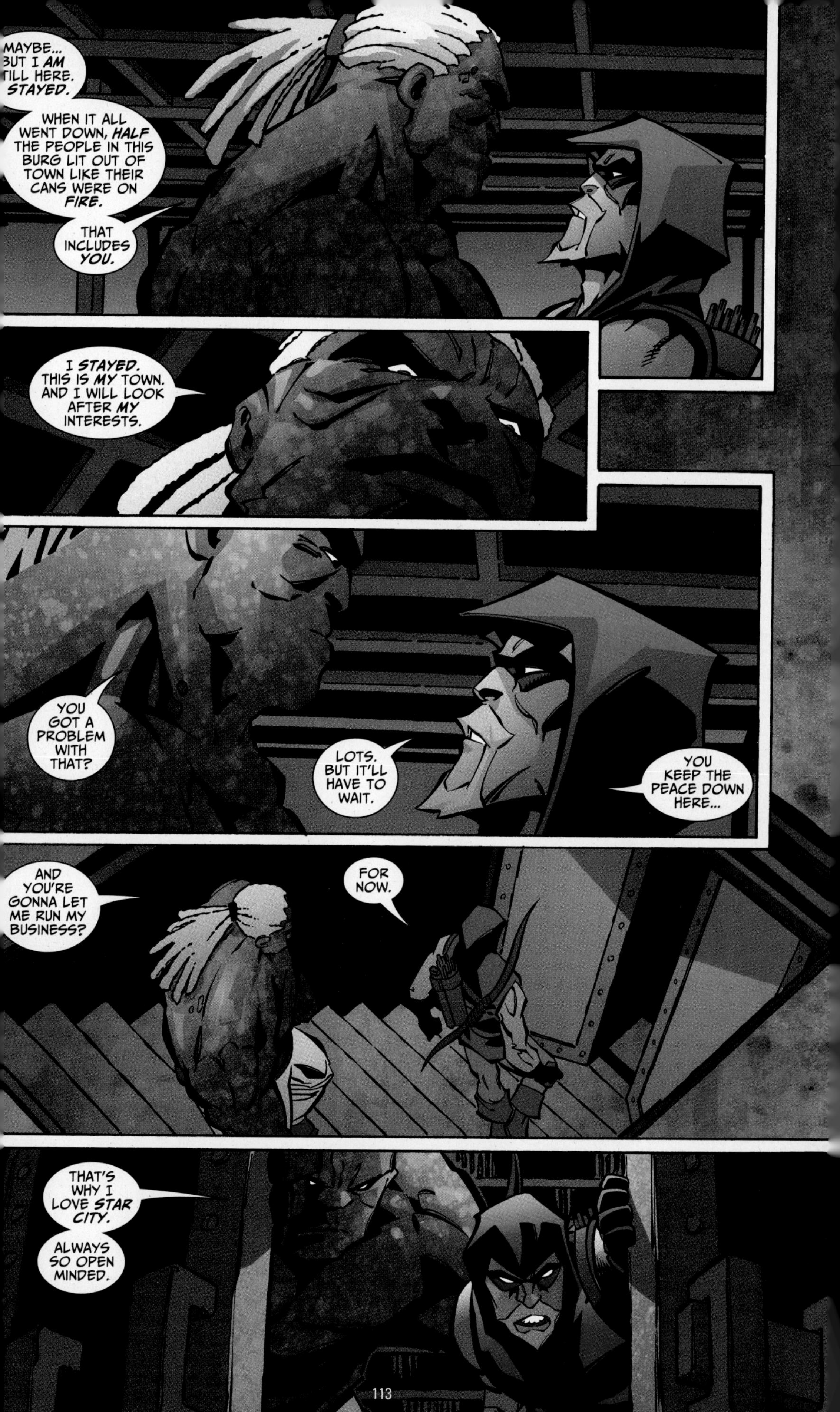

MAYBE... BUT I AM STILL HERE. STAYED.
WHEN IT ALL WENT DOWN, HALF THE PEOPLE IN THIS BURG LIT OUT OF TOWN LIKE THEIR CANS WERE ON FIRE.
THAT INCLUDES YOU.
I STAYED. THIS IS MY TOWN. AND I WILL LOOK AFTER MY INTERESTS.
YOU GOT A PROBLEM WITH THAT?
LOTS. BUT IT'LL HAVE TO WAIT.
YOU KEEP THE PEACE DOWN HERE...
AND YOU'RE GONNA LET ME RUN MY BUSINESS?
FOR NOW.
THAT'S WHY I LOVE STAR CITY.
ALWAYS SO OPEN MINDED.

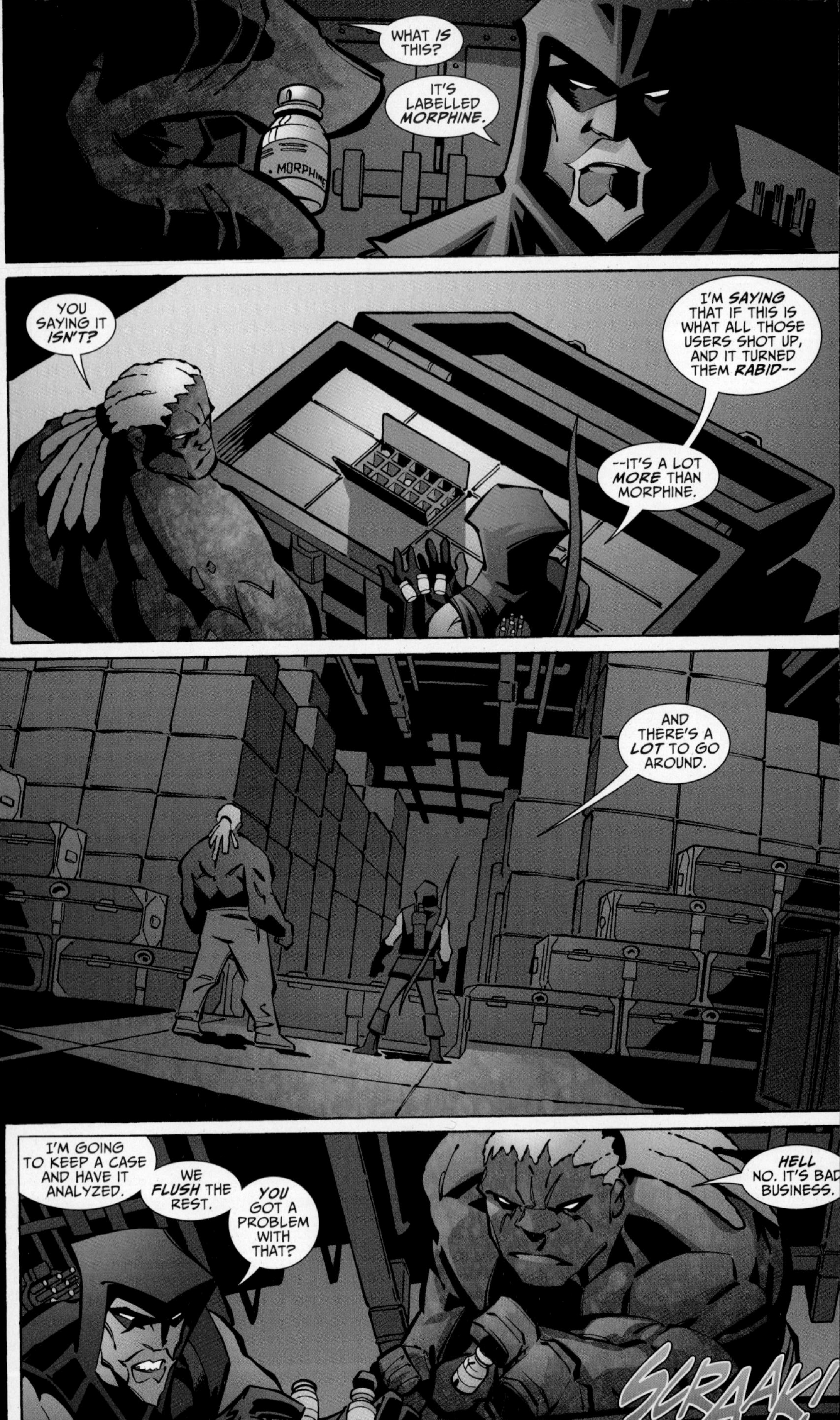

WHAT IS THIS?
IT'S LABELLED MORPHINE.
MORPHINE
YOU SAYING IT ISN'T?
I'M SAYING THAT IF THIS IS WHAT ALL THOSE USERS SHOT UP, AND IT TURNED THEM RABID--
--IT'S A LOT MORE THAN MORPHINE.
AND THERE'S A LOT TO GO AROUND.
I'M GOING TO KEEP A CASE AND HAVE IT ANALYZED.
WE FLUSH THE REST.
YOU GOT A PROBLEM WITH THAT?
HELL NO. IT'S BAD BUSINESS.
SCRAAK!

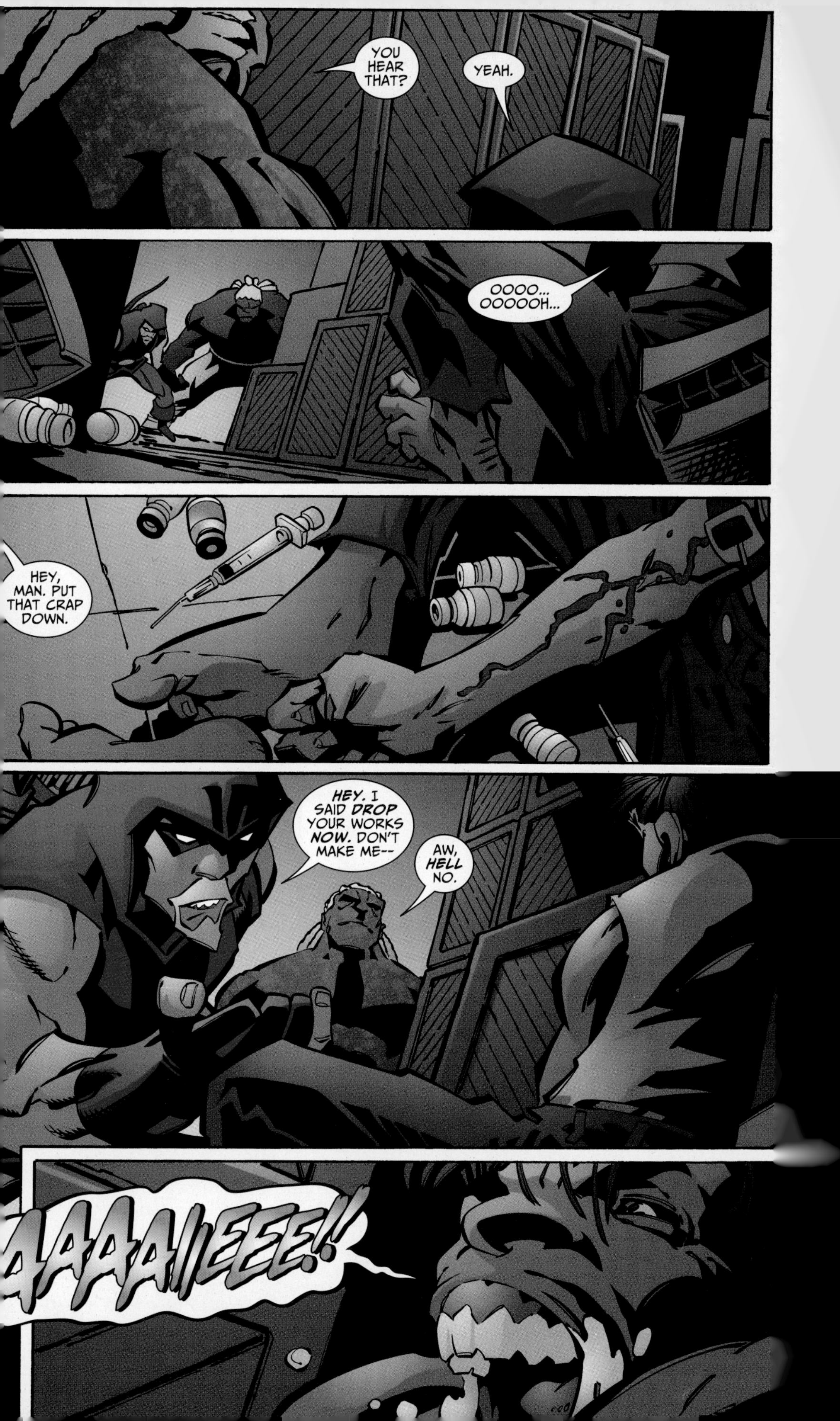
YOU HEAR THAT?
YEAH.
OOOO... OOOOOH...
HEY, MAN. PUT THAT CRAP DOWN.
HEY. I SAID DROP YOUR WORKS NOW. DON'T MAKE ME--
AW, HELL NO.
AAAAIIEEE!!

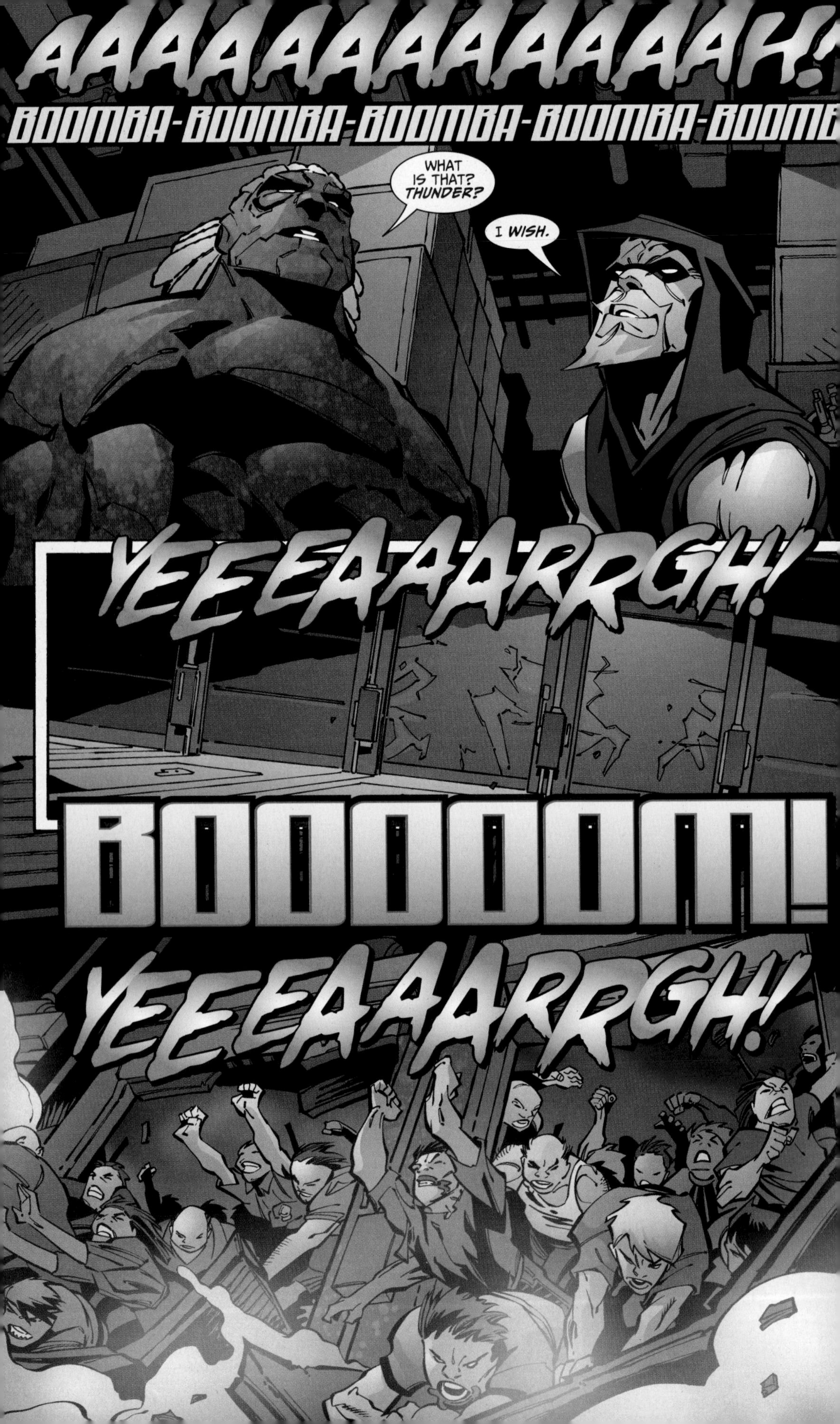
AAAAAAAAAAAAH!
BOOMBA-BOOMBA-BOOMBA-BOOMBA-BOOMB
WHAT IS THAT? THUNDER?
I WISH.
YEEEAAARRGH!
BOOOOOM!
YEEEAAARRGH!

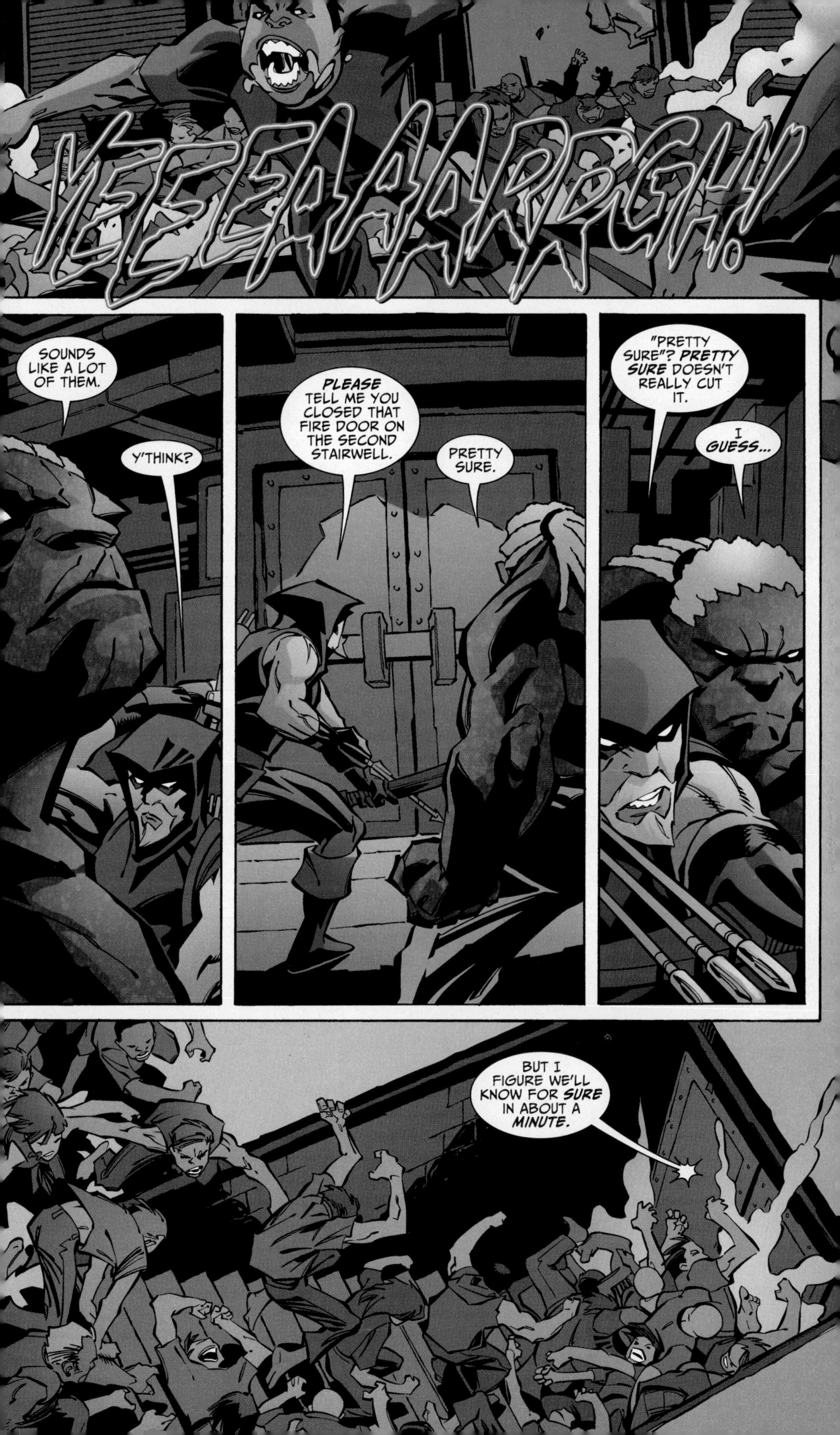
YEEEAAARRGH!
SOUNDS LIKE A LOT OF THEM.
Y'THINK?
PLEASE TELL ME YOU CLOSED THAT FIRE DOOR ON THE SECOND STAIRWELL.
PRETTY SURE.
"PRETTY SURE"? PRETTY SURE DOESN'T REALLY CUT IT.
I GUESS...
BUT I FIGURE WE'LL KNOW FOR SURE IN ABOUT A MINUTE.

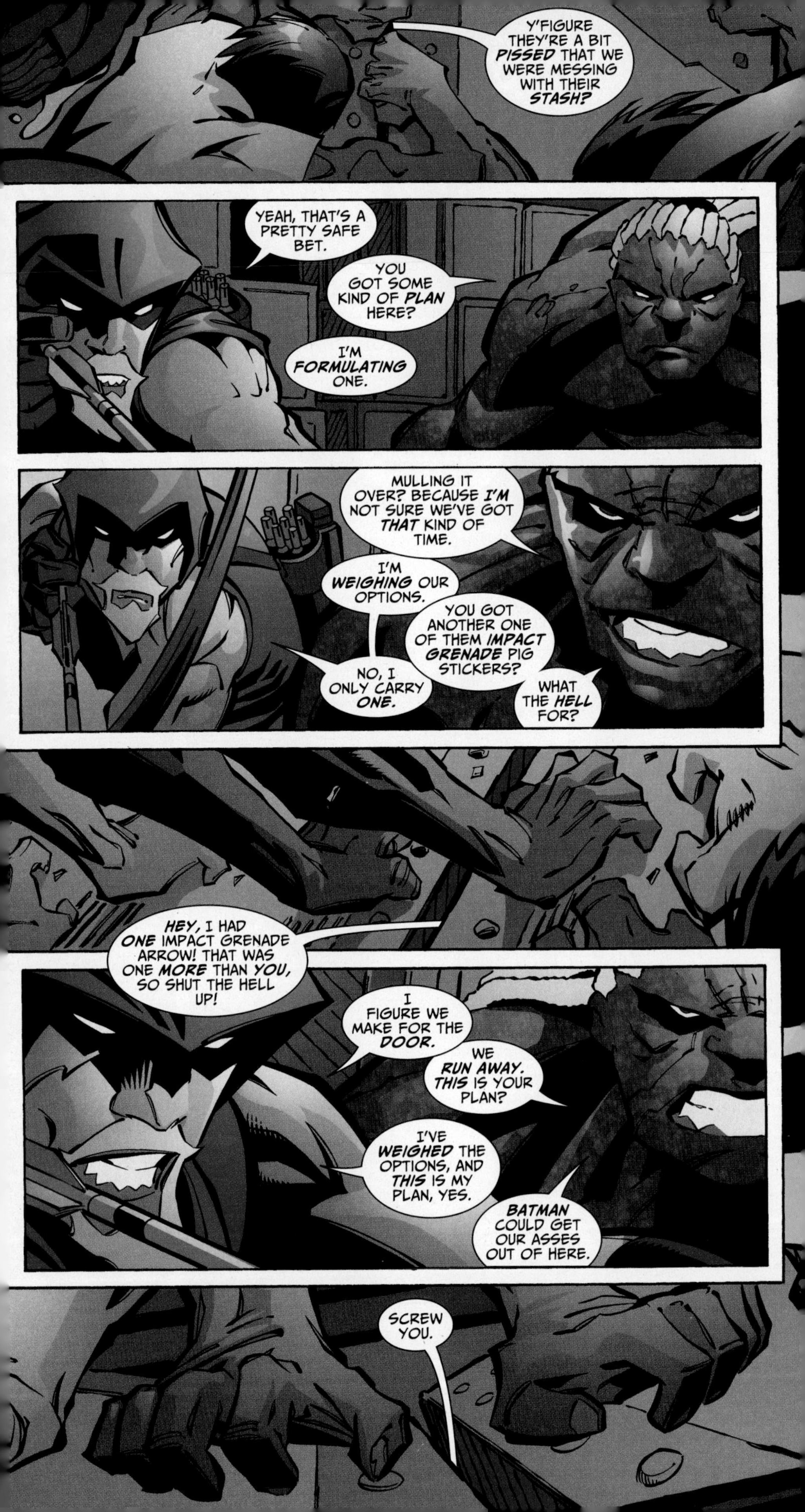
Y'FIGURE THEY'RE A BIT *PISSED* THAT WE WERE MESSING WITH THEIR *STASH?*
YEAH, THAT'S A PRETTY SAFE BET.
YOU GOT SOME KIND OF *PLAN* HERE?
I'M *FORMULATING* ONE.
MULLING IT OVER? BECAUSE *I'M* NOT SURE WE'VE GOT *THAT* KIND OF TIME.
I'M *WEIGHING* OUR OPTIONS.
YOU GOT ANOTHER ONE OF THEM *IMPACT GRENADE* PIG STICKERS?
NO, I ONLY CARRY *ONE.*
WHAT THE *HELL* FOR?
HEY, I HAD *ONE* IMPACT GRENADE ARROW! THAT WAS ONE *MORE* THAN *YOU,* SO SHUT THE HELL UP!
I FIGURE WE MAKE FOR THE *DOOR.*
WE *RUN AWAY. THIS* IS YOUR PLAN?
I'VE *WEIGHED* THE OPTIONS, AND *THIS* IS MY PLAN, YES.
BATMAN COULD GET OUR ASSES OUT OF HERE.
SCREW YOU.

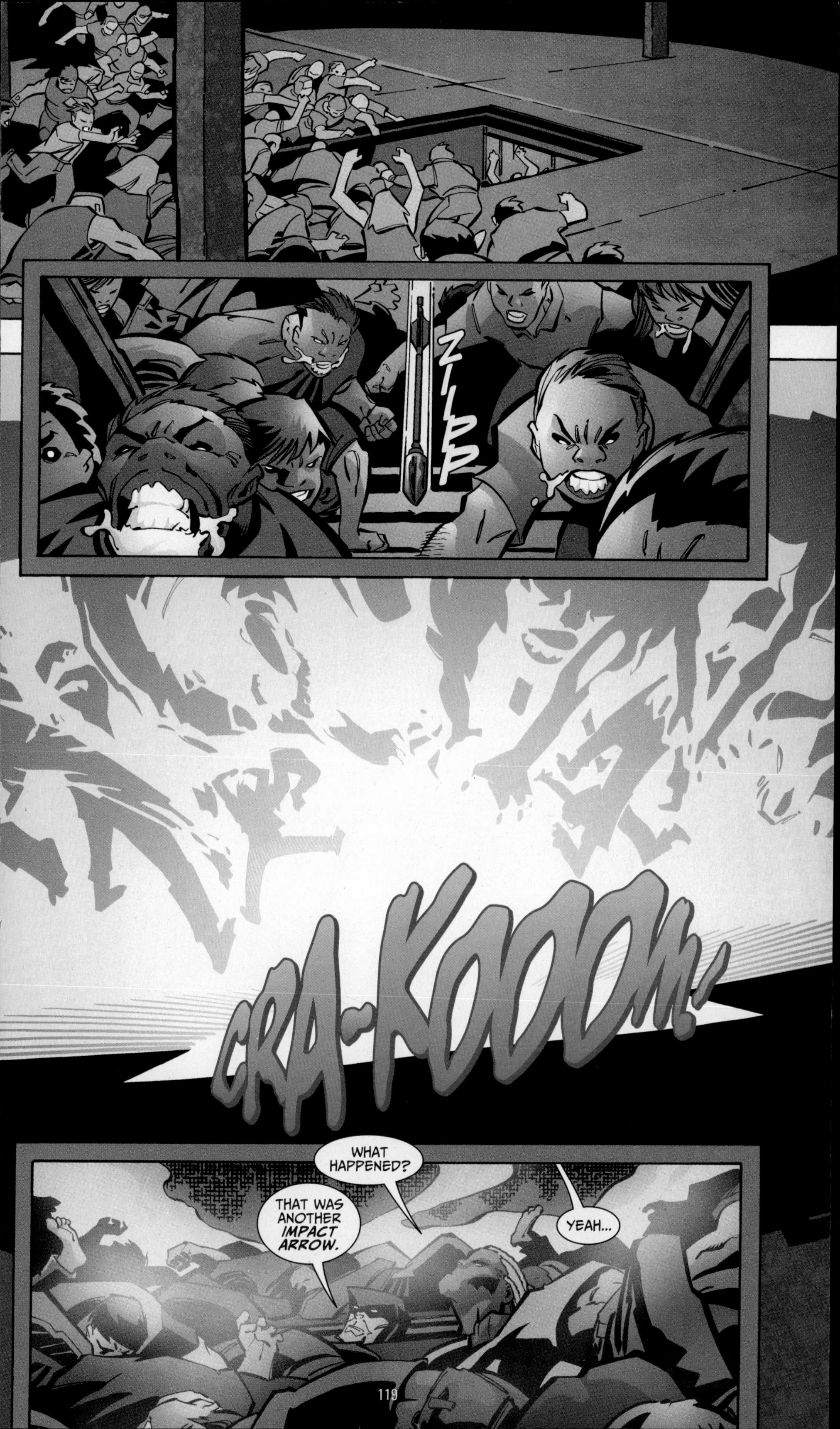
ZIPP
CRA-KOOOM!
WHAT HAPPENED?
THAT WAS ANOTHER *IMPACT ARROW.*
YEAH...

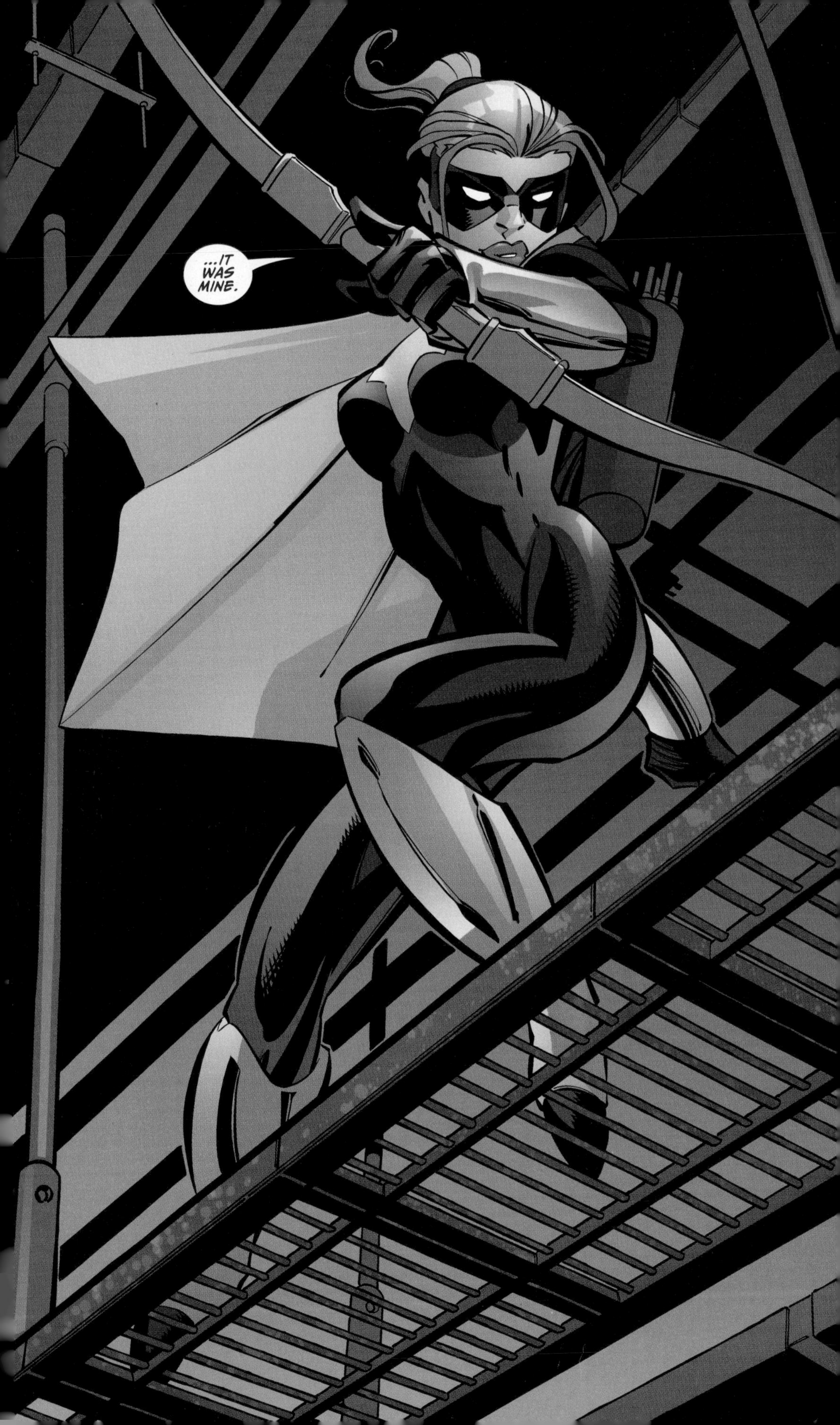
...IT WAS MINE.

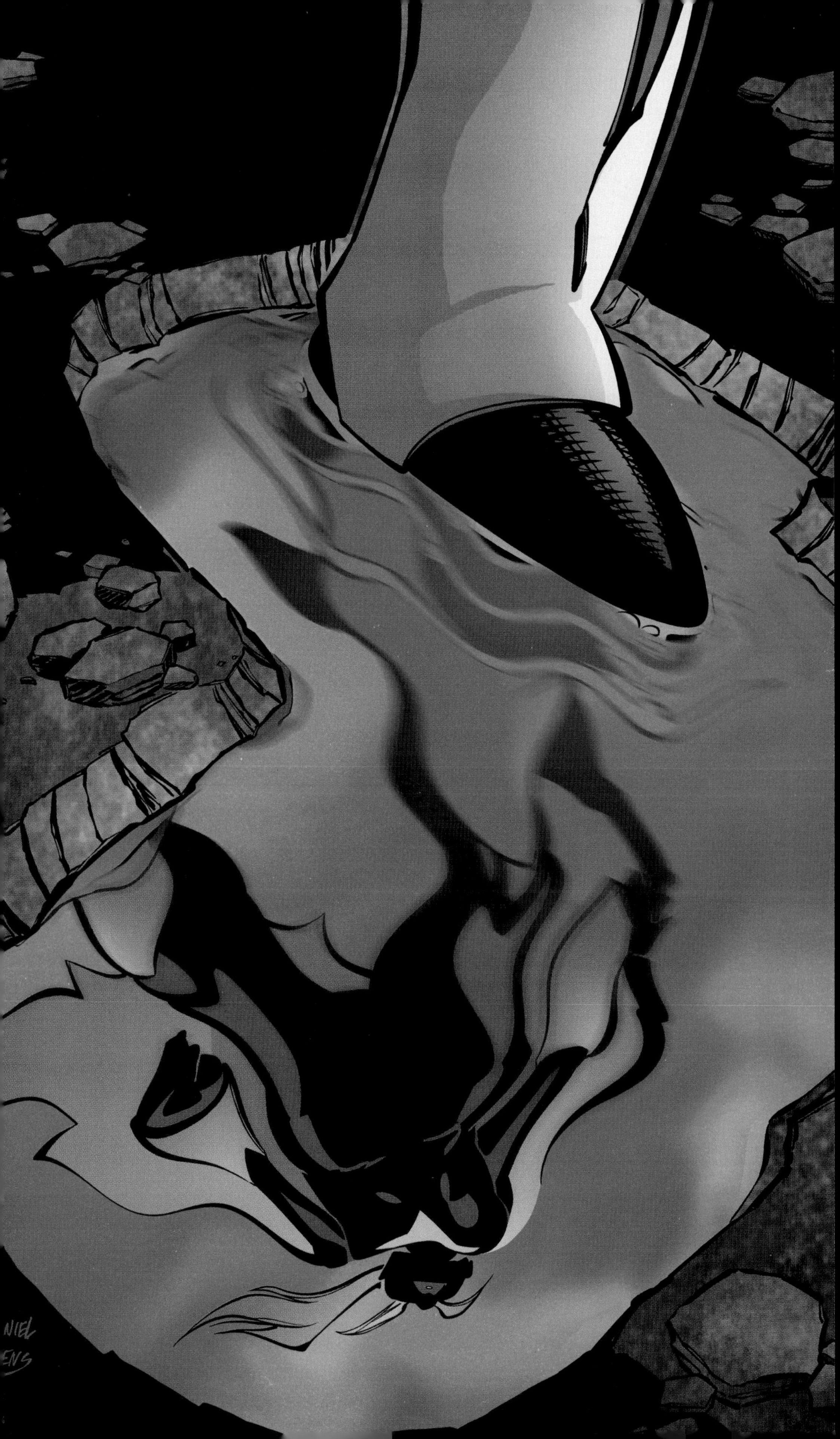

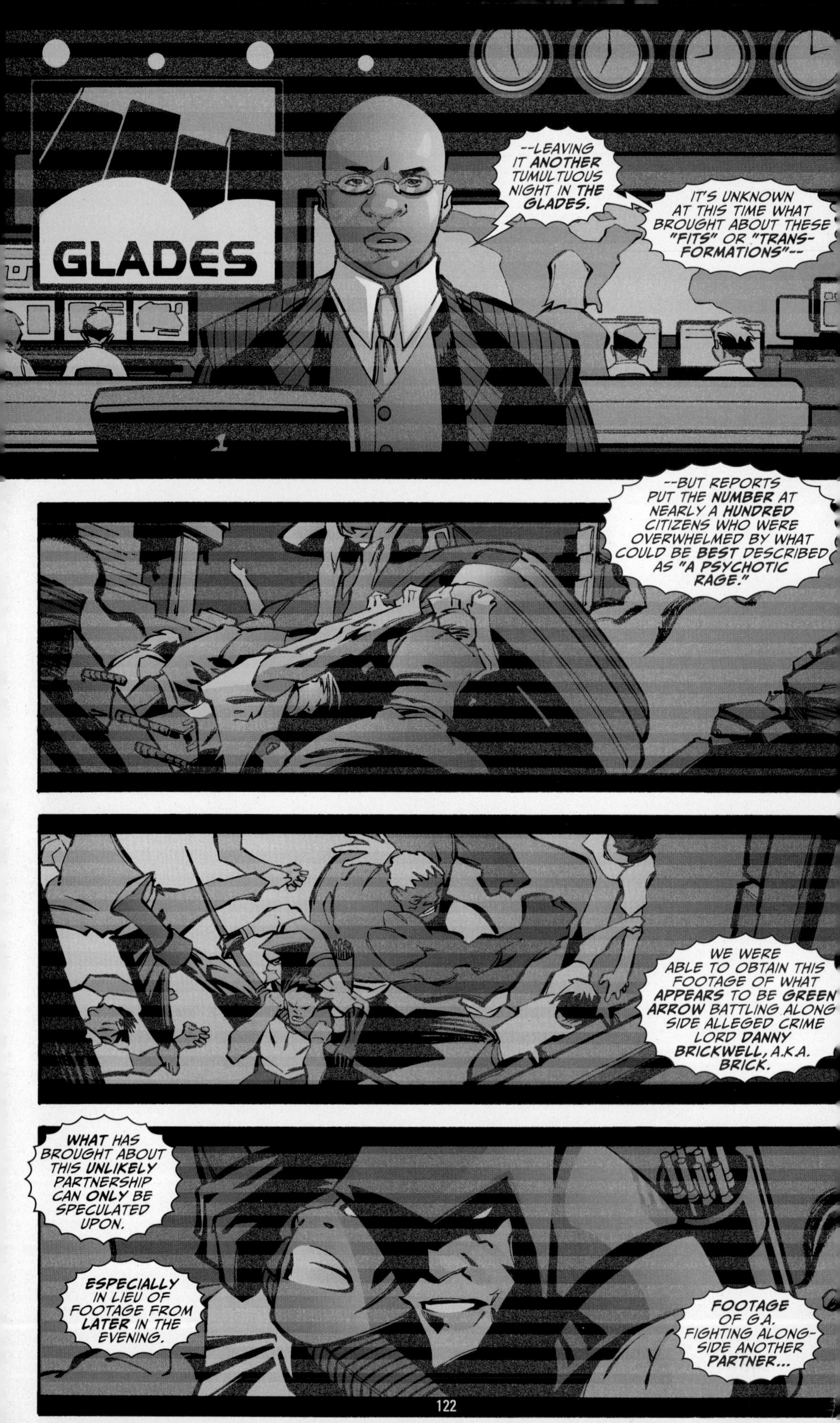
GLADES
--LEAVING IT ANOTHER TUMULTUOUS NIGHT IN THE GLADES.
IT'S UNKNOWN AT THIS TIME WHAT BROUGHT ABOUT THESE "FITS" OR "TRANS-FORMATIONS"--
--BUT REPORTS PUT THE NUMBER AT NEARLY A HUNDRED CITIZENS WHO WERE OVERWHELMED BY WHAT COULD BE BEST DESCRIBED AS "A PSYCHOTIC RAGE."
WE WERE ABLE TO OBTAIN THIS FOOTAGE OF WHAT APPEARS TO BE GREEN ARROW BATTLING ALONG SIDE ALLEGED CRIME LORD DANNY BRICKWELL, A.K.A. BRICK.
WHAT HAS BROUGHT ABOUT THIS UNLIKELY PARTNERSHIP CAN ONLY BE SPECULATED UPON.
ESPECIALLY IN LIEU OF FOOTAGE FROM LATER IN THE EVENING.
FOOTAGE OF G.A. FIGHTING ALONG-SIDE ANOTHER PARTNER...

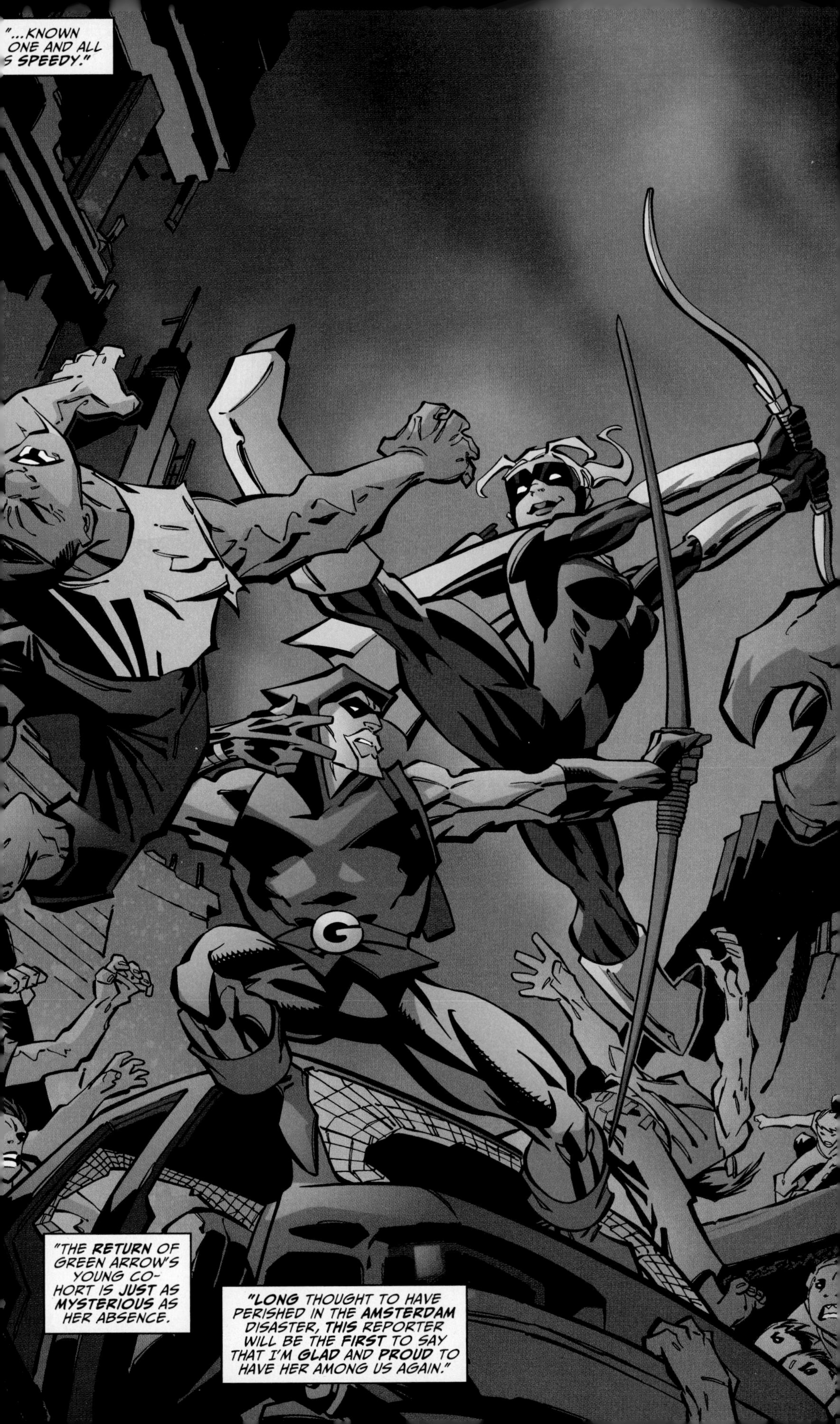
"...KNOWN ONE AND ALL S SPEEDY."
"THE RETURN OF GREEN ARROW'S YOUNG CO-HORT IS JUST AS MYSTERIOUS AS HER ABSENCE.
"LONG THOUGHT TO HAVE PERISHED IN THE AMSTERDAM DISASTER, THIS REPORTER WILL BE THE FIRST TO SAY THAT I'M GLAD AND PROUD TO HAVE HER AMONG US AGAIN."

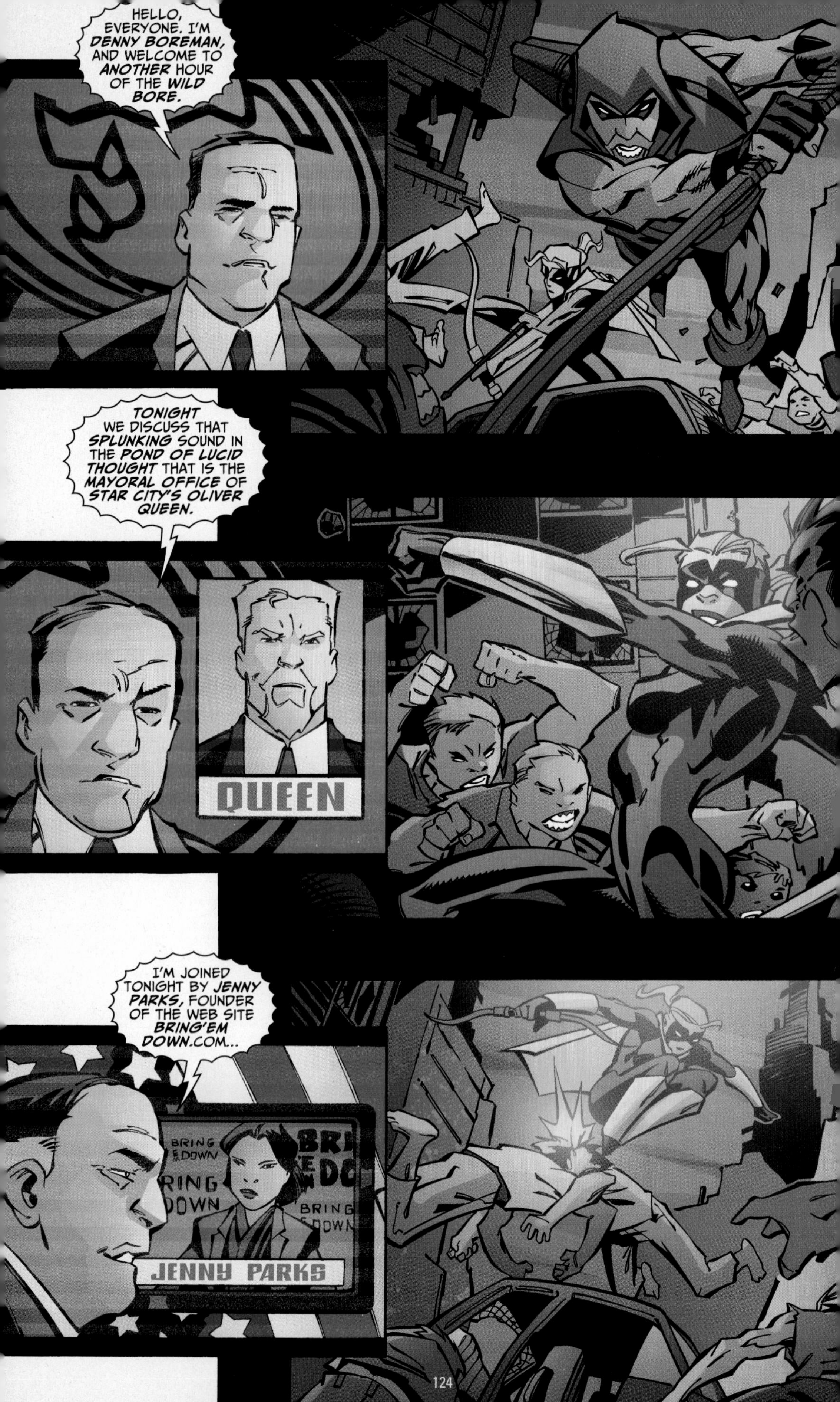
HELLO, EVERYONE. I'M DENNY BOREMAN, AND WELCOME TO ANOTHER HOUR OF THE WILD BORE.
TONIGHT WE DISCUSS THAT SPLUNKING SOUND IN THE POND OF LUCID THOUGHT THAT IS THE MAYORAL OFFICE OF STAR CITY'S OLIVER QUEEN.
QUEEN
I'M JOINED TONIGHT BY JENNY PARKS, FOUNDER OF THE WEB SITE BRING'EM DOWN.COM...
BRING 'EM DOWN
BRING DOWN
BRING DOWN
JENNY PARKS

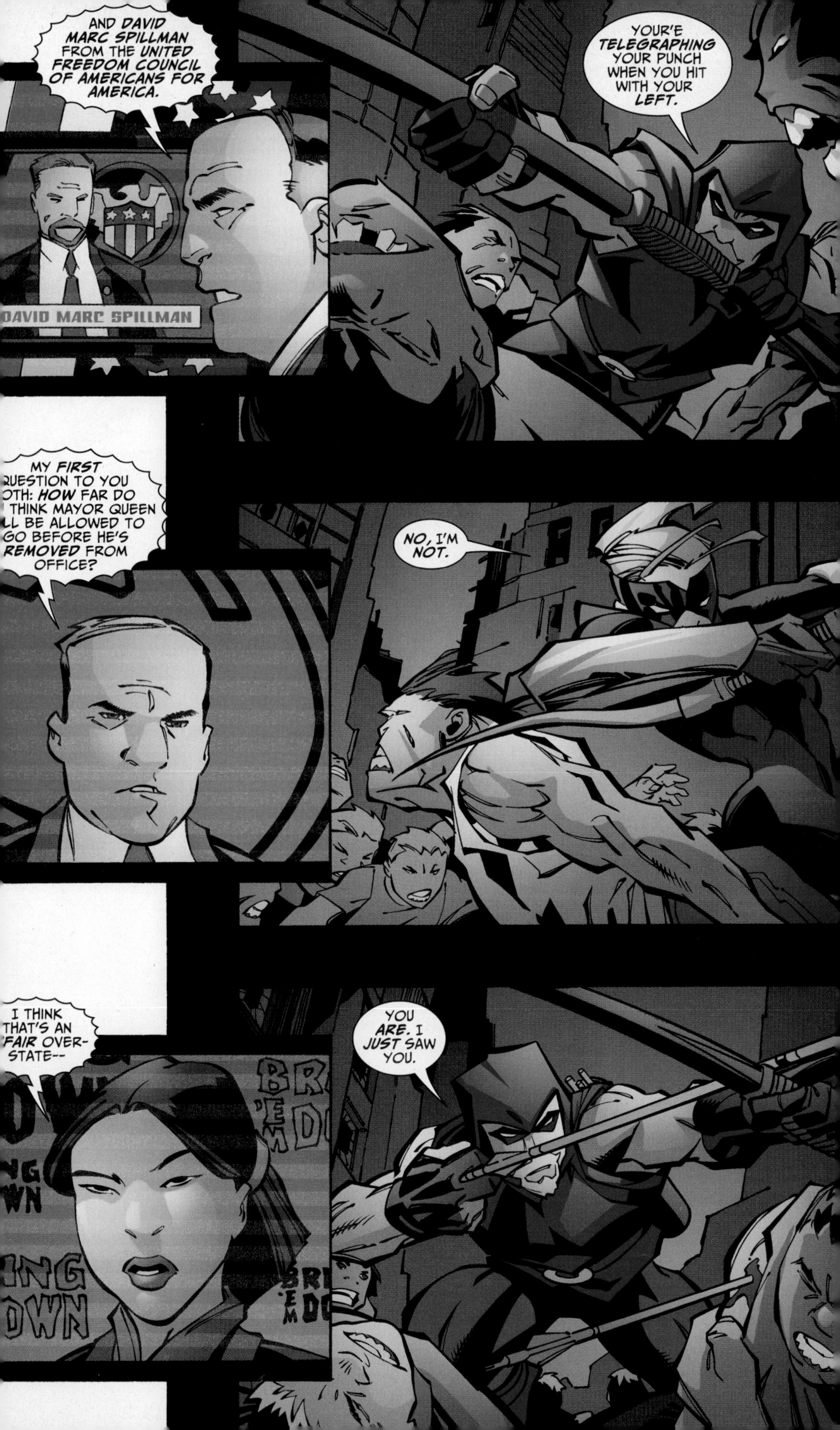
AND DAVID MARC SPILLMAN FROM THE UNITED FREEDOM COUNCIL OF AMERICANS FOR AMERICA.
DAVID MARC SPILLMAN
YOUR'E TELEGRAPHING YOUR PUNCH WHEN YOU HIT WITH YOUR LEFT.
MY FIRST QUESTION TO YOU OTH: HOW FAR DO THINK MAYOR QUEEN LL BE ALLOWED TO GO BEFORE HE'S REMOVED FROM OFFICE?
NO, I'M NOT.
I THINK THAT'S AN FAIR OVER-STATE--
YOU ARE. I JUST SAW YOU.

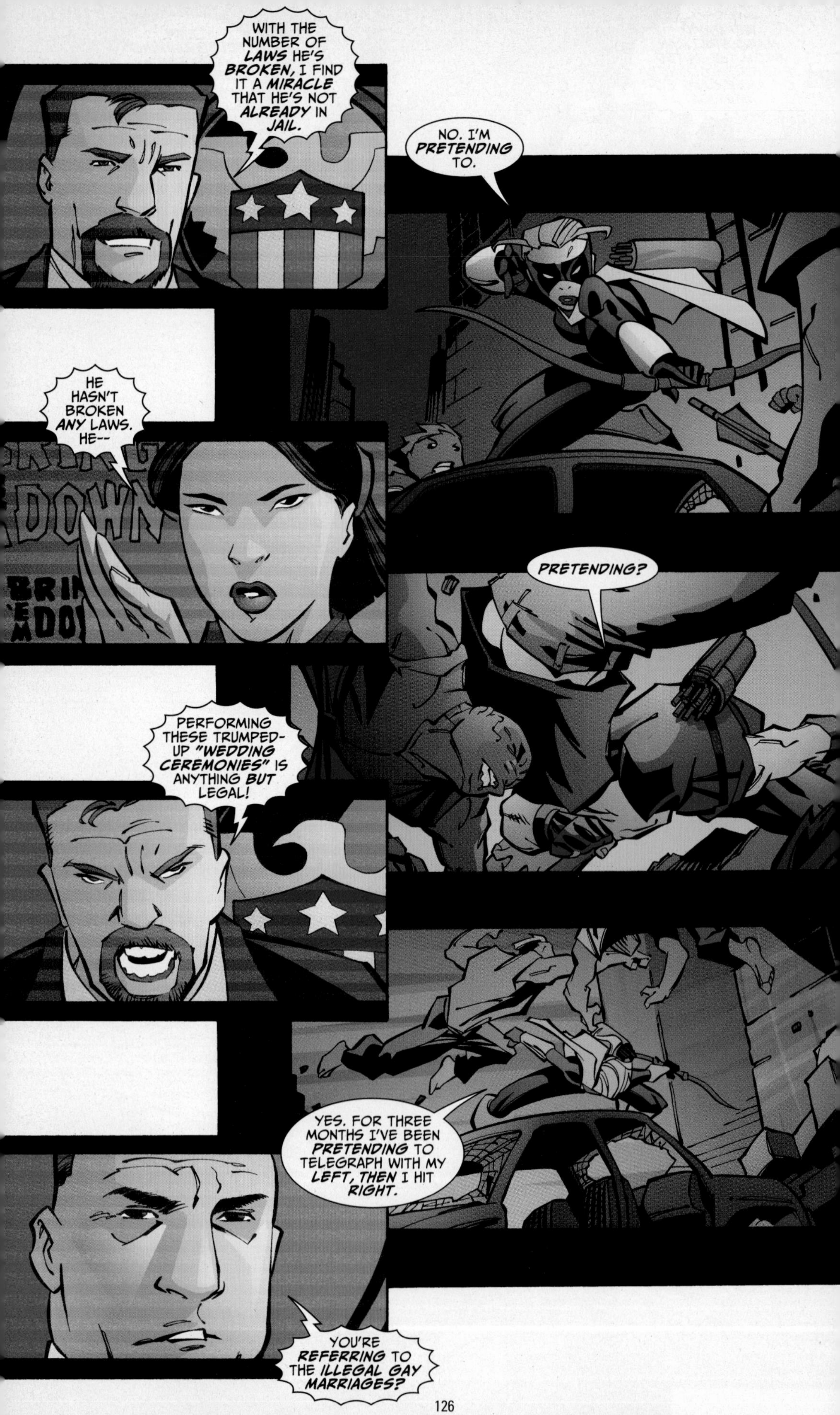
WITH THE NUMBER OF *LAWS* HE'S *BROKEN*, I FIND IT A *MIRACLE* THAT HE'S NOT *ALREADY* IN *JAIL*.
NO. I'M *PRETENDING* TO.
HE HASN'T BROKEN *ANY* LAWS. HE--
PRETENDING?
PERFORMING THESE TRUMPED-UP *"WEDDING CEREMONIES"* IS ANYTHING *BUT* LEGAL!
YES. FOR THREE MONTHS I'VE BEEN *PRETENDING* TO TELEGRAPH WITH MY *LEFT*, *THEN* I HIT *RIGHT*.
YOU'RE *REFERRING* TO THE *ILLEGAL GAY MARRIAGES?*

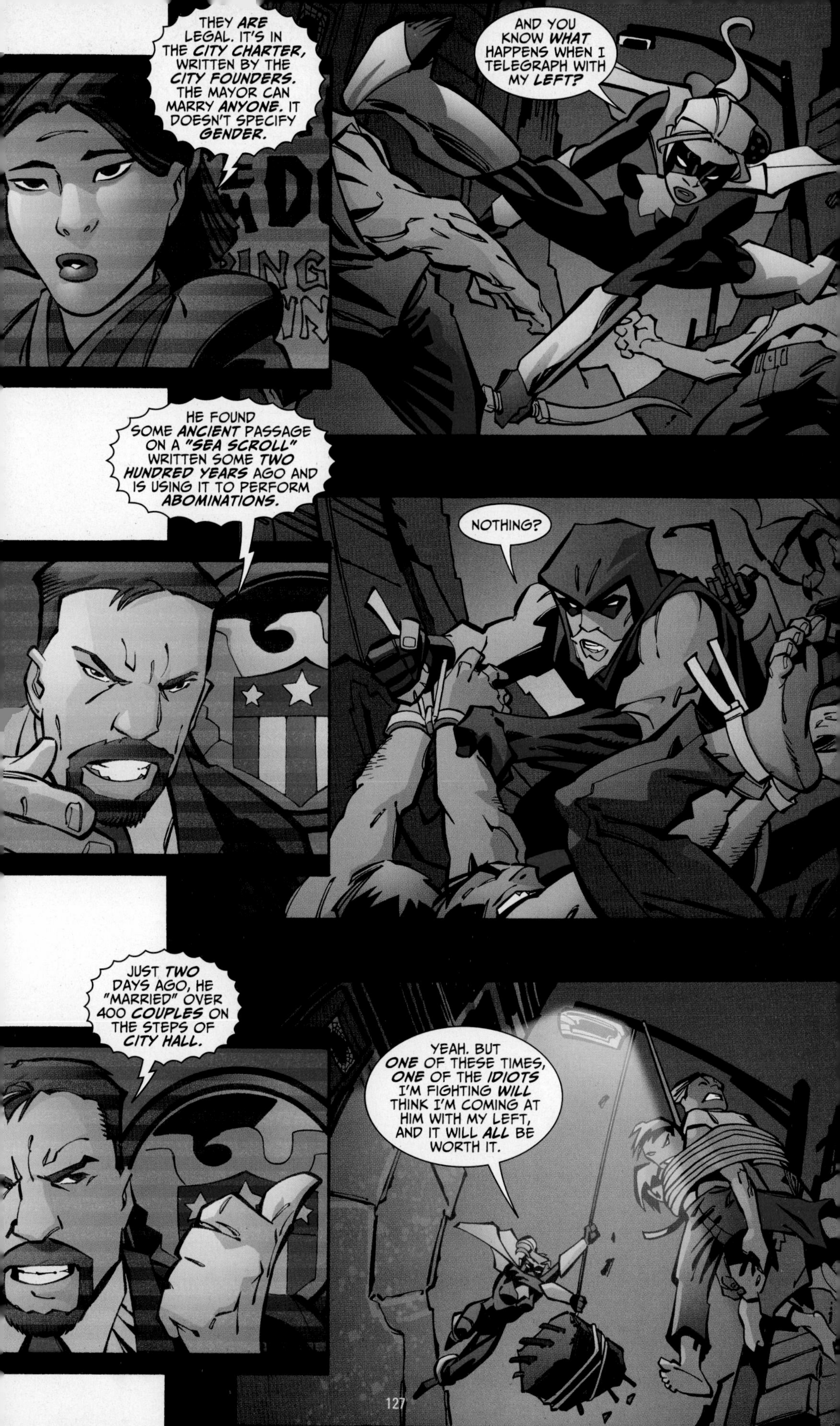
THEY ARE LEGAL. IT'S IN THE CITY CHARTER, WRITTEN BY THE CITY FOUNDERS. THE MAYOR CAN MARRY ANYONE. IT DOESN'T SPECIFY GENDER.
AND YOU KNOW WHAT HAPPENS WHEN I TELEGRAPH WITH MY LEFT?
HE FOUND SOME ANCIENT PASSAGE ON A "SEA SCROLL" WRITTEN SOME TWO HUNDRED YEARS AGO AND IS USING IT TO PERFORM ABOMINATIONS.
NOTHING?
JUST TWO DAYS AGO, HE "MARRIED" OVER 400 COUPLES ON THE STEPS OF CITY HALL.
YEAH. BUT ONE OF THESE TIMES, ONE OF THE IDIOTS I'M FIGHTING WILL THINK I'M COMING AT HIM WITH MY LEFT, AND IT WILL ALL BE WORTH IT.

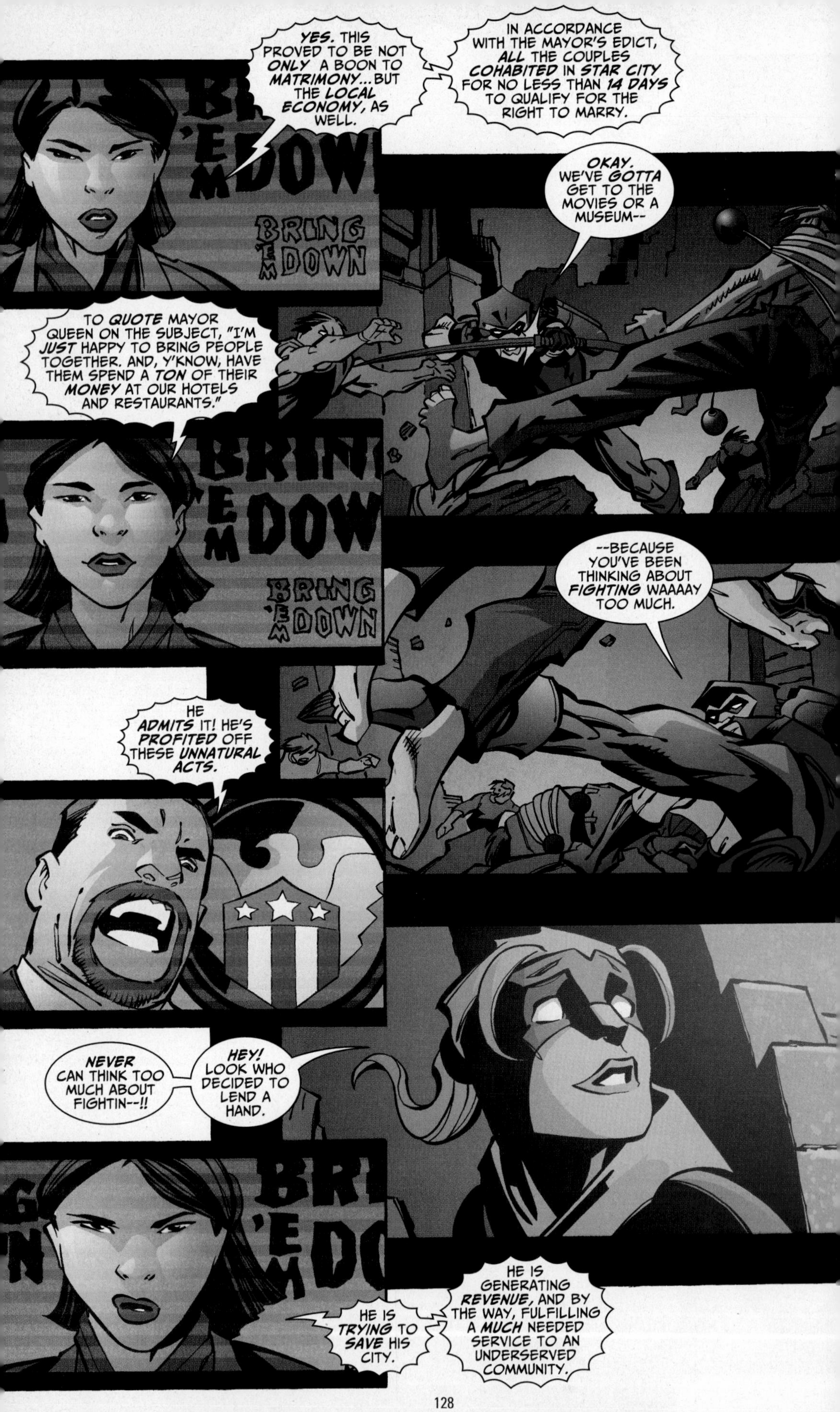
YES. THIS PROVED TO BE NOT ONLY A BOON TO MATRIMONY...BUT THE LOCAL ECONOMY, AS WELL.
IN ACCORDANCE WITH THE MAYOR'S EDICT, ALL THE COUPLES COHABITED IN STAR CITY FOR NO LESS THAN 14 DAYS TO QUALIFY FOR THE RIGHT TO MARRY.
BRING 'EM DOWN
OKAY. WE'VE GOTTA GET TO THE MOVIES OR A MUSEUM--
TO QUOTE MAYOR QUEEN ON THE SUBJECT, "I'M JUST HAPPY TO BRING PEOPLE TOGETHER. AND, Y'KNOW, HAVE THEM SPEND A TON OF THEIR MONEY AT OUR HOTELS AND RESTAURANTS."
BRING 'EM DOWN
--BECAUSE YOU'VE BEEN THINKING ABOUT FIGHTING WAAAAY TOO MUCH.
HE ADMITS IT! HE'S PROFITED OFF THESE UNNATURAL ACTS.
NEVER CAN THINK TOO MUCH ABOUT FIGHTIN--!!
HEY! LOOK WHO DECIDED TO LEND A HAND.
HE IS TRYING TO SAVE HIS CITY.
HE IS GENERATING REVENUE, AND BY THE WAY, FULFILLING A MUCH NEEDED SERVICE TO AN UNDERSERVED COMMUNITY.

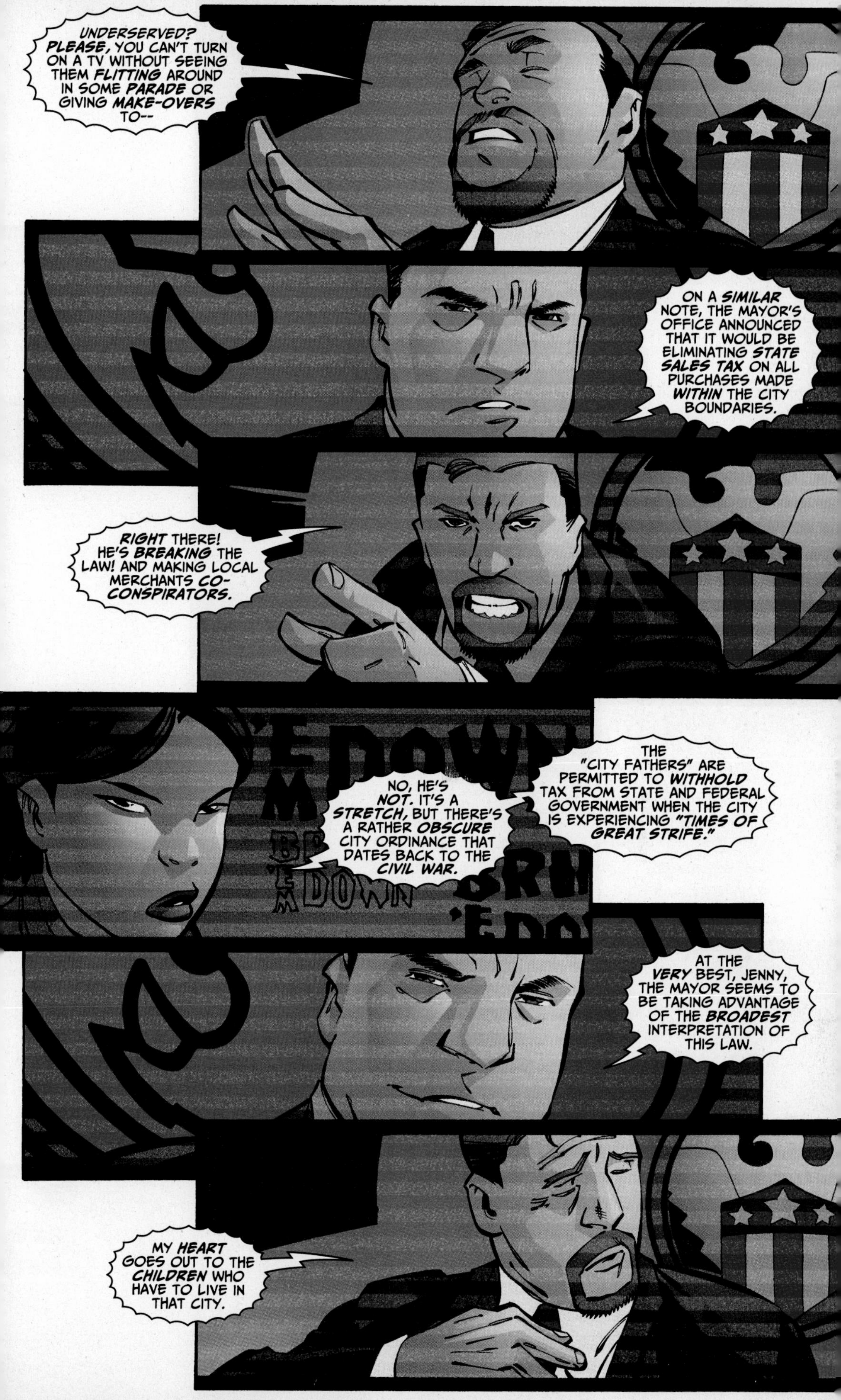
UNDERSERVED? PLEASE, YOU CAN'T TURN ON A TV WITHOUT SEEING THEM FLITTING AROUND IN SOME PARADE OR GIVING MAKE-OVERS TO--
ON A SIMILAR NOTE, THE MAYOR'S OFFICE ANNOUNCED THAT IT WOULD BE ELIMINATING STATE SALES TAX ON ALL PURCHASES MADE WITHIN THE CITY BOUNDARIES.
RIGHT THERE! HE'S BREAKING THE LAW! AND MAKING LOCAL MERCHANTS CO-CONSPIRATORS.
NO, HE'S NOT. IT'S A STRETCH, BUT THERE'S A RATHER OBSCURE CITY ORDINANCE THAT DATES BACK TO THE CIVIL WAR.
THE "CITY FATHERS" ARE PERMITTED TO WITHHOLD TAX FROM STATE AND FEDERAL GOVERNMENT WHEN THE CITY IS EXPERIENCING "TIMES OF GREAT STRIFE."
AT THE VERY BEST, JENNY, THE MAYOR SEEMS TO BE TAKING ADVANTAGE OF THE BROADEST INTERPRETATION OF THIS LAW.
MY HEART GOES OUT TO THE CHILDREN WHO HAVE TO LIVE IN THAT CITY.

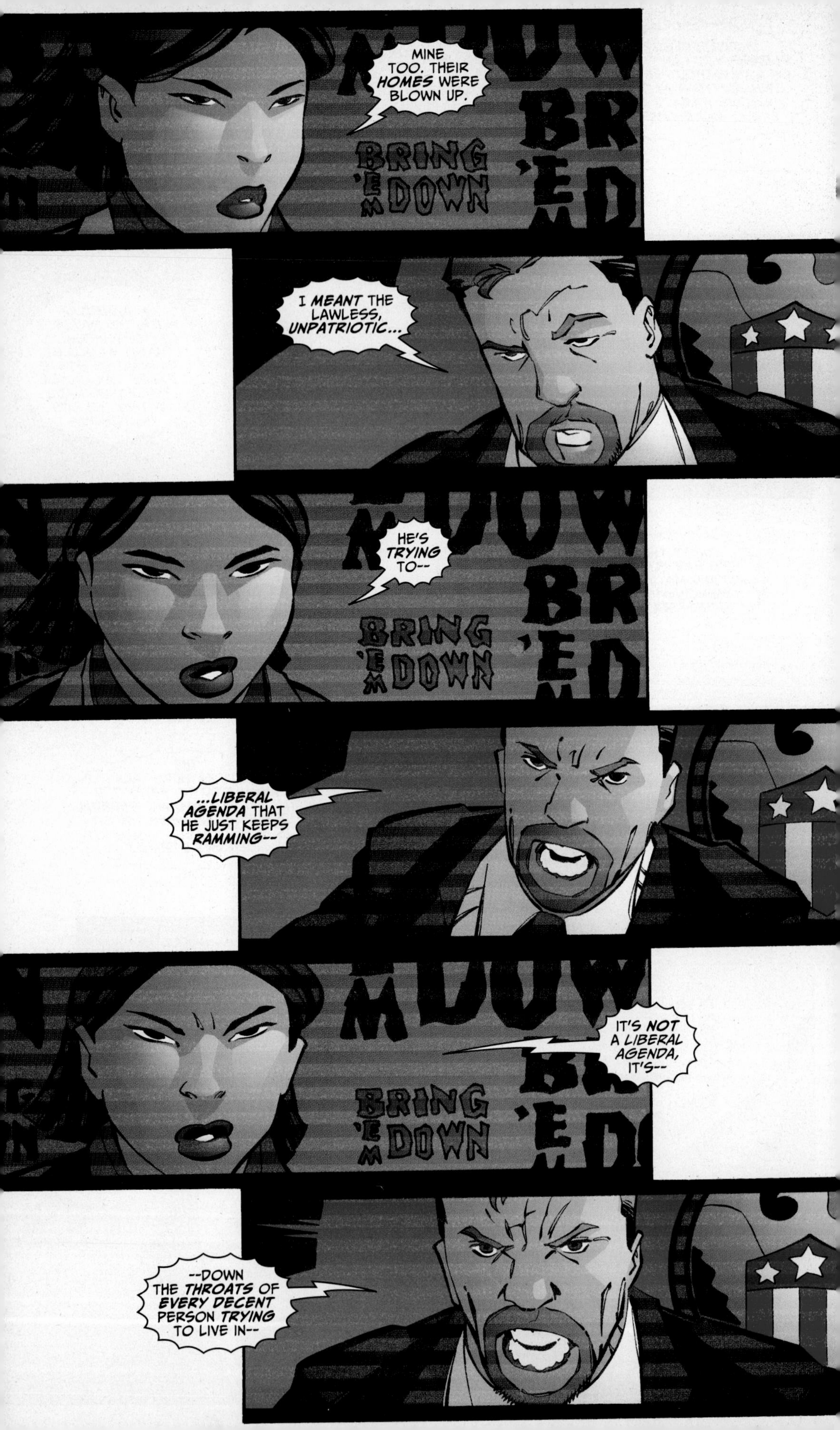
MINE TOO. THEIR HOMES WERE BLOWN UP.
BRING 'EM DOWN
I MEANT THE LAWLESS, UNPATRIOTIC...
HE'S TRYING TO--
BRING 'EM DOWN
...LIBERAL AGENDA THAT HE JUST KEEPS RAMMING--
IT'S NOT A LIBERAL AGENDA, IT'S--
BRING 'EM DOWN
--DOWN THE THROATS OF EVERY DECENT PERSON TRYING TO LIVE IN--

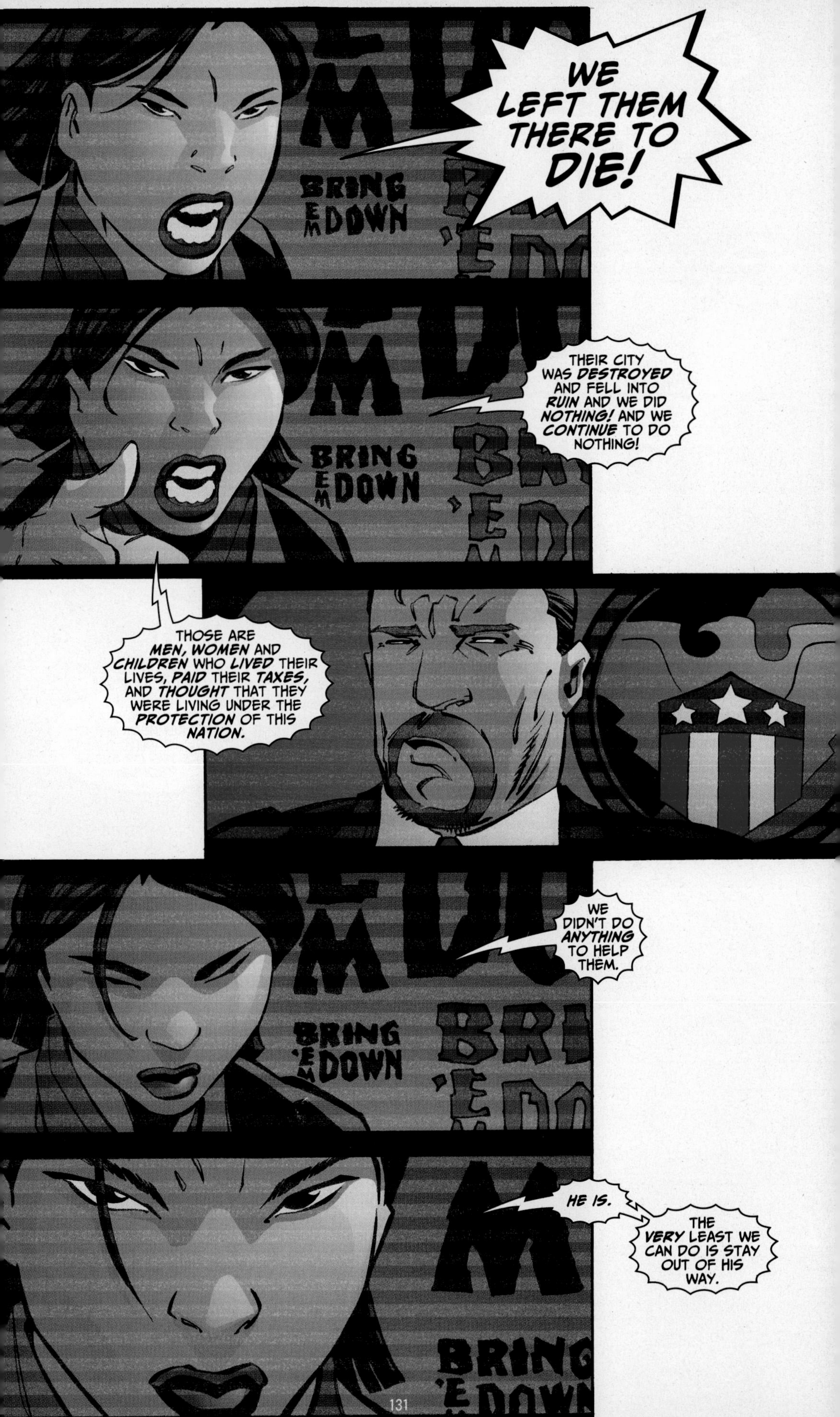
WE LEFT THEM THERE TO DIE!
BRING 'EM DOWN
THEIR CITY WAS DESTROYED AND FELL INTO RUIN AND WE DID NOTHING! AND WE CONTINUE TO DO NOTHING!
BRING 'EM DOWN
THOSE ARE MEN, WOMEN AND CHILDREN WHO LIVED THEIR LIVES, PAID THEIR TAXES, AND THOUGHT THAT THEY WERE LIVING UNDER THE PROTECTION OF THIS NATION.
WE DIDN'T DO ANYTHING TO HELP THEM.
BRING 'EM DOWN
HE IS.
THE VERY LEAST WE CAN DO IS STAY OUT OF HIS WAY.

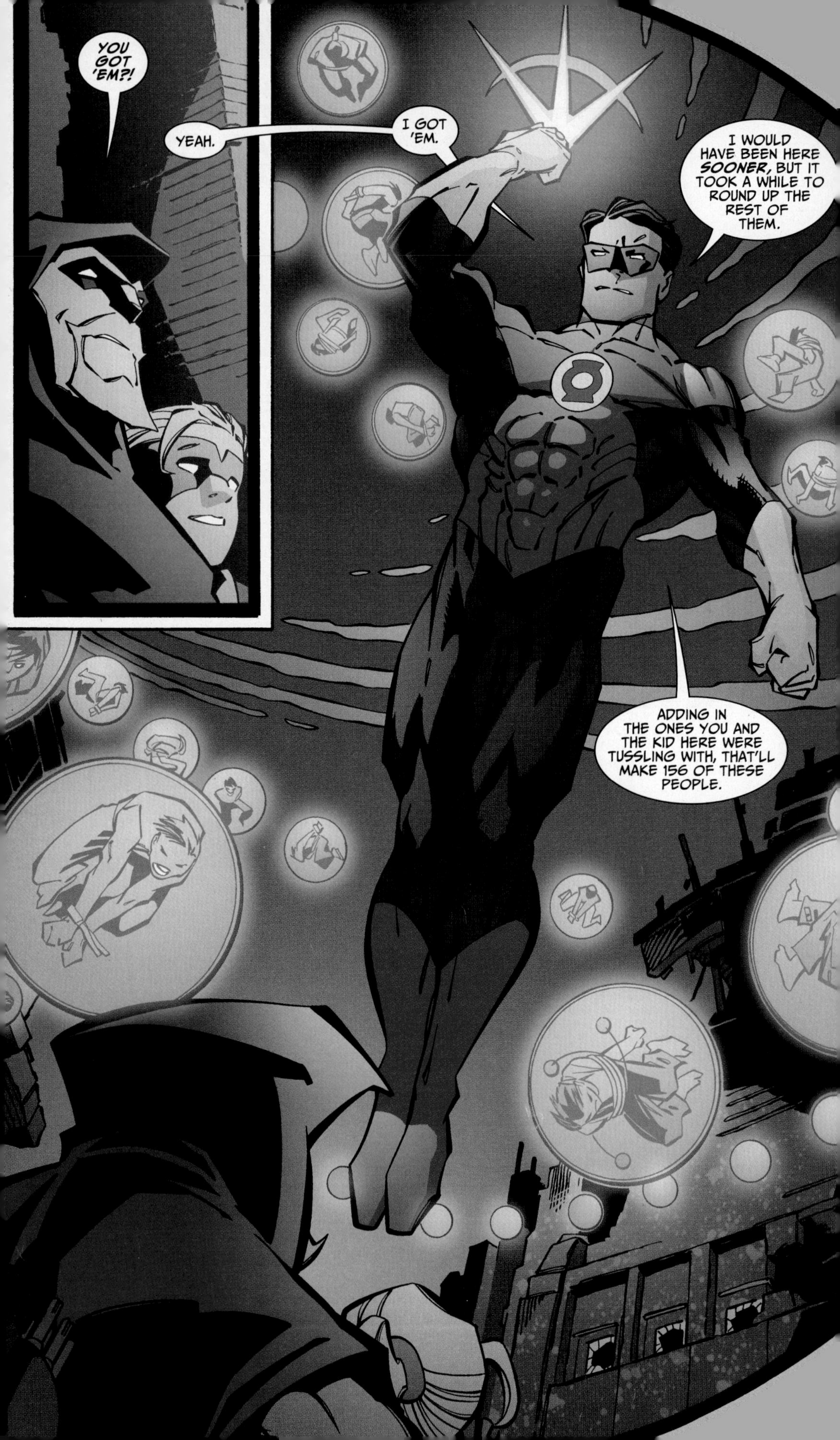
YOU GOT 'EM?!
YEAH.
I GOT 'EM.
I WOULD HAVE BEEN HERE SOONER, BUT IT TOOK A WHILE TO ROUND UP THE REST OF THEM.
ADDING IN THE ONES YOU AND THE KID HERE WERE TUSSLING WITH, THAT'LL MAKE 156 OF THESE PEOPLE.

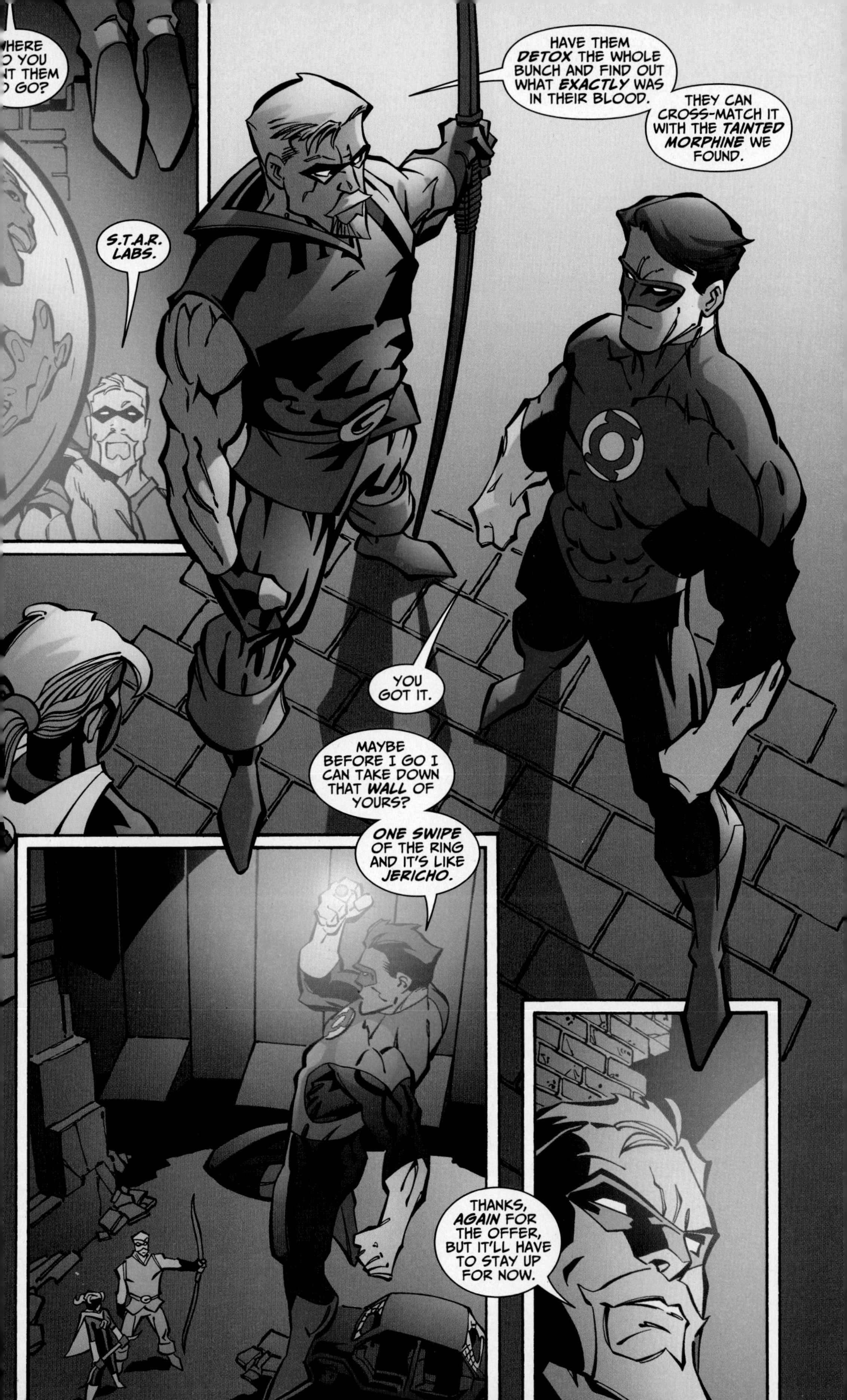
HERE O YOU IT THEM O GO?
S.T.A.R. LABS.
HAVE THEM DETOX THE WHOLE BUNCH AND FIND OUT WHAT EXACTLY WAS IN THEIR BLOOD.
THEY CAN CROSS-MATCH IT WITH THE TAINTED MORPHINE WE FOUND.
YOU GOT IT.
MAYBE BEFORE I GO I CAN TAKE DOWN THAT WALL OF YOURS?
ONE SWIPE OF THE RING AND IT'S LIKE JERICHO.
THANKS, AGAIN FOR THE OFFER, BUT IT'LL HAVE TO STAY UP FOR NOW.

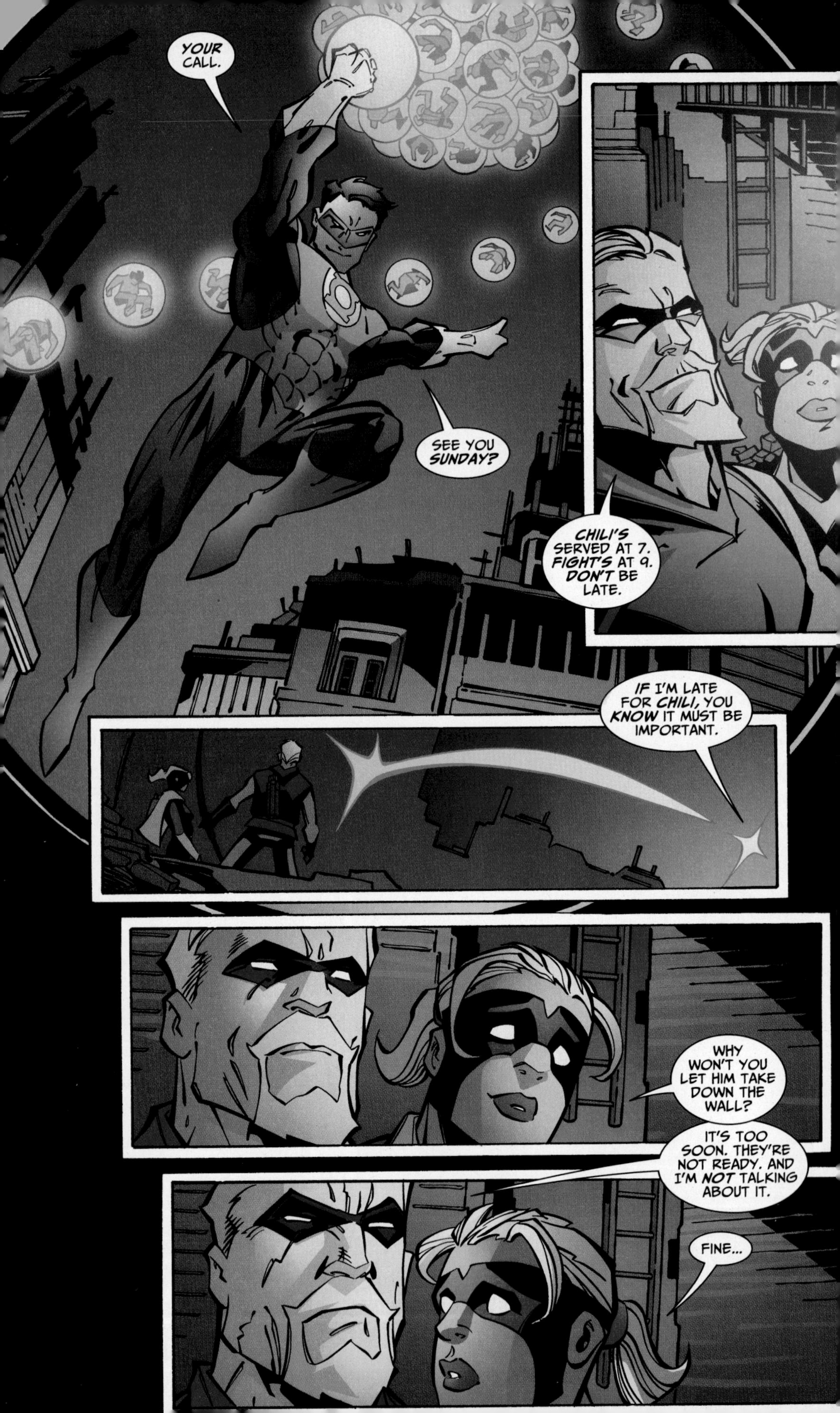
YOUR CALL.
SEE YOU SUNDAY?
CHILI'S SERVED AT 7. FIGHT'S AT 9. DON'T BE LATE.
IF I'M LATE FOR CHILI, YOU KNOW IT MUST BE IMPORTANT.
WHY WON'T YOU LET HIM TAKE DOWN THE WALL?
IT'S TOO SOON. THEY'RE NOT READY. AND I'M NOT TALKING ABOUT IT.
FINE...

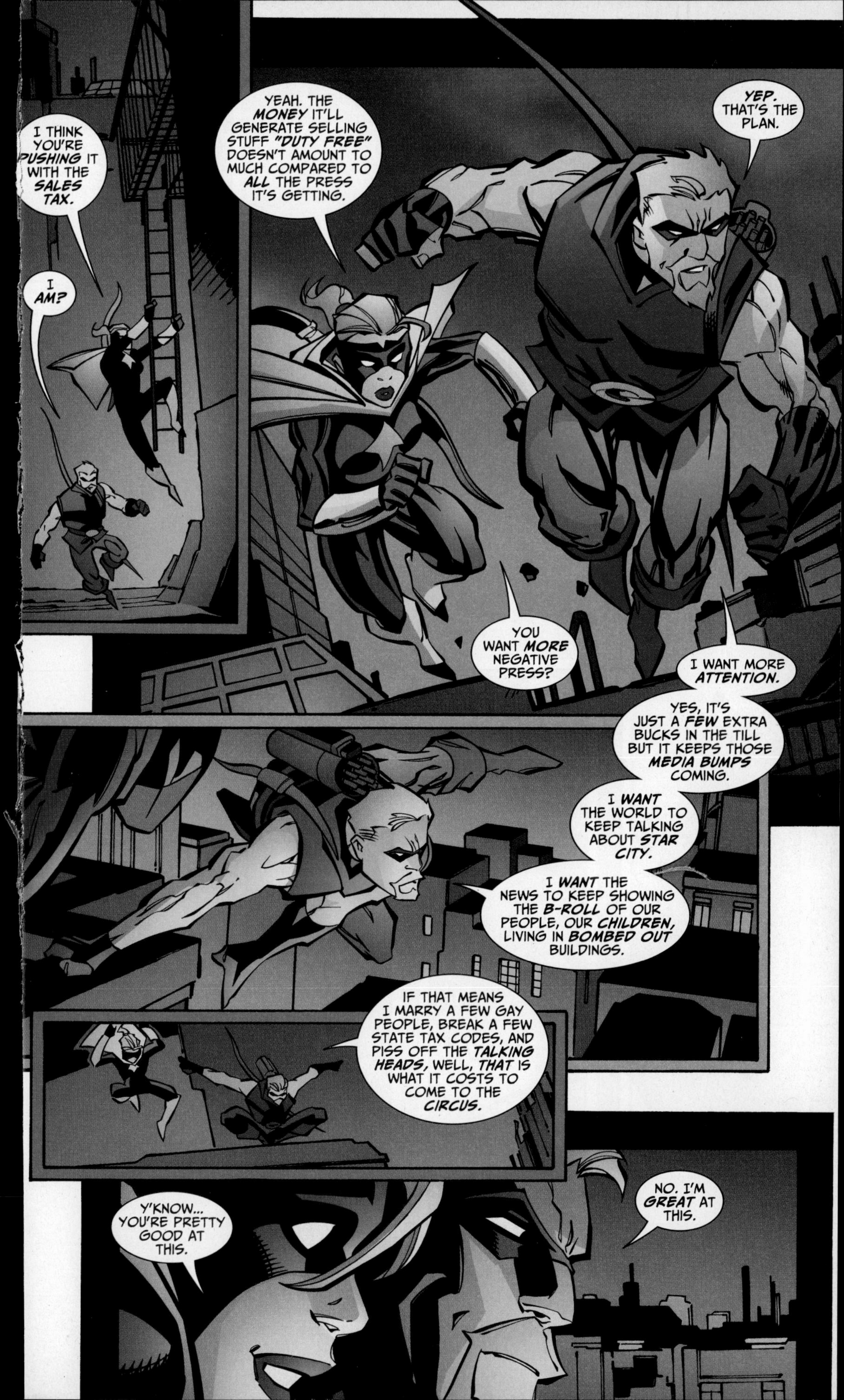
I THINK YOU'RE PUSHING IT WITH THE SALES TAX.
I AM?
YEAH. THE MONEY IT'LL GENERATE SELLING STUFF "DUTY FREE" DOESN'T AMOUNT TO MUCH COMPARED TO ALL THE PRESS IT'S GETTING.
YEP. THAT'S THE PLAN.
YOU WANT MORE NEGATIVE PRESS?
I WANT MORE ATTENTION.
YES, IT'S JUST A FEW EXTRA BUCKS IN THE TILL BUT IT KEEPS THOSE MEDIA BUMPS COMING.
I WANT THE WORLD TO KEEP TALKING ABOUT STAR CITY.
I WANT THE NEWS TO KEEP SHOWING THE B-ROLL OF OUR PEOPLE, OUR CHILDREN, LIVING IN BOMBED OUT BUILDINGS.
IF THAT MEANS I MARRY A FEW GAY PEOPLE, BREAK A FEW STATE TAX CODES, AND PISS OFF THE TALKING HEADS, WELL, THAT IS WHAT IT COSTS TO COME TO THE CIRCUS.
Y'KNOW... YOU'RE PRETTY GOOD AT THIS.
NO. I'M GREAT AT THIS.

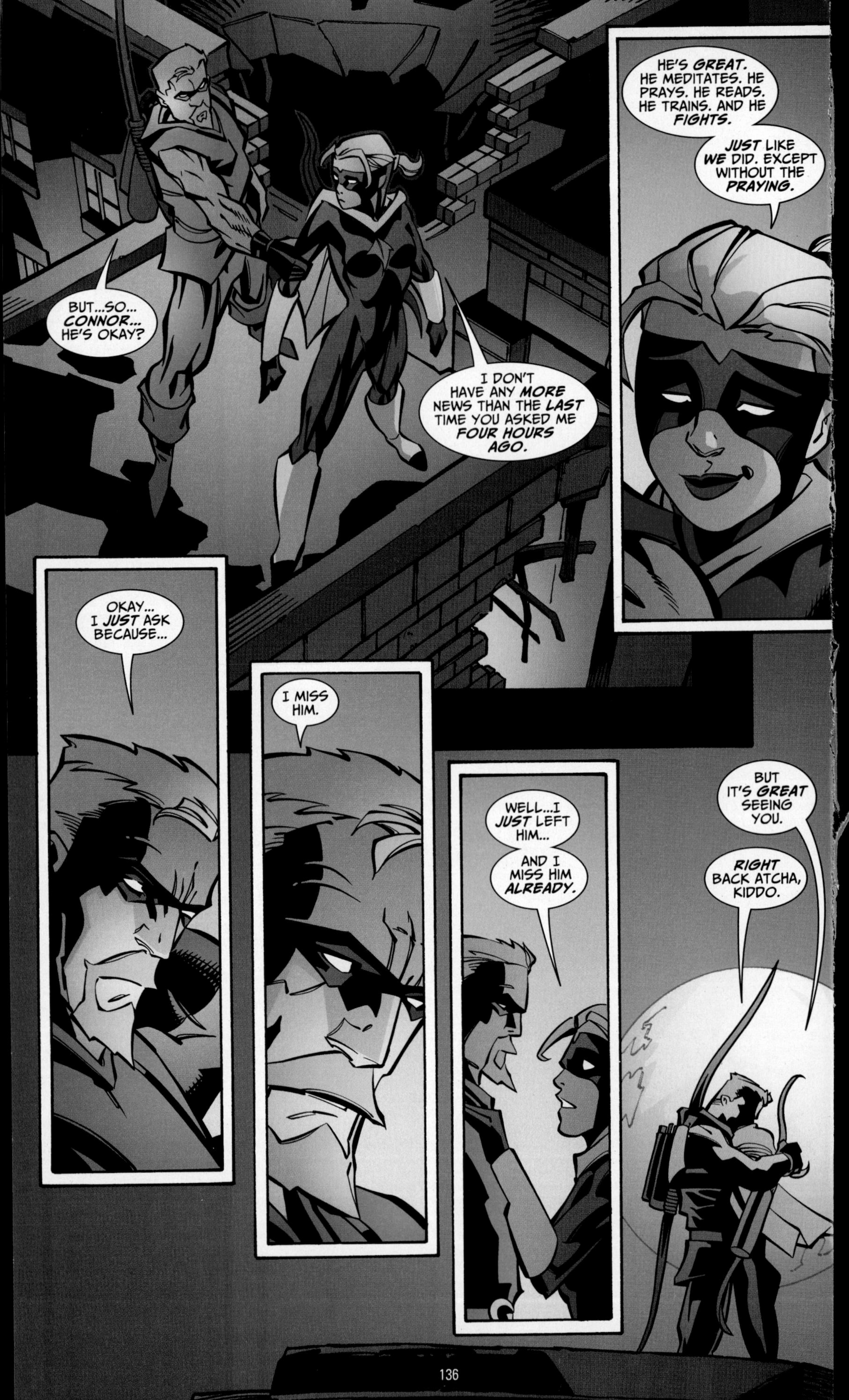

BUT...SO... CONNOR... HE'S OKAY?
I DON'T HAVE ANY MORE NEWS THAN THE LAST TIME YOU ASKED ME FOUR HOURS AGO.
HE'S GREAT. HE MEDITATES. HE PRAYS. HE READS. HE TRAINS. AND HE FIGHTS.
JUST LIKE WE DID. EXCEPT WITHOUT THE PRAYING.
OKAY... I JUST ASK BECAUSE...
I MISS HIM.
WELL...I JUST LEFT HIM...
AND I MISS HIM ALREADY.
BUT IT'S GREAT SEEING YOU.
RIGHT BACK ATCHA, KIDDO.

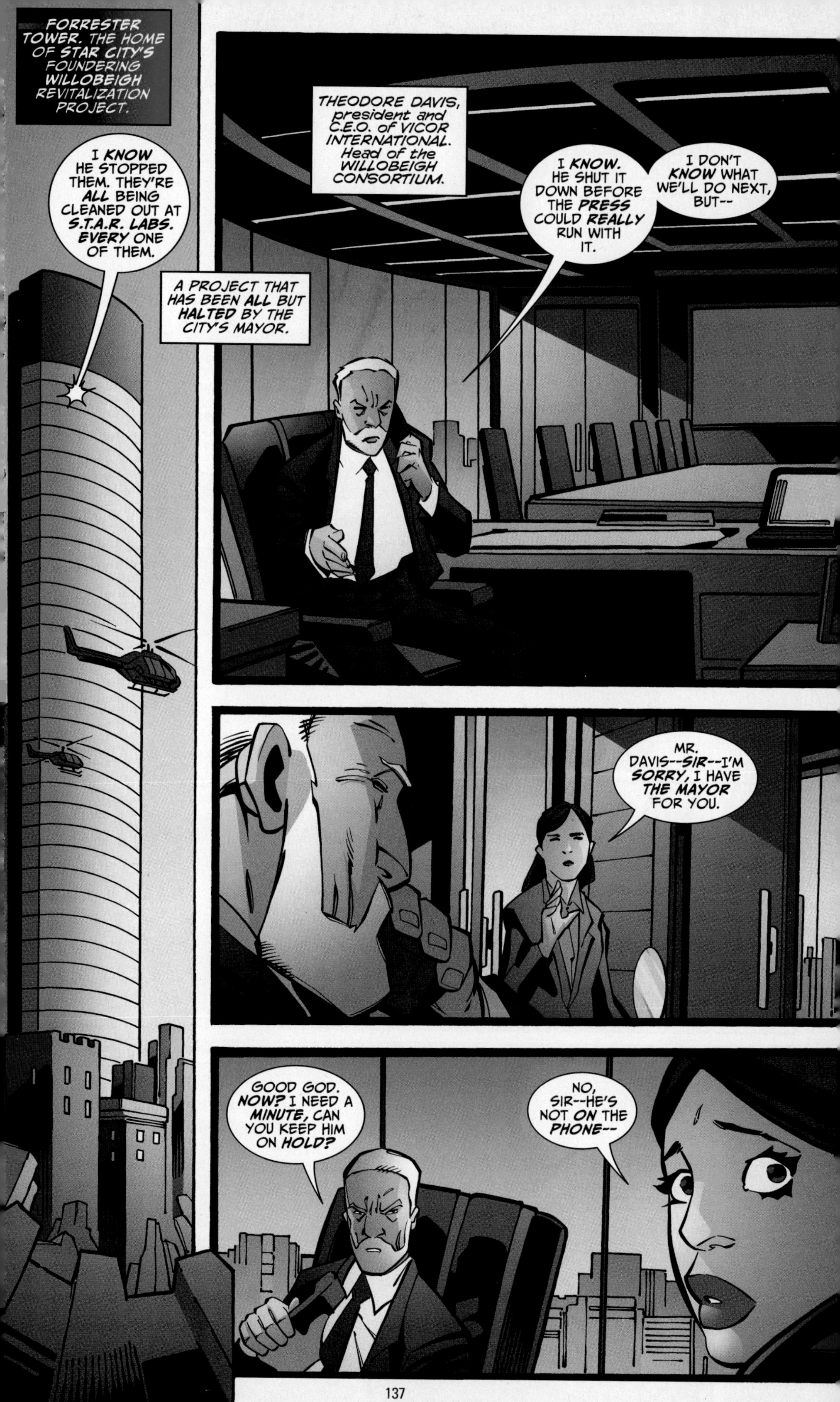
FORRESTER TOWER. THE HOME OF STAR CITY'S FOUNDERING WILLOBEIGH REVITALIZATION PROJECT.
I KNOW HE STOPPED THEM. THEY'RE ALL BEING CLEANED OUT AT S.T.A.R. LABS. EVERY ONE OF THEM.
A PROJECT THAT HAS BEEN ALL BUT HALTED BY THE CITY'S MAYOR.
THEODORE DAVIS, president and C.E.O. of VICOR INTERNATIONAL. Head of the WILLOBEIGH CONSORTIUM.
I KNOW. HE SHUT IT DOWN BEFORE THE PRESS COULD REALLY RUN WITH IT.
I DON'T KNOW WHAT WE'LL DO NEXT, BUT--
MR. DAVIS--SIR--I'M SORRY, I HAVE THE MAYOR FOR YOU.
GOOD GOD. NOW? I NEED A MINUTE, CAN YOU KEEP HIM ON HOLD?
NO, SIR--HE'S NOT ON THE PHONE--

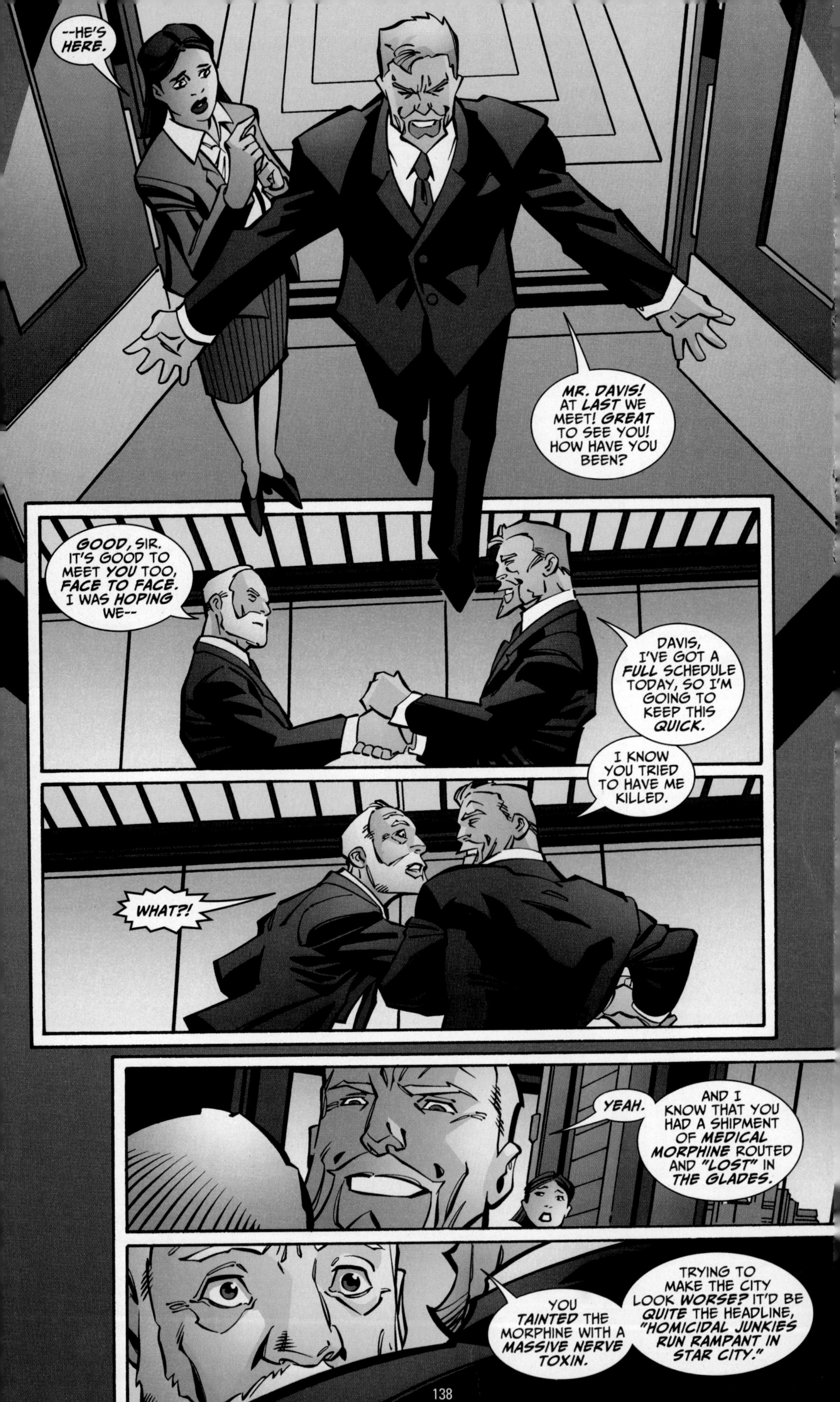
--HE'S HERE.
MR. DAVIS! AT LAST WE MEET! GREAT TO SEE YOU! HOW HAVE YOU BEEN?
GOOD, SIR. IT'S GOOD TO MEET YOU TOO, FACE TO FACE. I WAS HOPING WE--
DAVIS, I'VE GOT A FULL SCHEDULE TODAY, SO I'M GOING TO KEEP THIS QUICK.
I KNOW YOU TRIED TO HAVE ME KILLED.
WHAT?!
YEAH.
AND I KNOW THAT YOU HAD A SHIPMENT OF MEDICAL MORPHINE ROUTED AND "LOST" IN THE GLADES.
YOU TAINTED THE MORPHINE WITH A MASSIVE NERVE TOXIN.
TRYING TO MAKE THE CITY LOOK WORSE? IT'D BE QUITE THE HEADLINE, "HOMICIDAL JUNKIES RUN RAMPANT IN STAR CITY."

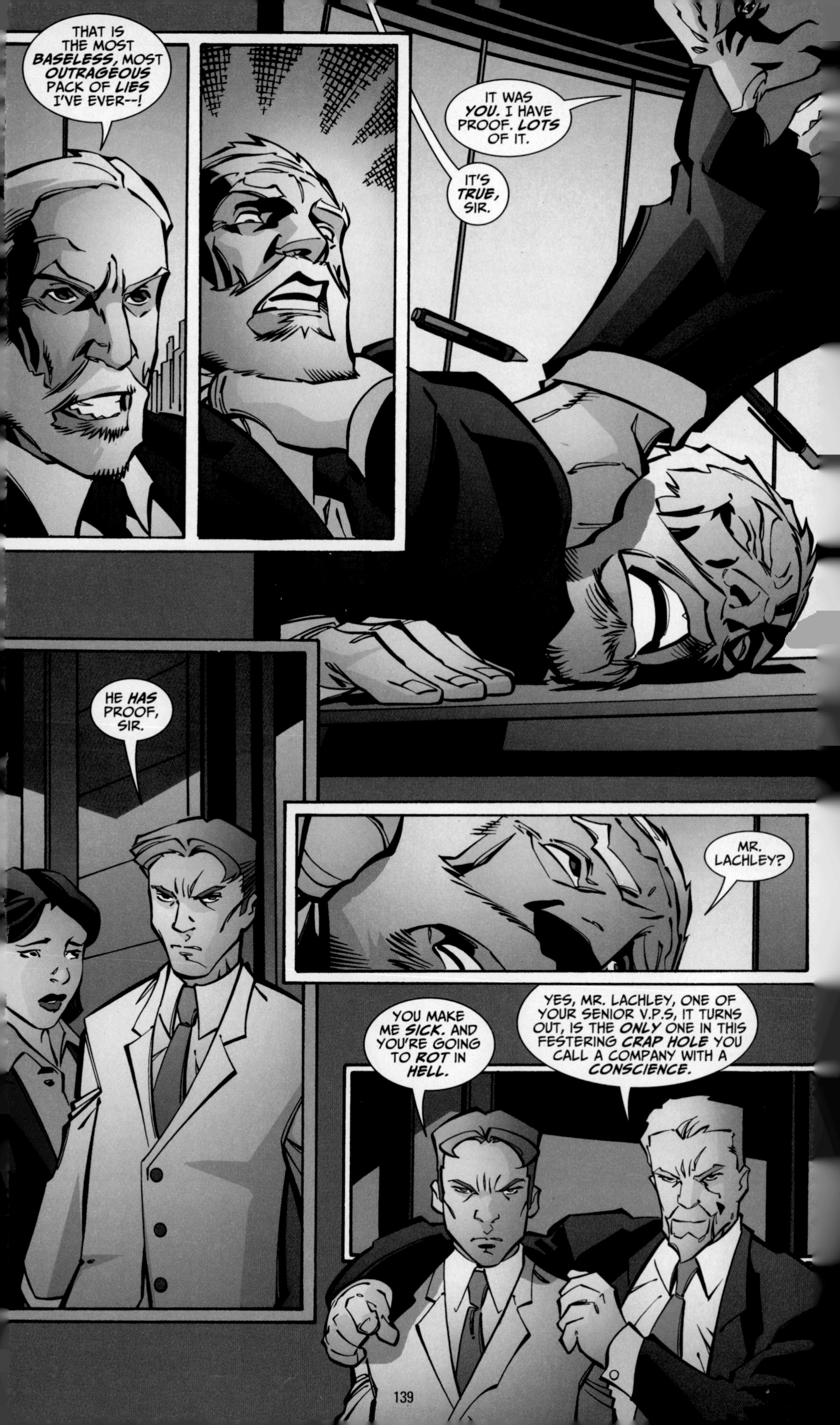
THAT IS THE MOST BASELESS, MOST OUTRAGEOUS PACK OF LIES I'VE EVER--!
IT WAS YOU. I HAVE PROOF. LOTS OF IT.
IT'S TRUE, SIR.
HE HAS PROOF, SIR.
MR. LACHLEY?
YES, MR. LACHLEY, ONE OF YOUR SENIOR V.P.S, IT TURNS OUT, IS THE ONLY ONE IN THIS FESTERING CRAP HOLE YOU CALL A COMPANY WITH A CONSCIENCE.
YOU MAKE ME SICK. AND YOU'RE GOING TO ROT IN HELL.

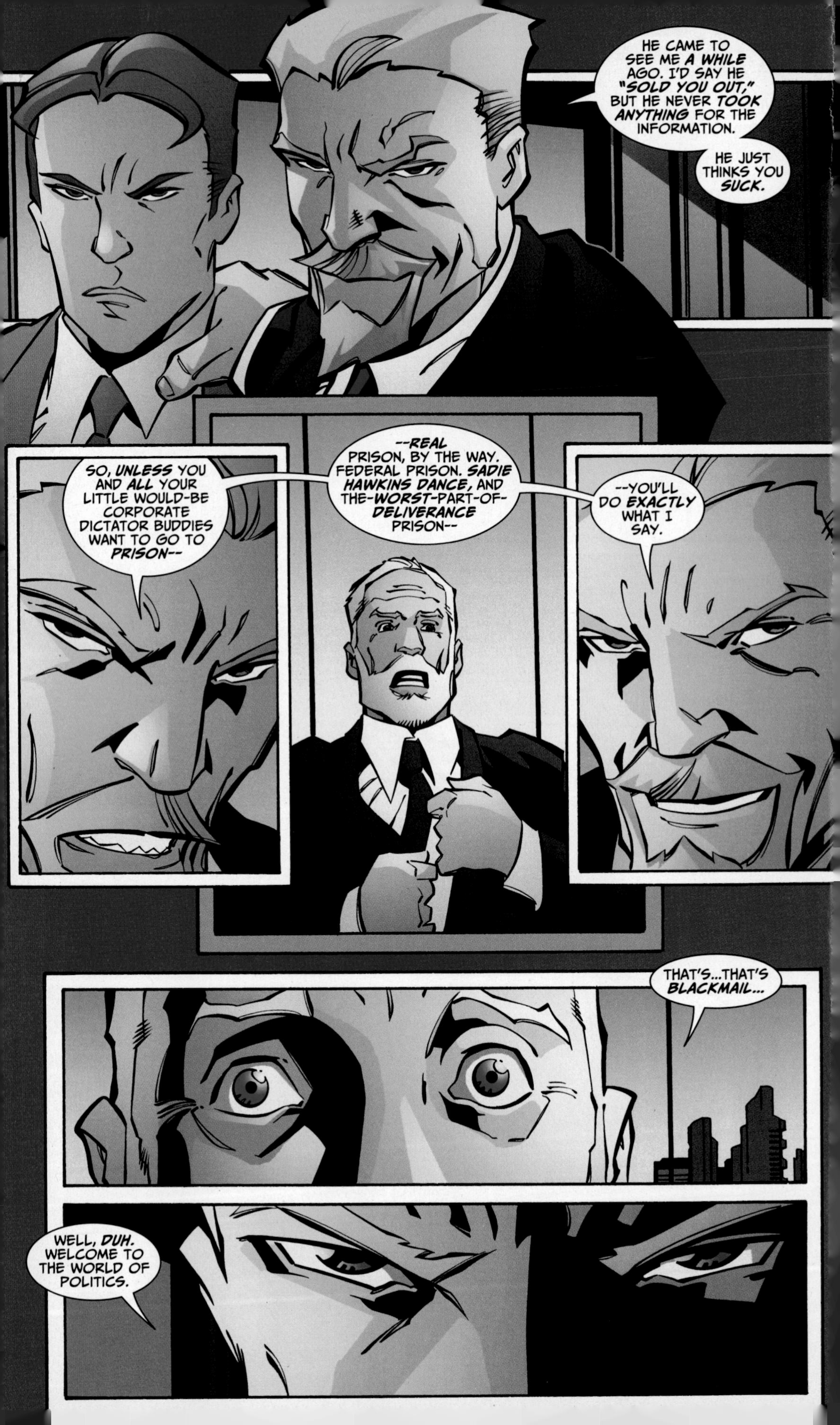
HE CAME TO SEE ME A WHILE AGO. I'D SAY HE "SOLD YOU OUT," BUT HE NEVER TOOK ANYTHING FOR THE INFORMATION.
HE JUST THINKS YOU SUCK.
SO, UNLESS YOU AND ALL YOUR LITTLE WOULD-BE CORPORATE DICTATOR BUDDIES WANT TO GO TO PRISON--
--REAL PRISON, BY THE WAY. FEDERAL PRISON. SADIE HAWKINS DANCE, AND THE-WORST-PART-OF-DELIVERANCE PRISON--
--YOU'LL DO EXACTLY WHAT I SAY.
THAT'S...THAT'S BLACKMAIL...
WELL, DUH. WELCOME TO THE WORLD OF POLITICS.

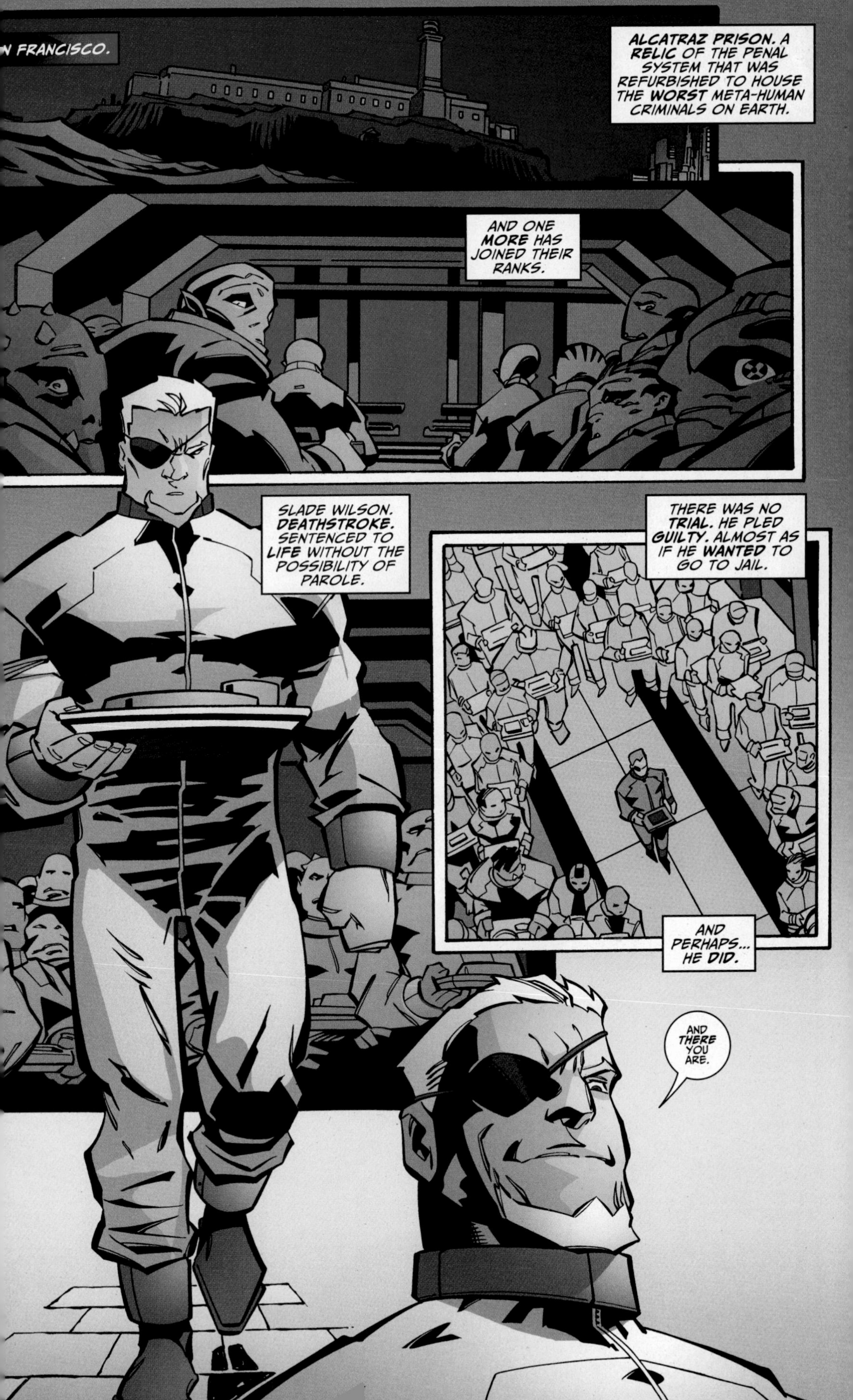

N FRANCISCO.
ALCATRAZ PRISON. A RELIC OF THE PENAL SYSTEM THAT WAS REFURBISHED TO HOUSE THE WORST META-HUMAN CRIMINALS ON EARTH.
AND ONE MORE HAS JOINED THEIR RANKS.
SLADE WILSON. DEATHSTROKE. SENTENCED TO LIFE WITHOUT THE POSSIBILITY OF PAROLE.
THERE WAS NO TRIAL. HE PLED GUILTY. ALMOST AS IF HE WANTED TO GO TO JAIL.
AND PERHAPS... HE DID.
AND THERE YOU ARE.

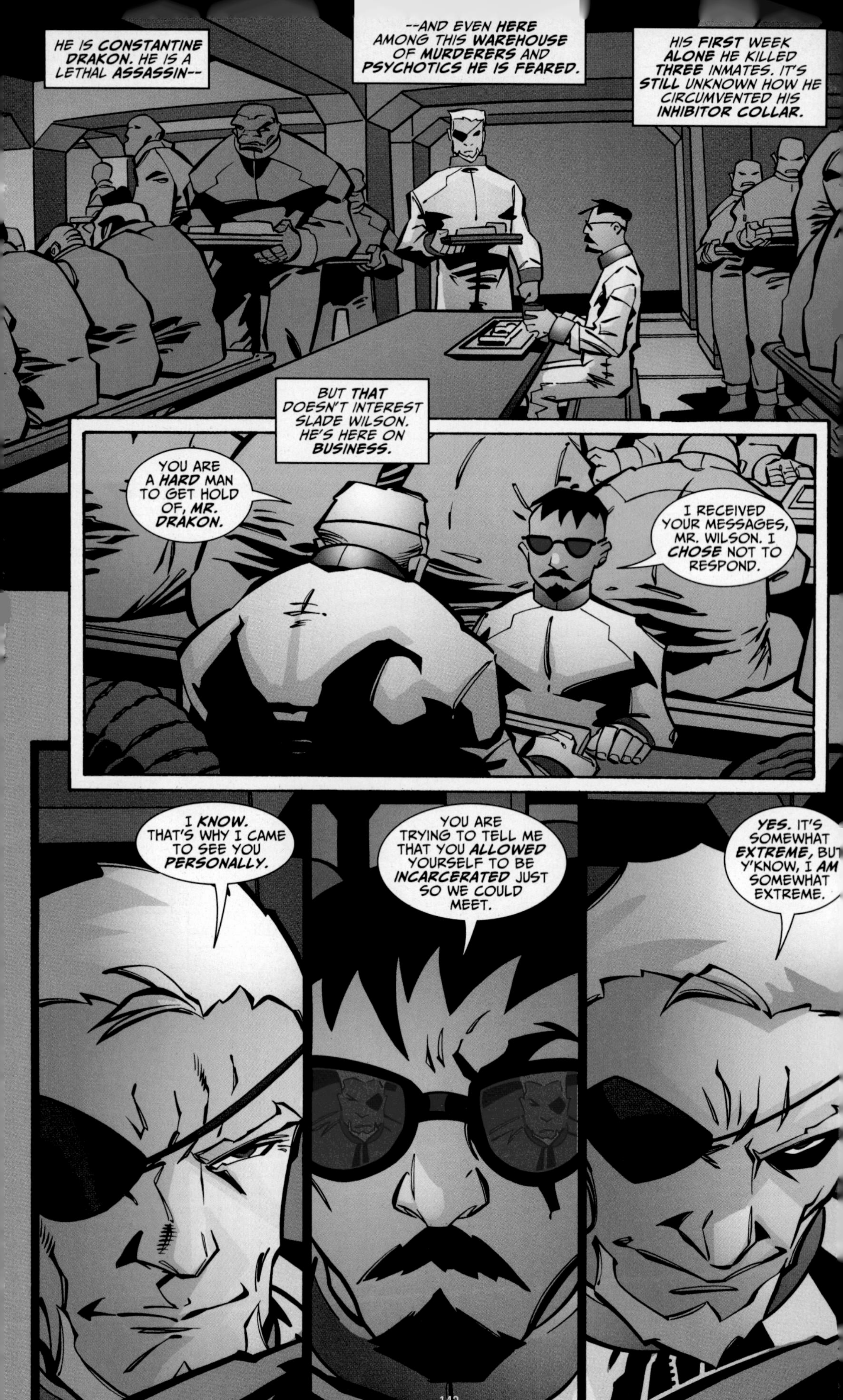

HE IS CONSTANTINE DRAKON. HE IS A LETHAL ASSASSIN--
--AND EVEN HERE AMONG THIS WAREHOUSE OF MURDERERS AND PSYCHOTICS HE IS FEARED.
HIS FIRST WEEK ALONE HE KILLED THREE INMATES. IT'S STILL UNKNOWN HOW HE CIRCUMVENTED HIS INHIBITOR COLLAR.
BUT THAT DOESN'T INTEREST SLADE WILSON. HE'S HERE ON BUSINESS.
YOU ARE A HARD MAN TO GET HOLD OF, MR. DRAKON.
I RECEIVED YOUR MESSAGES, MR. WILSON. I CHOSE NOT TO RESPOND.
I KNOW. THAT'S WHY I CAME TO SEE YOU PERSONALLY.
YOU ARE TRYING TO TELL ME THAT YOU ALLOWED YOURSELF TO BE INCARCERATED JUST SO WE COULD MEET.
YES. IT'S SOMEWHAT EXTREME, BUT Y'KNOW, I AM SOMEWHAT EXTREME.

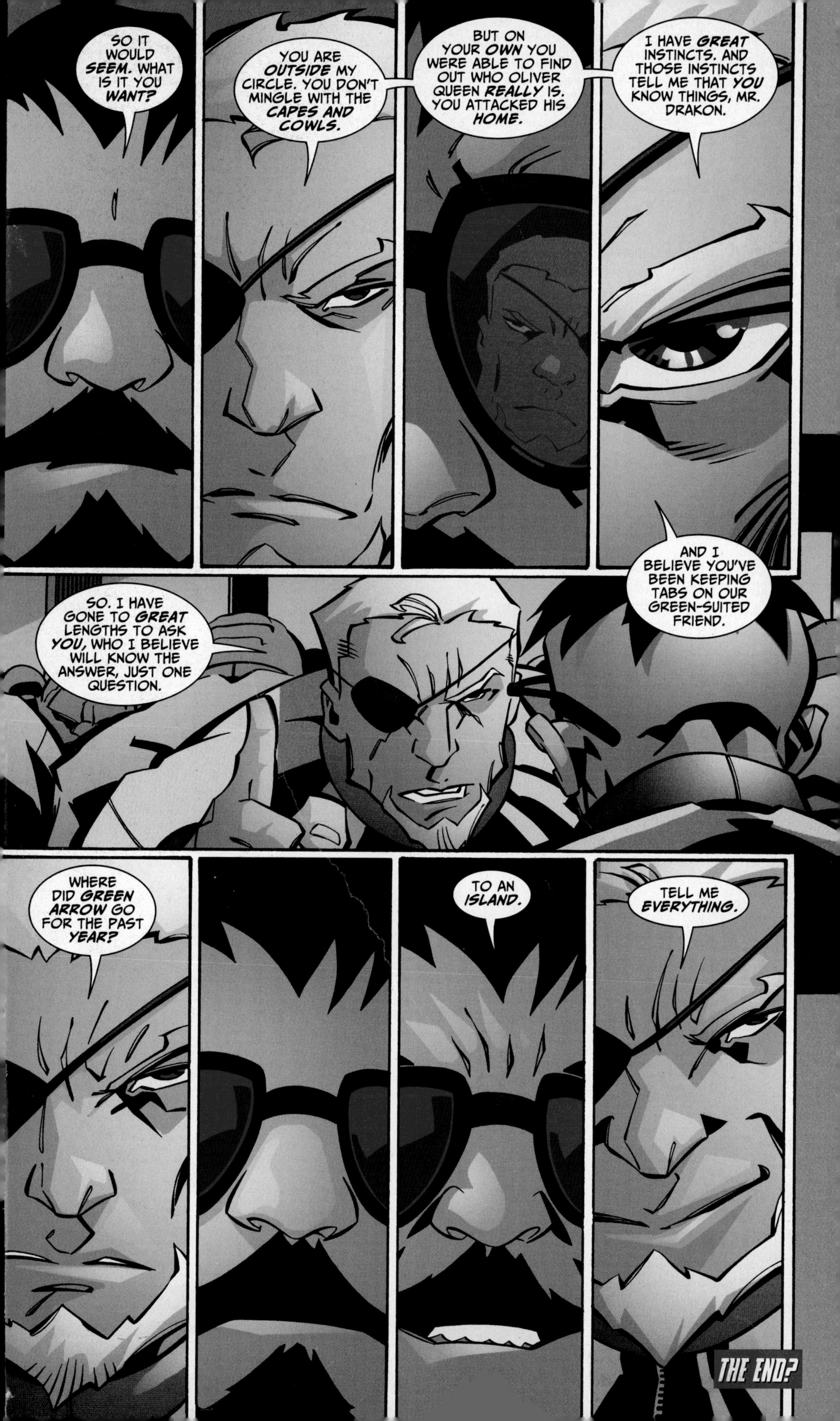
SO IT WOULD SEEM. WHAT IS IT YOU WANT?
YOU ARE OUTSIDE MY CIRCLE. YOU DON'T MINGLE WITH THE CAPES AND COWLS.
BUT ON YOUR OWN YOU WERE ABLE TO FIND OUT WHO OLIVER QUEEN REALLY IS. YOU ATTACKED HIS HOME.
I HAVE GREAT INSTINCTS. AND THOSE INSTINCTS TELL ME THAT YOU KNOW THINGS, MR. DRAKON.
AND I BELIEVE YOU'VE BEEN KEEPING TABS ON OUR GREEN-SUITED FRIEND.
SO. I HAVE GONE TO GREAT LENGTHS TO ASK YOU, WHO I BELIEVE WILL KNOW THE ANSWER, JUST ONE QUESTION.
WHERE DID GREEN ARROW GO FOR THE PAST YEAR?
TO AN ISLAND.
TELL ME EVERYTHING.
THE END?

READ MORE ADVENTURES OF YOUR FAVORITE HEROES IN THESE COLLECTIONS FROM DC COMICS:

KINGDOM COME

THE GREATEST SUPER HERO EPIC OF TOMORROW!
ELSEWORLDS
KINGDOM COME
Mark WAID Alex ROSS

Mark Waid and **Alex Ross** deliver a grim tale of youth versus experience, tradition versus change and what defines a hero. KINGDOM COME is a riveting story pitting the old guard — Superman, Batman, Wonder Woman and their peers — against a new uncompromising generation.

WINNER OF FIVE EISNER AND HARVEY AWARDS, INCLUDING BEST LIMITED SERIES AND BEST ARTIST

IDENTITY CRISIS

NEW YORK TIMES BEST-SELLING AUTHOR OF THE ZERO GAME
BRAD MELTZER
RAGS MORALES MICHAEL BAIR
IDENTITY CRISIS
Introduction by JOSS WHEDON, creator of BUFFY THE VAMPIRE SLAYER and FIREFLY
— The New York Times

BRAD MELTZER
RAGS MORALES
MICHAEL BAIR

CRISIS ON INFINITE EARTHS

CRISIS
ON INFINITE EARTHS
MARV WOLFMAN
& GEORGE PÉREZ

MARV WOLFMAN
GEORGE PÉREZ

DC: THE NEW FRONTIER VOLUME 1

DC: The New Frontier
VOLUME ONE
BY DARWYN COOKE WITH DAVE STEWART

DARWYN COOKE
DAVE STEWART

SEARCH THE GRAPHIC NOVELS SECTION OF

www.DCCOMICS.com

FOR ART AND INFORMATION ON ALL OF OUR BOOKS

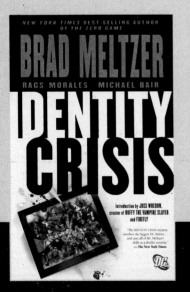